The

WAY OF THE HEART

This work was transcribed from the original tape recordings made of Jeshua in communion with Jayem. References by Jeshua to 'tapes' are therefore specific to the time when the recordings were made and the technology used.

If you wish to obtain the audio recordings please visit *www.wayofmastery.com*.

The

WAY OF THE HEART

Jeshua (Jesus)

IN COMMUNION WITH

Jayem

The Way of the Heart

Fourth Edition

WAY *of* MASTERY
www.wayofmastery.com

PO Box 204
Ubud, Bali 80571
Indonesia
admin@wayofmastery.com
www.wayofmastery.com

ISBN: 978-602-98911-0-2

CONTENTS

Study Suggestions from Jeshua

Jeshua has also given the following specific suggestions about how to "listen" to the recordings or transcripts of these Lessons:

1. Select a separate *'Way of'* notebook with a cover that has meaning for you, and a pen that you love; use them only for this work. Keep your notebook in a sacred space (such as on your altar, if you have one) wherever you live.

2. Always settle down, relax and allow the breath to flow deeply and fully before you start listening to the recordings or reading the transcripts.

3. Allow the words to simply land within you, without any effort to understand all of this information at once.

4. Notice which passages cause feelings to arise within your being.

5. Make selective notes and identify in your *'Way of'* notebook those passages which touch your feeling nature.

6. Later (or on a different day) copy the passages from your notebook which elicited a strong feeling. Write them several times on a separate sheet of paper in a state of innocence and playfulness.

7. Whenever a question is asked it is useful to pause and reflect on it, before moving on.

These Lessons were first given with the intention of each being lived with, and deeply absorbed, for at least thirty days. In reality you will find that each Lesson keeps teaching you, and taking you further into your own spiritual awakening!

Listen to each recording or read the Lesson several times in different locations at different times of the day. Stay with each Lesson until you feel complete with it.

Doing the exercises as given is also very important. Many of these exercises are the same ones that were given to Jeshua by his Essene elders over 2000 years ago.

Feel free to use these suggestions as you wish, but most of all have fun with the material.

Foreword
by Jayem

I write to you from a bit of an odd position. On the one hand, I have been the conduit through which these rich, rare, and transformative Teachings have flowed to bless us all. I am also a ceaseless student of them, and of the Being Who has given them to us all: Jeshua ben Joseph, better known in the West as 'Jesus,' which is but a transliteration of his original Aramaic name. (You may see it spelled as 'Yeshua' or Y'shua).

When Jeshua first appeared to me in a field of brilliant golden-white light in August of 1987, I was thrust into a radical path of awakening. But first I had to go through a fear of such gut-wrenching depth, for I was sure I had lost my mind. I recounted my initial year of contact with Him in my book, *The Jeshua Letters.* I demanded of Him that He provide proof that He is, indeed, separate from any projection of my own mind, and—over a period of nine years—He did just that, finally defeating my own deeply held (and probably fear-based) skepticism.

In hindsight, the sheer magnificence and profundity of wisdom in these Teachings should have been enough for me to accept it was clearly not my own mind creating it! As these communications began, I had had some experience teaching, primarily yoga and meditation. The classes and workshops I gave were well scripted days in advance. By contrast, at no time have I ever known what Jeshua was going to speak about.

When he began, in 1994, the first recording of *The Way of the Heart*, He gave no indication to me it would be the first chapter in a three year training course in awakening to Christ Mind (initially mailed as audio tapes to hundreds of folks around America). I merely did what, by then, I had grown accustomed to…

I sat down, closed my eyes, began repeating a short prayer He had given me to do whenever I joined with Him, and allowed the vibrational patterns, colors, and sense of leaving my body to occur. He would then communicate His message, and utter "Amen." Then I would be aware He was telling me He was finished. I would sense my body again, and 'land' in it, often to feel radically energized for hours.

I recall one night having a fever, swollen throat, and no voice at all. He said it would not be a problem, because He (unlike me) did not believe in limits or sickness! There was no trace of it as He spoke, and I felt liberated from the symptoms for hours afterward. But as they crept in, I cried to Him: "How do I prevent this?" His reply?

That, my brother, is what you must come to know in and for yourself.

From the beginning of His contact of me, it has been indicated by Him that He was actively creating through and with me a PathWay "never done on the earth before," and that it was dedicated to flowering a million souls into Christ Mind as part of the coming radical transformation of Mankind we are feeling pressing upon us at this time.

The Way of the Heart is the first in His PathWay Trilogy (comprised of *The Way of the Heart*, *The Way of Transformation* and *The Way of Knowing*), fondly known to thousands as the *'Way of'* teachings. Only recently (2005) did I discover in a scholarly documentary that the very first Christians referred to His teachings as "The Way." A mere coincidence? I don't think so, for one thing I have discovered in my now twenty-four year apprenticeship with, and service to, Him is this: nothing is without Plan and Purpose.

The PathWay Trilogy itself is simply one of the most exquisite and masterful teachings I have ever come across, and that includes all of my studies in yoga, world religions and philosophy. How He could 'plant seeds' in *The Way of the Heart*, and then masterfully weave them to deeper levels as the student becomes ready for their fuller fruits through the subsequent consecutive works, *The Way of Transformation* and *The Way of Knowing*, still leaves the teacher in me humbled and astonished. However, they are yet only a part of the PathWay He has been developing through me over many years; other key texts include *The Jeshua Letters* and *The Way of the Servant*. A further step in the student's journey is the experiential and transformative energies in the *Aramaic Lord's Prayer* and, especially, the *Beatitudes*, which are the basis of the deep healing and awakening work utilized at retreats, intensive trainings and pilgrimages. Along with the essential Aramaic teachings are the supportive practices of *LovesBreath, Radical Inquiry*, and the unique meditation entitled *In the Name*.

It is important for the student to know that these formal teachings found in the three '*Way of*' texts lay an important groundwork for deeper levels of the alchemy of radical transformation. You may note how often he refers to both *breath* and *feeling* in these teachings. From before these formal teachings were given, He was already guiding me deeply into fully understanding—in the laboratory of my own being—the importance of Breath (which He calls the presence of the Holy Spirit) and how to fully penetrate the layers of 'frozen feeling' held in the subconscious and into the soul; how the soul falls into what He calls the Dream of Separation, how these patterns are recapitulated in womb and birth, and even our choices of parents and time-frames for incarnation. Without these deeper, personal, experiential journeys, the 'Word' does not fully incarnate and 'land in the cells,' precisely the only place we can know our healing is complete: here, in this world, now, in this moment.

Therefore, the current volume you hold in your hand, together with all the other 'parts' mentioned, form one of the most exquisite, and all-encompassing spiritual Pathways to grace our world. As He put it years ago:

> *Our one goal is to establish a complete PathWay that can carry a soul from its first stirrings to awaken, all the way into a mature manifestation of Christ Mind.*

Interested readers can learn more about the PathWay at the website, *www.wayofmastery.com*.

One further note: These are the only authorized versions of these Teachings, given precisely as they were first offered, including the original question and answer sections, some of which are priceless Teachings meant for all of us. Great care has been taken to ensure editors have not altered anything in the transition from audio to text. No chapter titles appear, nor are sub-sections given themes, for He gave none. Words emphasized by Him originally are shown in italics.

What you have in your hands is a Master Key, but a key is only useful to the degree we wrap our hands around it, insert it into the locks upon our hearts and mind, and 'turn it'—by fully engaging what has been given us by one of the supreme Master Teachers ever sent by Love to make Love known yet again in our sleeping souls.

It is in your hands now, and not by accident. He has said no one will come to this Work "in whom all preparation for it is not complete." If you are reading these words, grace has wed the secret longing of your soul, and placed you here, and these Teachings, in your hand.

Now, it is up to you. God bless, and may you know the radiance of the Grace that loves you beyond all comprehension, and come to know the Soul's Completion as it works through you to coat this world in Love.

Streams of Joy,
Jayem
May, 2011

Lesson One

Now, we begin.

And indeed, once again, greetings unto you, beloved and holy friends. I come forth in this hour, yet again, to abide with you where you *believe* yourself to be. For in Truth, if it were not for the fact that you are choosing to turn your attention to the world of physicality through the vehicle of the body, our communication would not require the device of what you might call "channeling," nor the devices of the technologies of this world in which to record and capture spoken words that are themselves but the reflection of what the words would point your mind toward.

Therefore, beloved friends, I come not for myself, but for you. I come not to teach you, but to love you, until you choose, from the depth within your own being, to set aside every illusion you have ever given credence to, and to remember the Truth which alone is true. For indeed, in that hour, there is a transcendence of all that knows limitation. There is a transcendence of all that knows coming and going, birth and death. There is but the Mind of Christ within which each of us, as a spark of Divine Light, as a sunbeam to the sun, rests eternally in perfect communion and communication, always. Now of course, the great secret is that *that is* the state of your reality. That in each and every moment, you abide in perfect communion with the whole of creation, since all things are but temporary modifications of the one fundamental energy which I have chosen to call the *Christ Mind,* the offspring of the Father.

And so, beloved friends, *I* come to where *you* choose to be. And if you would choose to open that place within the heart and within the mind in which you can communicate with me directly, I will meet you there as well. What is important, then, by way of our beginning, is to consider the simple fact that your *experience* is always the *effect* of where you choose to focus the attention of your consciousness, its Self being unlimited forever, embracing all the many dimensions of creation. You abide in that which embraces all things, in all ways, and at all times. And in Truth, you do not know separation, birth or death, gain or loss.

In this hour, as you have taken the tape from its envelope and put it into your machinery, recognize how you, as an infinite being, have deliberately chosen to participate in a form of experience. You have, therefore, called to yourself the sensory apparatus of the body through which to filter the energies of this physical domain, that you might hear vibrations against vocal chords that create words that carry certain meanings for each and every one of you. And each and every one of you will color that meaning according—*according*—to the perceptions that *you* have chosen to place value upon.

Does this mean that some are ahead and some behind? It only seems that way. In reality, each of you is equal; each of you, choosing from your infinite freedom to attract to yourself certain vibrational frequencies, if you will—certain forms or qualities of experience. That freedom is what you abide in *always*, from before the foundations of this world, and long after this world ceases to be. In each and every moment, then, you cannot be a victim of what you see, and nothing is outside of you. What you experience you have directly and deliberately called to yourself. And if you hold the thought that, "Well, I don't like what I've called to myself," that's perfectly okay, too. For then, you have called to yourself the experience of being in judgment of yourself. Merely look with the wonder of a child and see what it feels like and ask yourself,

Is this an energy I wish to continue in, or would I choose something else?

For ultimately, when all possible choices within the dream of separation have been made, have been tasted, have been felt, have been known, then finally there emerges the still, quiet Voice of Spirit that speaks through the soul—and we'll come back to that—whispering of the one Truth and the one reality, the one Love, the one peace, the one bliss that is continual.

Then, the soul begins to turn from the things of this created world. It begins to withdraw its attention, as it were, from its attachments to all of the things it has called to itself. It begins to transcend its sense of identification with the vibrational frequencies it had only meant to play with, and then took seriously. For it is seriousness within the mind which is the creation of ego, and it is great seriousness that holds the vibrations of what you would no longer experience within

10

the field of your being, within the field of your soul.

And as you, as the soul—the individual divine spark—begins to choose to withdraw the attention, to withdraw the value you have placed upon all things, and as you learn to simplify the nature of your own consciousness, as you begin to realize that you can *surrender* into something that seems beyond you, that you can entertain the insane thought of trusting the invisible, you come more and more to be less and less. And as you become less and less of what you thought you were, conversely, you become more and more of what your Father created you to be—*the Thought of Perfect Love in form*, a channel, a simple vehicle through which that Love of Spirit can shine forth. And your only task becomes the cleaning of your windows, the polishing of your floors, the weeding of your garden, so that that Light can pour forth unimpeded.

No longer will you find the need to defend perceptions you had identified with in error. And you will, indeed, know when you have come to that state of awakening, for you will be able to look upon all created things that you have ever experienced, all reactions you have ever held within the mind, all perceptions, all judgments, all desires that you have ever held for anyone or anything, and as they arise in your mind, they will not disturb your peace. And you will smile. And you will see that within your consciousness has arisen all saintlihood and all devilishness. You have been both saint and sinner, and your happiness and your unhappiness has been merely an effect of where you would choose to place your attention.

Indeed, beloved friends, I come forth to meet you wherever you are, because I have chosen to use the infinite power of consciousness, given me of the Father, as equally as it is given unto you, to discover how deep delight can be when the mind is focused only on seeing from, and seeing only, the Mind of Christ. I have, therefore, called to my Self all multitude of experiences, even when I walked upon your beloved Earth as a man—in order to challenge myself, in order to test myself, in order to condition myself, to rise above, to transcend all possible experiences that could distract me from the remembrance of who I am.

You could say, by the way, that my crucifixion was simply the climax of my own direct choice to be challenged by the events of space and time, so that I could cultivate, within myself, the ability to see from, and to see only, the perfect purity of the Mind of Christ.

The point that I'm seeking to make with you is that, in each and every moment, what you are experiencing in the realm of your emotions and mind, and the effects, to a latter degree, within the body, are there because you—from your infinite freedom—have simply selected that experience, that energy, to focus your attention on, so that you can see what the effects are.

The insanity, you see, does not come from having chosen to see something other than the Mind of Christ. The insanity, which you experience as your pain and as your suffering and your seeking and your dramas, comes only from your mistaken choice to become *identified* with what arises in the field of your awareness. You, therefore, lose the sight of innocence. For, indeed, all events are perfectly neutral, and you are free to see them any way you want.

When a child is born—and many of you who are mothers know this—you can experience a depth of joy that is unspeakable. Likewise, you can also experience fear and contraction at the thought of having to be responsible for a child. When a loved one dies, and you experience grief and suffering, rest assured it is because you have chosen to contract your attention, so that all you can see is the loss of an animated body, and thereby convince yourself that you have become separated from the loved one.

I speak from experience when I share with you that separation is an illusion. And when death occurs in your plane, in that very moment, you still have the *power* to choose to recognize that something has changed, and to shift your attention to a different faculty that the body could never possibly contain, in which you perceive and hear and communicate with that spark of Divine Light—the soul—that seems to have given up the idea of trying to keep a physical form animated.

It is, therefore, imperative and, in fact, it is the very first step on what we are going to begin to call *The Way of the Heart*. The first step in awakening is to allow into the mind the thought, the axiom, the Truth, that *nothing which you are experiencing is caused by anything outside of you.* You experience only the effects of your own choice.

For you see, during this coming year, we will be building, month by month, on what I'm choosing now to call *The Way of the Heart.* It is the way unknown to the world. It is a way unknown to many that would call themselves spiritual teachers, for it is not a way of resting on, or becoming dependent on, magical means. It is, rather, that pathway which cultivates within you the decision to turn your attention upon your own mind, upon your own behavior, upon what is true and real for you, moment to moment—to study it, to consider it, to feel it, to breathe the Light of Spirit through it, and to constantly retrain the mind so that it assumes complete responsibility in each moment.

And why is this necessary? Because, without it, there can be no peace. Without it, you can not transcend the false identifications that you have chosen. To use, perhaps, a simpler form of your language, you need to come to the point where you say to yourself,

> *I've done this to myself. I did it, I must correct it. No one is to blame. The world is innocent.*

And in the coming months, we will be communicating with you more and more deeply, the finer points, if you will, of *The Way of the Heart.* For it is that way that was taught to me, and it is that way to which I have pointed you with many, many clues. It is that way that brings about the reversal of every thought you have ever had about any one or any thing. It is that way, alone, which allows you to pass back through the eye of the needle, and to come to rest in the Perfect Peace from which you have sprung forth.

The Way of the Heart is not the way of the intellect; for, indeed, that aspect of the mind was never designed to be your master. It was designed to be the humble, and—if you will pardon the expression—very stupid servant of the Awakened Heart. The Heart is that which feels all things, embraces all things, trusts all things, allows all things. The Heart is that in which the soul rests eternally. The Heart is that which is beyond space and time and is that spark

13

of Light in the Mind of God, which is called *Christ*. And only in That will you find the peace that you seek.

You will discover, then, that the pathway of awakening is not a pathway of avoidance, but a pathway of truthfulness. It is not a pathway of accomplishment and pride, but a pathway of releasing from the consciousness every hope and every wish to be special—to see yourself as having "made progress," so that you can pound a fist upon the chest and spread the tail feathers. It is a transcendence of the hope of somehow getting God's attention, so that he will look upon you and say,

> *Oh, you've been such a good person. Oh, my goodness, yes. Well, I think we'll allow you into the Kingdom now.*

It is a way in which you will come to cultivate—regardless of your inner experience or degrees of awakening—to cultivate the willingness and the art of returning to the simplicity of empty-headedness and not-knowingness, with each and every breath. It is a way of life in which all things and all events become an aspect of your meditation and your prayer, until there is established, once again within you, the Truth that is true always:

> *Not my will, but Thine be done. For of myself, I do nothing. But my Father does all things through me.*

Imagine, then, a state of being in which you walk through this world, seemingly appearing like everyone else, and yet, you are spacious within; you are empty within. In Truth, you desire nothing, though you allow desire to move through you, and you recognize it as the Voice of the Father, guiding your personality, your emotions, and even the body, to the places, to the events, to the people, to the things, to the experiences through which the tapestry of the Atonement is being woven, through which all of the Children of God are called home again. And you trust the complete flow of that, whether you are asked to give a speech in front of ten thousand people, or you're asked to tell a friend the truth of your feelings, or whether or not you are, perhaps, asked to sweep the streets and live penniless. For in Truth, that mind that *trusts* the Source of its creation allows all things, trusts all things, embraces all things, and transcends all things.

Rest assured, then, whenever you feel frustration and anxiety, it is because you have decided not to trust the Truth. And the Truth is simply this: Only God's plan for salvation can work for you. Your way must always fail, for your way begins with the illusory and insane assumption that you are a separate being from the Mind of God and must, therefore, direct your own course. For if you are sick and diseased and not at peace, why would you decide that you know how to create peace? It requires great humility to accept the first step of the path:

> *I have done all this; I must undo it. But I have no idea how I did this. Therefore, I must surrender to something else.*

I want to give you this thought, even as I gave it to this, my beloved brother, some time ago. And the thought is this (and I would ask that you consider it well):

What if the very life you are living, and each experience that is coming to you now, since the moment you decided, "I've got to awaken here"—what if everything was being directly sent to you of your Father, because your Father knows what is necessary to unravel within your consciousness to allow you to awaken? What if the very things you are resisting are the very stepping stones to your homecoming? What if you achieved a maturity along this pathway in which you were finally willing to let things be just as they are?

And if it was necessary to sweep the streets, you simply took a deep breath and said, "Father, you know the way home," and therefore began sweeping. And up into the mind comes the thought,

> *Oh, my God, I won't be recognized. I won't stand out. People won't think I'm special if I'm just a street sweeper.*

And you recognize,

> *Ah-ha, no wonder my Father wants me to do this. I've got to flush this up so that I can look at it, dis-identify from it, and learn to be the presence of Love in the sweeping of the street.*

For in Truth, I tell you, the least of these among you, according to your perception, is already equal to the greatest. And there is none among you who is less than I am.

And so, *The Way of the Heart* begins there. It begins by accepting the humility that you've created quite a mess within your consciousness. You've created a labyrinth and gotten lost within it, and you don't know the way back—that *of yourself, you can do nothing.* For all you've managed to achieve is the creation of a whole lot of insane dramas that are, in Truth, occurring *nowhere* except within the field of your mind. They are like chimeras, like dreams. In Truth, there is no difference between a waking state, in which you would be the director of your life, and the dreams you have when the body sleeps at night. They are both the same thing.

I wish to direct you to peace, even that peace which forever transcends the understanding and comprehension of the world. I desire—because my Father desires it through me—to bring you wholly to where I am, that you might discover there is someone that got there ahead of you. And when you look closely, you go,

Ahhh, it's my Self. I've always been there, but I forgot.

And in the end of all journeying, in the end of all purification—and, indeed, purification is still necessary—you will discover that to awaken means to have journeyed nowhere. It means to have arrived at a goal that has never changed.

Awakening is only remembrance—but it is a remembrance not just of the intellect, for it is not an idea, as you would understand ideas. It is an idea that vibrates through the whole field of your beingness, so that even the cells of the body—while yet the body remains coalesced together in its present form—even the cells of the body *awaken* and *relax* into the Truth that is true always.

The Way of the Heart . . . If you were a gardener, would you not cultivate the art of weeding your garden? Would you not look to see that the soil is just the correct dampness? Would you not keep your eye on the clouds on the horizon and the heat of the day? Would you not cover the delicate plants that need protection while they grow strong? And if those that would come would not respect your garden, would you not ask them to leave, or build a temporary fence until the garden is strong enough—until it bursts forth with enough fruit so that you can give to even those who do not respect it?

Be you, therefore, a wise gardener. Cultivate a deep love and respect for *yourself*, for you are not here to "fix" the world. You are not here to "fix" your brother or sister. 'Tis only Love that heals. And until you have loved *yourself* wholly, by having purified the mind of every erroneous thought you've ever held—until you've loved—you do not, in Truth, love anyone or anything, save in those brief moments when you let your guard down and the Love of God shines forth, through you, so quickly you don't even know what happened. For the wise gardener cultivates a state of consciousness in which the Love of God is unimpeded.

Beloved friends—those of you that have elected to answer a call to participate in this pathway, with this Family—if you would make your commitment to trusting your Creator for having set before you a pathway that can, indeed, lead you home, you will, indeed, arrive at home. But commitment means that you don't get to leave the room when the shouting begins. The shouting we're speaking of is the shouting within your own mind, within your own body, within your own emotions. That you will stay with these things by being honest about them, and loving yourself for ever having the power to even create such insane perceptions of yourself and the world around you.

The Way of the Heart is the final pathway that any soul can enter. There are many stages of awakening. There are many pathways that can be followed, but ultimately, "All roads lead to Rome," so they say. Eventually each soul must find its way into *The Way of the Heart*, and come back to the Truth that it's time to take responsibility, to learn to cultivate the ability to look upon the deep and vicious blackness of what I have called ego, which is nothing more than the cesspool of denial—it is that which lacks Light—and begin to bring Light back to it by simply observing your own mind, your own behavior, your own reactions with a sense of wonder, with a sense of innocence, with a sense of childlikeness.

For is it not written that you must again become a little child to enter the Kingdom? The little child simply marvels at all that they see: "Well, how about that?" Can you imagine looking upon the deepest, darkest parts of your own shadow, your own denials and being able to say, "Oh, how about that!"? Hmm. Remember, then, that everything is neutral, and in Truth all that which arises within your consciousness *has no effect* upon the Truth of your reality.

The Way of the Heart, then, is a way of cultivating the decision to become identified with the Light that can shine away all darkness—not by fighting with it, but by recognizing it, embracing it as your own creation, and choosing again. *The Way of the Heart* is the way that I teach. And now we begin a more focused—shall we say—year-long study, a year-long cultivation together, that *The Way of the Heart* might become established within your *holy* mind. And we will be drawing, indeed, upon many sources. And there may be some surprises according to who may choose to speak to you through this vehicle.

But rest assured, at all times and in all ways, I have committed myself to gently directing the birthing and the manifestation of what you have come to call Shanti Christo. The idea was given by me. And what I give, I nurture. And what I create, together with you, I do not abandon. Therefore, you will find that I will be here always. We will have yet to see whether you will be.

Remember then, always, that the Truth is true always. Is it not time, beloved friends, to truly step into ownership of your only reality? *The Way of the Heart* does not know the word *avoidance*. *The Way of the Heart* does not know deception, manipulation, or control. *The Way of the Heart* does not know blame, although it watches these things arise as echoes of old patterns now outgrown. It learns to see them, to recognize them, like you might recognize certain kinds of clouds that pass through the sky, and then to turn the attention of the mind, that a new choice might be made.

The Way of the Heart is the way that calls you home. And the call comes from that deep part of your soul that is still like unto the Spirit, which abides as Christ in the Holy Mind of God. Trust, then, that you are as a sunbeam to the sun. And trust not the perceptions you have cultivated in error. For you are not alone on the way that you journey, and you journey not apart from your brothers and sisters. This Family cannot know separation, though some may seem to come and go. For once the call to awaken through *this* lineage has been acknowledged, though bodies may not communicate in space and time, rest assured, communication remains, and there is no way to avoid it.

And so, we begin *The Way of the Heart.* We enter, now, a stage where it's time to stop listening out of polite kindness or out of curiosity, and to step into the willingness to don the mantle of that one *committed to healing every obstacle to the presence of Love* that may yet remain secretly hidden in the depth of that part of your mind which would struggle to be separate from God, and to remember that you are truly the Light that can come to shine, lovingly, upon every aspect of darkness you have known.

So along this pathway this year, you are going to learn how to shake hands with the devil, and to do a little jig with him, and recognize his face to be your own. For when you can dance with the darkness that you have created, that darkness is transformed into an angel. And Light abides with Light.

We will be giving you, and bringing forth, certain meditations, if you will, certain energetic practices to help cultivate within you a quality of *feeling* that will allow you to recognize energies that do not serve you, in a way that transcends what your mind may choose to think of these energies, so that you learn more and more to lead with the body, if you will, to lead with your feeling nature, not your intellect. For your intellect does not know anything except the trivialities that you have shoved into it, like garbage into a garbage can. The intellect can *never* bring the healing of the Heart that *is* the Atonement. It can only be utilized to argue against the insane perceptions you are used to, so that you might come to see that perhaps there is a greater good in giving up your insistence on treating the intellect as your god.

Therefore, indeed, beloved friends, dance often, rejoice, play often. Let this year be that year in which you bring up within yourself everything unworthy of the Mind of Christ every thought of scarcity, every sense of unworthiness, every fear. Let them come up, look at them, embrace them, transmute them through your own love of self and through your honesty. Accept where you are and don't pretend to be otherwise, for the wisest are always the humblest.

Be you, therefore, at peace, beloved friends. Be you, therefore, at peace in all things. For we delight—and I speak here of the many "we" who are in what you might call a disembodied state, who are electing to participate with you that are asking to be helped this year, through this way. We delight in joining with you! We delight in loving you! We delight in waiting on you to welcome your Self home!

Therefore, indeed, we will begin to end this message of this hour now. But as we close, I would ask that you would close your eyes for just a moment and take a deep breath into the body and let it go. And as the breath leaves the body, hold the thought that there is nothing worth holding onto any longer that keeps your peace and happiness at arm's length. Become committed—become *fully* committed—to the experience of happiness, even as you've been fully committed to unhappiness, and limitation, and lack. Give your Creator full permission this year to sweep the basement clean. There really isn't anything down there worth defending or protecting.

And it will come to pass that you will know the perfect peace of empty-headedness, not-knowingness. You will know what it means to be relieved of time and to be comforted by what is eternal.

Peace be unto you always. And never once let yourself think that you are alone. It is what they call—what is this word you have—"haberdash." Hmm. What is this haberdash? That is an interesting term. It is nonsense for you to think that I'm not with you. You have asked. I picked up the phone. We are in communication. That is the way it is. That is the way it will be until the end of all illusion.

Amen.

Lesson One
Question and Answer Section

*Following completion of the lesson, Jeshua often answers
questions read to him on behalf of students.*

Question: What motivates you? How does an enlightened person
move throughout his or her day? Apparently you have moved into
a state of Oneness with Source, yet you still have a distinct, unique
personality. You are still a Self, yet you are also One with God. Can
you describe what this state is like for us?

Answer: Beloved friend. What motivates me? Worldly accolades.
Being hung on so many walls in so many churches across the world.
Hmm . . . All of the many priests and ministers who make a very
good living professing to teach my teaching, although they teach
fear, and guilt, and judgment. Hmm. What motivates me? The bets
that I have placed with my "comrades in arms," who often believe
that I'm wasting my time with humanity. For there are, indeed, many
Masters in many dimensions that wouldn't touch this plane with a
ten-thousand foot pole. And yet, I say unto you, beloved friend, I
speak somewhat tongue-in-cheek, although I don't have one.

What motivates *me* is what must come to motivate *you* when the
Christ Mind is awakened within your being, and has come to
outshine any other possibility. For what will motivate you is the
deep appreciation for the Grace that has healed your mind, the great
Mystery from which you have arisen, that somehow reaches into
your illusions and brings you Home. You know not how. *Love* of your
Creator will motivate you as you become more and more empty of
self, empty of fear, empty of the need to survive, empty of everything
unlike Love, and more and more conformed to the *instrument of peace.*

Beloved friend, what motivates me is the very fact that you exist, and
that, at times, within you, your soul has cried out to come Home.
And because my Father has brought me home, because I know how
perfect it is, how can I not extend myself to you? So to my many
comrades, who seem to wish to avoid ever taking on the human
experience, I simply, politely, nod my non-physical head and say,

Well yes, but you see, I know that no one goes Home until everyone goes Home.

I am merely your brother. And I seem to have gone ahead of you a little while. And yet, I say this unto you, *The Way of the Heart* must cultivate within you—and will—the recognition that there is no one and nothing outside of you, and that only Love has the power to heal. And, therefore, everyone that comes into your life is an aspect of your savior, teaching you to cultivate the forgiveness, and the patience, and the willingness to hear not the voice of ego within you, but to trust the guidance of the Holy Spirit in all matters, regardless of how insane it may seem to the world. What motivates me is the Grace that released me from all illusion, even as that Grace is already at work accomplishing the same within you.

What does it mean to go through the day in an enlightened state? I would be happy to tell you, only I have no days, for a day is a function of time. Time is something I no longer know anything about. It is not something that pervades my beingness. I abide only in what is eternal. And when fear has been completely uprooted from within your beingness, you, too, will know timelessness. There is a message in that answer. I hope you're listening.

Beloved friend, what is it like to be One with the Source of all Creation, and yet to hold an individuated consciousness? Why not ask yourself? You know perfectly well. For in Reality, you *are* One with the Source. And again, as the message of this hour has shared, you are acting from your infinite perfection at all times, to call qualities of experience, qualities of energy to yourself. That is exactly what I do. The only difference is, I have chosen to call only that of the *highest possible vibrations*, while you are choosing to say to yourself and to me,

Well, yes, yes. All that bliss stuff is fine, but I'd still like to get a little taste of drama and suffering. I just want to make sure I've got this down before I leave this plane.

In all respects, the choosing mechanism within you is equal to that within me. Therefore, understand well, if you would know what it means to know you are One with your Creator, while yet exhibiting an individuality, simply begin to observe your own mind, your own choices, your own experiences, with perfect innocence, constantly reminding yourself that the Truth is true always. As a sunbeam can never escape the sun, as a wave can never escape the ocean, you remain as you are created to be. And you are given *infinite* and *perfect freedom*, because you are made in the image of God.

Therefore, beloved friend, consider well what you would desire and what your intention will be. Ask yourself, moment to moment,

> *What am I truly committed unto? For what I am committed to is the focus of my intention. And the intention that I focus on brings to me the fulfillment of my desire. And what I am experiencing, like it or not, is* always *the* effect *of my* desire.

Question: Would you please comment on the world of sexuality and sexual expression for those of us committed to a path of spiritual evolution?

Answer: Well, indeed, beloved friend, if you would be committed to a role of genuine spiritually, you must put that which is called, I believe, the *chastity belt* upon the body. You must separate yourself from all those who seem to elicit little tickles of sensations in your body. Hmm. You must banish from yourself all thought of another body next to yours. Hmm. And if these things arise, by all means, whip yourself! Hmm!

Beloved friend, I've said many times that *all events are neutral, all experiences are neutral.* They will be, therefore, precisely what *you choose* them to be. Sexuality . . . In your world, most minds take this to mean that there is some sort of juxtapositioning of physical bodies, some groping of the hands, and the lips, and the tongues, and what have you. But, indeed, this is only the outer reflection, or the symbolic expression, of the energies being held within the mind.

It is most appropriate to say that all of Creation is an act of sexuality. It is an expression of energy which wishes to birth forth with *great passion—Creation!* And all relationships between two bodies, or between the moon and the sun, between the Earth and the sky—all forms of relationship are inherently the same. They hold within

23

themselves the promise, and the purpose, and the challenge of discovering the *unity* between the two or the three or the ten. It doesn't matter.

Therefore, sexuality, as you understand it in your world, is only what you will choose it to be. It does not, *necessarily*, accelerate your awakening. And it does not, *necessarily*, impede it. What you approach with sanctity and purity of heart, what you approach in every relationship, what you approach from the recognition that Creation streams forth only from the Mind of God and, therefore, the Light of Love, the presence of Christ is present in that one before whom you stand or, perhaps, whom you lay next to. What you approach with *sanctity* is sanctified. What you approach with *secretness*, what you approach with *neediness*, is demoralized and destroyed.

I would say unto you, beloved friend, you cannot transcend what is not first embraced. Therefore, search the soul well, to see if there is any *fear* of the great *intimacy* and *vulnerability* that can be experienced in sexuality. Is there something in you conflicted that is not allowing you to truly drink in the beauty of the physical form of another, to pause over every curve and every dimple, and even every little hair upon the body? Can you see within *this*, grand Mystery? Can you pause long enough to lose the false self? Can you *sanctify* the touching of flesh? For I say unto you, you are the creator of what you experience.

Sexuality is a grand thing! Let no one tell you that I avoided it when I was a man. After all, that's the whole point. I was, after all, a man. But I *sanctified* it to keep it holy. And sexuality can be experienced in its totality merely by looking into the eyes of another and setting yourself aside, and asking only to see the Face of Christ. For sexuality, the great longing within humanity, is to find some method, some way to transcend the *fear*, the *guilt*, the *deep contraction* which is ego, to find some way to slip through the cracks and experience some momentary bliss of the unity of Oneness.

But I say unto you, cultivate the Reality of your Oneness within yourself. And, indeed, you will find that all relationships, whether you be with a body, with a blade of grass, or with the wind that touches your skin, will feel like a sexual experience, as long as the body lasts. Let then, this energy *fill* you. Feel the *bliss* and the *pleasure* and the *joy* of sensuality and sexuality. See it happening all over the place on your planet because, without it, the planet wouldn't even exist.

Beloved friend, have you not ever watched little children who run naked through the fields and play with their genitals without the least bit of thought? They derive from it a moment of pleasure and occasionally, they may touch each other. There is no judgment in this. There is only innocence. And the adults look and go,

> *Oh, isn't that cute?*

And some of them go,

> *Oh! Oh my God! Charlie, please, cover that up! You can't do that!*

Hmm.

> *Mary, put your dress back down!*

Why? What is the adult afraid of, if not Life itself?

And make not of sexuality a specialness, but rather, cultivate within it the sanctified state of consciousness in which you are deliberately choosing to set aside yourself, to *let Christ love Christ.* Sexuality is a rather good thing, if you choose to use the power of your beingness to *sanctify* it, that it may be *holy.* For what is *holy* gives rise to *wholeness.* And what is fragmented through fear, through guilt, through neediness, through mere lust, what is thus fragmented leads to fragmentation within one's consciousness.

Bless sexuality. Let it become sanctified. And set aside all of those incarnations you held as a nun in monasteries, listening to false ideas out of someone else's fear of the body. It is only a communication device. What would you, therefore, choose to communicate through your experience of sexuality?

Be at peace, beloved friend, and while the body lasts my suggestion to you would be: Enjoy it!

Question: I understand healing as Jeshua speaks of it in *A Course in Miracles*, yet what needs to occur for bodily symptoms to no longer be in one's experience?

Answer: Beloved friend, as I have spoken of healing in that text which you know as *A Course in Miracles*, is, indeed, the fundamental definition of healing. By considering it, it must flush up within you all the deeply held hopes and prayers and beliefs and need to have healing be something that also manifests the perfection of the function of the body, according to your desire of what that perfection should be.

What is necessary, then, for the removal of physical symptoms? The miracle. But the miracle is not something which is under your control. Listen well to the message of this session, for I've indicated already to you, and *deliberately* indicated, the answer to your question and you will find it there. For, rest assured beloved friend, when there arises within the mind the hope or the wish that a physical symptom would leave the body, there must already be the enactment of an ancient belief that the body is what you are. And that, therefore, disease of some kind, as you would call it this, limits your ability to extend Love, to communicate with all of Creation, and to be at peace.

You may rest assured that when my many friends saw me with a crown of thorns upon my head, they thought,

> *Oh, poor Loved One,*

out of the belief that certainly spirituality must mean the power to overcome everything the mind has judged as a dis-ease.

The point that I'm seeking to reach with you is an attempt to dig deep within the depth of your psyche, to bring to the surface with you an ancient belief that true spirituality is recognized by all absence of disease, and that if you were truly whole, it would never arise within the body. Yet I say this unto you: What if every moment of your experience was literally being brought to you of the Father, Who alone knows the perfect plan for the healing of your mind?

Remember: *It is not possible to transcend what is not wholly loved.* Therefore, place the attention on deepening the *love of Self,* the exploration of the experience that has been called to the consciousness, through the form of dis-ease, of whatever kind. Learn to look upon it with the perfect innocence that you would look upon anything else. And see through it to see that it does not limit you in any way from being the unlimited presence of Love. It is not a weakness. And it is not to be compared to what may appear to be a diseaseless body. For the eyes of the body do not show what is within another's soul.

Beloved friend, there is a part of you that carries an ancient tear. Let it be released and healing will come.

Lesson Two

Now, we begin.

And indeed, greetings unto you, beloved and holy friends. Again, it is with great joy that I come forth to abide with you in this hour. Indeed, it is with great joy that we come forth to abide with you in this hour. For in Truth, I come not alone to join in communion with this, my beloved friend, in order to commune-i-cate with you through a medium that you understand, and that you accept.

For, it is a great Truth that I come often unto many. But often, because of what you have learned in your world, you have believed me to be but a figment of your imagination. And the voice that steals quietly through the space between your own thoughts, you would think to be but an illusion. Yet, I say, I come often unto many. And yet, when I come forth to abide with this, my beloved brother, to speak with you, I come not alone, for there is, in Truth, a host of friends that come to create a vortex, a circumference if you will, of energy. We have come even in this hour into this space, and we have set that tone. If you would well receive it, there are many friends, unseen by physical eyes, that are gently encircling those that have come forth to contribute, to support, to abide in the creation of this work. And what is this work, but to create a medium of communication?

Why is that important? Because always, in each and every moment of your experience, what, in Truth, is occurring is that you, as a soul, as a divine spark of consciousness, are deliberately choosing to create mediums of communication. You do it with the raiment that you place upon the body. You do it with your gestures, the sound of your voice. You do it with the very culture and time frame in which you incarnate. You are constantly and only creating mediums through which you communicate. And is communication anything but the attempt to rest in communion with Creation? That through you, what you are choosing to perceive, and believe, and accept as true will be radiated through your communication devices (which, of course, includes the body), that you might transfer your perceptions to another, that they might therefore know who you are and which Voice you are committed to.

I have said often that the body is a teaching and learning device, and all forms of communication affect the process of teaching and learning. When you arise in the morning, the first thought that makes a home in your mind, you will act on. You may stretch the body; you may smile; you may frown; you might be filled with peace, or you might feel the weight of the world. These things come, not because you have perceived them outside, but because you have allowed them inside the depth of your consciousness, that remains pure and undefiled and radiant beyond all boundaries forever. And as that thought makes a home in your mind, you literally begin to transform the communication device called the body into that which carries, expresses, and reflects what has come to make a home within your mind. Remember please, that the mind is not where the body is. It does not abide within the body, but the body does abide within the field of your mind.

Communication is creation. These two are one and the same. Therefore, if you would create well, ask only,

> *What am I committed to communicating? What will my creations express? What will my creations convey to others? For what I seek to convey reveals the Truth of my Self to the world.*

Therefore, indeed, beloved friends, as we begin this year to focus on, to refine, to deepen, to mature in what we have chosen to call *The Way of the Heart*, it is wise to begin at the beginning. And the beginning of this pathway is simply this: *You are as God has created you to be.* You are an *infinite focus of consciousness.* Your very sense of existence is nothing more than a feedback loop, or feedback mechanism, so that you can witness the effects of the choices you are making in the very deep, deep depth of your mind that rests right along the Mind of God.

Therefore, in each moment of your existence, which includes this bodily incarnation, you are literally allowing, through deliberate choice (though perhaps unconscious), to bring forth vibration of thought, vibration of creation, and to *commune-i-cate* it to the world in an attempt to experience *communion* with all of Life—with a friend, with a parent, with a child, with a beloved, with the clouds that pass through the sky, with the earth itself. Each gesture, each thought, the way that the body breathes, all of these things are going on constantly, and they are communicating, or revealing, the effect of what you have allowed to make a home in your mind.

Understand well, then, <u>The Way of the Heart requires that you allow yourself to rest into the simplicity of this Truth:</u>

✳ *I am Pure Spirit, undefiled and unaffected by anything or anyone. I am given full power to choose and, therefore, to create my experience as I would have it be.*

Not quite the "I" that is the egoic part of the mind, for that is just one of your creations that came along somewhere down the line. It is a very small part of the mind. We are speaking of the "I" of you that is Pure Spirit, that knows it exists, even though it does not know the time of its own creation.

You are Pure Spirit. Therefore to know,

✳ *I am only this, and in each moment, regardless of what I believe I see, regardless of the feelings that arise within my awareness, I, and I alone, am wholly one hundred percent responsible for them. No one has caused them, no great force in the universe has made this perception well up within my consciousness. I have selected it.*

Just as you would go to a grocery store and say "Well, what will I have for dinner?" And you own a perception, you lodge it in the mind, and then it expresses itself through the body, through the environment that you create around yourself, through the friends that you would call into your awareness. Every aspect of the life you live is the symbol of what you have chosen to experience and, therefore, to convey throughout Creation.

The Way of the Heart begins with the acceptance of the simple Truth that,

<u>*I am as God created me to be. Made in His image, I am a creator always.*</u>

What, then, would you ask your creations to communicate? Why do you make the choices you are making? You all know perfectly well that sometimes you seem to be compelled, and the mind wants you to believe—now we are speaking of the egoic part of the mind—the ego wants you to believe that you are compelled to certain actions, certain feelings, certain choices, certain perceptions, certain statements, by something that surely exists outside yourself. This is never true. In no circumstance is there anything of Creation that has the power to dictate to you the choice you will make.

Therefore, the pathway of awakening, *The Way of the Heart*, must begin with the decision to embrace the Truth that is true always,

> *I am a creator of all that I think and see and experience. I am free always. Nothing impinges upon me but the thoughts I have chosen to hold within. Nothing imprisons me but my own perception of imprisonment. Nothing limits me at any level or dimension of experience save that which I have chosen.*

The Way of the Heart, then, embraces all things, trusts all things and, eventually, transcends all things. But why? Because it begins by assuming complete and total *responsibility* for what is being *channeled* through it. And so you see, it is not just this, my beloved brother, who serves as a channel. That is, in Truth, all that you do, from the moment you arise until the moment you arise. For even during your sleep you are yet choosing that which flows through your consciousness.

The goal that we seek has never changed. It is, in Truth, a journey without distance. It is merely the return to where you are always, that you might begin anew to create deliberately, clearly, and with the perfect knowledge that if you are experiencing something, it is because you are the source of it—no other reason.

The Way of the Heart, then, is not a way of gaining power. *The Way of the Heart* is not a way in which you will finally be able to make the world be what you want it to be. But rather, *The Way of the Heart* is that pathway in which you learn to transcend and to dissolve from your consciousness every perception, every thought, that is out of alignment with what is true. The thought of death is out of alignment. The thought of fear is out of alignment. The thought of guilt is out of alignment. The thought of eternal Life is in alignment.

The thought of perfect fearlessness is in alignment. The thought of peace is in alignment. The realization of innocence is in alignment. The thought of joy and of forgiveness, these things are in alignment and reflect the Truth that is true always.

For, you see, although you are given complete free will to create as you choose to, the soul begins to learn that that which brings it the highest joy, that that which brings it the highest peace, that that which brings it the highest bliss imaginable, is that which flows *from* the Mind of God through the mind of the channel, the soul, and expresses itself in the field of experience. It is for this reason that your Father's Will is that you be happy. And your happiness is found in choosing to restore your perfect alignment with only the Voice for God.

The Way of the Heart, then, is that pathway that begins with a commitment to healing and awakening, and is founded on the premise, the axiom that we have given unto you, that you are perfectly free at all times. And everything that is experienced has been by your choice. And at no time has there been any other cause.

It seems simple, doesn't it?

Well, of course, okay. I'm creating my own experience.

And yet, what soul has not known a resistance to this idea? If you bake a cake and it turns out well, you will say, "I did that." But if you bake a cake and it turns out very bad,

It must have been the flour. It must have been the temperature of the oven. Surely there was something that caused this creation to not be what I would truly desire.

It takes great courage, great faith, to look upon all of your creations—your thoughts, your feelings, your manifestations—with Love, and with the innocence of a child. To plant a garden and to have all things wither and die, and yet to smile and say,

I planted this garden. I, and I alone, have done this. Well, I'll get a little hungry here, so I might as well go to the store.

Why is this important? Because the soul, a long time ago, began to create the perception that it was something *other* than it was created to be. And the *voice for ego* emerged within the garden of consciousness. And as the soul, as the deep mind that you have all known and, in fact, are—that deep mind began to identify with a voice that was other than the Voice for God. That voice has led you to believe that your creations determine your *worthiness*. Do you know that feeling?

And therefore, if what you create is not up to—what is this word, "snuff"?—hmm, is not up to snuff, that it means you, in the *core of your beingness*, are some kind of a failure. But I say unto you, in reality, *failure is not even remotely possible*. And why? If you plant a garden and the seed does not turn into the beautiful flower, it withers and dies, that experience is a creation, and you have done it. And because all events in space and time—everything you experience—because these things are *perfectly neutral*, there is, in reality, never failure.

The only failure occurs only within your own consciousness when you believe that it is not acceptable to receive and own and embrace your creation—with love and with innocence. To look upon it, to experience it, to recognize your perfect safety in doing so—from where you can decide whether to continue in that form of creation, or whether to think differently, to approach things differently. That is where the catch is—is that that part of the mind has begun to teach you a long, long time ago what to accept as acceptable creations and what not, what to take responsibility for, and what to deny responsibility for. And that *conflict* creates the illusion of *separation*. And when taken to its extreme, one discovers what you call your hospitals full of those in deep depression, paranoia, the feeling within the beingness, within the human mind, of feeling alienated and alone.

Helplessness, hopelessness, despair, anger, hatred—all of these are symptoms of a *fundamental delusion* that has occurred within the depth of the mind. It has occurred because there has been a long history of having *cultivated* the skill of listening to the *wrong voice*. The wrong voice is the voice of ego. It has taught you to judge, to pick, to select what you will be responsible for. The more you move into that consciousness, the harder it seems to ever hope for a chance of transcending the sense of separation, and conflict, and lack of peace.

For, how many of you have not known the feeling of resting your head upon the pillow at night and not being able to sleep because it's just not going the way you expected? The reason you cannot sleep is because you are in judgment of your creation. But it is *possible* to cultivate just the opposite, in which you learn to look with perfect innocence upon *all* things that arise in that field that is your experience—to look with innocence and what is called "wonder" at every feeling, from the place of curiosity, as you would look upon a cloud that passes through the sky. Look at it and marvel at it, its shape, its color, "Well where did that one come from? Hmm." And to embrace it, knowing that it does not affect the *purity* of the sky through which it temporarily floats by.

And each of your creations is exactly like this. It arises in the field of time and space, you experience it, and then it fades away. Every hurt that you have ever known is like a cloud that began to pass into the field of your awareness because you were *perceiving things* in a certain way. And if that hurt is still lodged within you, it is because you latched on to it. You followed the voice of ego, which caused you to believe that you are identified with that feeling, with that perception. And because that's you, if you let go of it, what's going to happen? You might disappear! You might die!

And the human mind, then, is that field within Creation, within Consciousness, that has learned to become so identified with perceptions, and experiences, and feelings that are not necessarily comfortable, it believes that if it lets go of them, it will die. And so, from our perspective, as we would look upon your energy fields, those of you who are still identified with this dimension, it looks as though you are gripping, causing to condense energy. And your knuckles are white, trying to hold on to limitation and guilt, to unworthiness and doubt.

You would, indeed, seek innocence and peace. You would seek abundance, and prosperity, and joy. But often, when you touch these things, it frightens you. And why? Because the Truth of the Kingdom requires openness, trust, expansiveness, spaciousness. It involves allowing, trusting, witnessing, letting things come and go, learning to cultivate a deep enjoyment of whatever arises, seeing that all things are just modifications of Consciousness Itself, and then letting them go when it's time for them to do so. And rest assured, there is no one, not a single soul, that has ever discovered something that was birthed in time that did not also *end* in time.

And how much of your suffering comes because you are clinging to a lifeless past and insisting that you carry it with you still? And you are doing that because, in that past, you became identified with the clouds that were passing by—claimed that as your own identity. And therefore, if you release it, it will mean that *you* must change, you must go on.

And creation, itself, that flows from the Mind of God is an *ongoingness*—forever! You will never cease to be! You will go on forever and forever and forever and forever and forever. You will go on forever exactly as you are now, or you can allow the Mind of God to flow through you, carrying you to an ever greater expansiveness, deepening your awareness of the infinite loveliness of the power of the Mind of God.

This year, then, we do, indeed, embark on *The Way of the Heart*. And though many clues have been given, we will come this year to refine those clues, to create what you might think of as a system or a pathway upon which you can walk—to *deliberately cultivate* the quality of awareness in consciousness necessary to *stabilize* that awareness, so that you can bring it to each and every moment of your experience.

Imagine, then, being able to experience whatever arises without losing the sense of spaciousness, and innocence, and ease that you now experience in fleeting moments. For instance, know you the experience when things are going well outside, around you, and you're singing a happy tune, and life seems to be moving ahead? Imagine that same quality of trust, and of faith, and of certainty of purpose, even when the buildings are crumbling around you, and the bank account has gone dry; being able to look at those events with the same sense of innocence and wonder with which you would look into the eyes of your beloved.

For, you see, such a quality of awareness is perfect mastery. Within it is discovered perfect peace and perfect freedom, perfect joy, and *uninterrupted communion* with all of Creation. And if you would well receive it, that quality of feeling intimately one with all of Creation is what you have been seeking as a soul since first the *identification* with a creation, called ego, began. For that creation, again, created conflict and separation. And everything you have ever attempted to do since has been an attempt to *overcome* separation, to gain back what you felt you had lost. It's just that the ways you have sought to do it don't work.

The eye of the needle that separates you in your consciousness from the world of conflict and fear and guilt and unworthiness—that world and the world of the Truth of the Kingdom lie side by side, within your own mind. And the eye of the needle that one must pass through is the recultivation of the innocence of a child. And it is for this reason that I often taught,

> *Become again as a little child, to enter the Kingdom.*

And the cultivation of *The Way of the Heart* is that pathway whereby you deliberately, consciously, choose to become again as an innocent child, as you were in the beginning, before you ever created, and then incarnated into, this dimension of experience that seems to be so permeated by a sense of conflict and separation.

So, it begins there. And I would ask you now to begin to put this into practice. So wherever you happen to be—whether you are viewing this with your eyes on what you would call your video, or whether you are listening to the words—stop for just a moment, and truly become aware of where you are. And where are you? Are you not having the experience of seemingly being within a body? Don't you seem to be abiding in a room somewhere? Aren't you within an environment in which there are certain weather patterns going on around you? Perhaps there are other sounds coming into your ears. Can you truly be aware of where you are *now*? Can you feel the weight of the body as you stand upon your feet or sit within your chairs? Do you notice the tension in the neck? Do you notice the racing of the mind if that's going on? Can you begin to bring awareness to exactly what is—from a place of innocence and non-judgment?

You have a saying in your world, "It is what it is." And *that* is the beginning of wisdom. You will, of course, discover that what is, is what you have chosen to make of it. Be, therefore, where you are now, and deliberately decide—*deliberately decide*—to accept wholly that what you are experiencing in this very moment has no cause whatsoever, except your choice to experience it. Rest assured, whatever the mind may try to say, if you did not wholly want to be right where you are, you wouldn't be there. And if you are in a body in the field of space and time, rest assured—you desired it, you chose it, and it's here.

Begin here. There is no need to judge it, no need to ask it to be different. Just truly be aware of what is. If you are feeling the body sitting in a chair, can you allow the thought to come into the mind,

> *I have literally created this experience. Something within me is so grand, so powerful, so vast, so beyond anything that scientists have ever come up with, that I have literally crystallized, in the field of experience, awareness of being a body in space and time! It has come forth from the Field of my Consciousness, the gift to me of God, Who asks only that I learn to create as God creates.*

I've said many times that the Father looks upon you and says,

> *This is My only creation and it is very good.*

For the Father *marvels* at what you are, knowing perfectly well that what you are emerged from out of *Her* Holy Mind.

Likewise look upon *your* creations and marvel. How is it that you could abide in this time frame on this planet? How could it be that you can place yourself behind the wheel of an automobile and actually get it from point A to point B? That is a mystery and a marvel, and no one knows how it's done! And yet it is done. The reason it's done is that all power has been given unto you and *what you decree is*. For a man or a woman shall decree a thing and *it shall be so*. You have decreed this moment. Own it! For by owning it, right now, you can begin to sense the *incredible* and *awesome* power that flows through you in each moment. It is the *power* to create!

So, begin there, by choosing each day, *now*, to cultivate the practice in this manner. <u>Set the intention so that in each hour of your day, for three to five minutes, you practice bringing this quality of awareness to exactly whatever you are experiencing,</u> when the thought arises to do the practice. You see, where does that thought come from? Imagine you're going through the day and you've been hustling and bustling about. You've gone to your office or your work. You've talked to friends. You've bought groceries. You've done all of these things, and suddenly the thought appears,

✱   *Oh! Focus on being aware that I am literally the creator of what I experience.*

Do you think it just happened by accident? No! The thought is penetrating what you call your conscious awareness from the *depth* of your *mind* that rests right next to the Mind of God.

Therefore, the power to generate that very thought is the effect of God's Will entering into your field of being and penetrating the veils of distraction and shining forth as the thought [snaps fingers],

    Oh! That's right, five minutes every hour.

Can you feel the *awesomeness* of that? For you are linked to the Mind of God, and God *knows* how to bring you back to complete freedom, and perfect peace, and mastery of this entire realm.

PRACTICE

Therefore, those who truly love God, those that would truly awaken, will feel something compelling them to master this simple practice for five minutes of each hour. They will learn to delight and they will look forward to it. And pretty soon those five minutes will stretch into six, and then ten, and fifteen, and fifty, until finally, there is established in their awareness—like a background, if you will—the awareness that everything that arises, they have decreed it, and so it is so. Five minutes every hour is not much to ask. For five minutes every hour, be you, therefore, as you are created to be—a creator, decreeing that which brings forth experience. And never again allow yourself to tell yourself,

> *Well I'm really here because I have to be. I'm really just doing this because, well, you know, it's what I have to do.*

Take the words "ought" and "should" and "must" and "have to"—write them on a piece of paper. Look at them. And then light a match, and light the corner of the paper, and let the paper burn and dissolve to dust. For it is a symbol of allowing the energy you've given those words to become again as the dust or the ash of the ground. Clear from your consciousness all identification with such words. For all of them are *denials* of reality.

Many times I have shared with you that you *need* do nothing. Listen to those words, and take them into yourself as though they are your own voice, because they are.

> *I need do nothing.*

You don't have to survive. Whoever told you you had to? You don't have to make everybody happy. Whoever told you you *had* to? Whoever told you that you *could* make anybody happy? You don't have to abide as a body in space and time. Whoever told you you *had* to? You don't have to pay your bills.

> *How irresponsible.*

Who told you that? You literally *need* do nothing.

It's quite different than *wanting* or *choosing* to do something. You don't need to love your parents, you don't need to honor your father and your mother. You don't need to worship me or love me. You don't need to love yourself. You literally *need* do nothing, for "need" is an expression of the perception that there is something you lack. And because you are One with God, there is never a moment when you lack anything at all.

> *I need do nothing.*

Can you allow the thought to emerge in the mind when you arise in the morning,

I don't have to get out of this bed. I don't have to go to an office. I don't need to fulfill that order. I don't need to say, "Good morning," to my mate. I literally need do nothing.

For how can there be the power of *freedom* to choose and to create when you are being governed by the belief of the world that you must be a certain way? That you *need* to be acceptable to others. That you *need* to conform and fit in. That you *need* to dress the way others dress. That you need to be committed to surviving an extra day upon this plane. There can be no freedom where there is need.

So, those are the first two axioms of *The Way of the Heart*—to be built on, to be remembered, to be cultivated daily:

AXIOMS

I am created as my Father created me to be. I am free. And nothing sources my experience but me, in each moment. Nothing has an effect upon me, whatsoever, save that which I choose to allow to affect me.

I need do nothing.   ← Everything built on these

PRACTICE

Again we would ask you, at least twice in each of your days—and in the beginning we would suggest here that, in the morning and in the evening, as you are arising and as you are retiring—to cultivate for five minutes the repetition of that thought so that you feel it in your bones.

I need do nothing.

It will come as quite a shock to your consciousness, and the mind will say,

But I have all these things I have to . . . Oh! What about this and what about that? Oh, my goodness! Well, will the world stop spinning if I stop needing?

That's up to the world, not up to you.

I need do nothing.

The power of these first two axioms will be what everything that follows is built on, and yet everything that follows is merely a way of watering those two axioms and making them the anchor of your awareness. For when the anchor is firmly in place, you will literally create whatever you so desire, from perfect freedom, from perfect deliberateness. You will even transcend miracle-mindedness. For miracles, you see . . . as you begin to open to miracle-mindedness, you marvel,

> *Wow! That was a miracle—how great!*

Miracle-mindedness is still a stage of perception just short of mastery. For mastery comes when you know that you are literally and deliberately creating. And there is nothing miraculous about it. You will decree a thing and it shall be so!

That is to create as God creates. For while He marvels at you, He knows perfectly well that your creation was not a miracle. It was very deliberate, born from the Pure Radiance of Love. God does not sit on His throne and say,

> *I wonder if I'm worthy to create My Children? I wonder if I'm worthy to express Myself through the Divine Spark of Consciousness that they are?*

Never does it enter into the Holy Mind of God,

> *I wonder if it's okay if I create a solar system?*

God receives a thought, or a thought emanates within His Holy Mind, He decrees it, and it is so! And He looks upon all things and says,

> *It is very good!*

The third and last exercise that we would give you in this hour is this: Choose something that you do every day, that you are convinced is so utterly ordinary that it certainly doesn't hold any power or any spiritual meaning whatsoever. It could be something as simple as having a glass of water, brushing your teeth, yawning. Pick something that you know you do every day and decide to make that the focus of your worship, so that when you do it, you stop and you go,

> *'Tis very good.*

Even if it's something as simple as raising your head from the pillow. Become aware of it, own it as self-created, and then say, within yourself, as you contemplate that action,

> *It is very good. I have done this, and it is good. I have created.*

And again, those that are truly committed will find that they begin to enjoy that process, and they begin to apply it more and more to other events in their lives. They begin to reawaken the childlike *joy* of building a castle in the sandbox. For in Truth, that's all you're doing here. Consciousness is your sandbox and you are creating castles. You've simply forgotten to enjoy them. And when you want to be rid of them, you now lament,

> *Oh, but if I give this up and change my mind and move on, what will happen to my creations? What will others think of me if I act like a child and just take my little plastic shovel and knock the castle down and go in and have a sandwich for lunch?*

> *What will people think of me? Will I fit in? Will I be accepted? Will I be judged? Will I be persecuted?*

Who cares? For the opinions of others *mean nothing*, unless, of course, you want them to mean something.

And now we come to what concludes this hour. *What blocks you in your mind?* For, even as you're listening to this, many of you are recognizing a resistance. That resistance is the energy of fear:

> *What will happen if I follow this path?*

That part of your mind, called the ego, will rise up to tell you that if you listen to the "crazy one" (that some have called the Savior of the world), it will take you to a path of destruction. That's because the voice of ego knows that it will be destroyed if this path is followed. *You* cannot be destroyed—the reality of who you are.

That resistance, then, is fear. And fear is one of the energies out of alignment with the Truth of the Kingdom. Therefore, indeed, fear not, but continue in faith. For I say unto you, what you will discover at the end of this pathway is the perfect *freedom*, the perfect *power*, the perfect *spaciousness*, the perfect *joy*, the perfect *peace* of living—literally—in the Kingdom of Heaven.

So, the choice is yours. And for those of you that will feel this resistance come up so strongly, for those of you that will yet call out unto me in your dreams and your prayers, "Help me through this," I say unto you that you walk not alone. For I cannot be further from you than the width of a thought. And yes, you are the creator of that thought.

I would share with you that I, too, embarked upon just such a path. And each, what you might call axiom, that I will share with you and refine for you—many of the exercises that we would give unto you in this coming year—are specifically exercises and truths that were given unto me from the time I was initiated by certain Essene teachers in *The Way of the Heart*.

And when my teachers said, "It is time for you to go spend forty days and forty nights in the desert," do you not believe that resistance came up within me, too? . . . That I, too, had to notice that I was creating a thought of fear and separating myself from the great protection and Love of God? . . . That I had to physically move the body into the wilderness to move through my own rings of fear, to discover what was on the other side?

The pathway, then, that I have walked is the pathway that you are walking. And if our pathway is the same, then we walk *together*—*to God*—and away from illusion, and pain, and weakness, and unworthiness, and guilt, and death.

So, engage in your exercises with great zeal, with great joy, and, above all, with great outrageous playfulness! Learn to look with *innocence* upon all that arises. And if you put these little exercises to work, much, indeed, *will* arise. Practice, then, well. And practice with joy. Know that you are loved, loving, and lovable, and that, in Truth, the only thing that's occurring is that an old dream is being released, that a new dream might replace it—the dream of worthiness, and of peace, and of wakefulness, and of union with all of Creation.

And during this coming year, again, there will be others who will have specific guidance to give to you through this, my beloved brother. For again, I say, I come not alone in this specific work, but I come with many who support your healing and your awakening.

Therefore, indeed, be at peace this day, beloved friends.

Abide . . . lovingly . . . with your creations.

Amen.

Lesson Two
Question and Answer Section

Question: What did you experience when you went to the desert for forty days and forty nights? And what was the purpose of doing a fast?

Answer: Beloved friend, first, the purpose of the fasting was two-fold. The body is, indeed, a communication device. It receives and transmits what you might think of as signals. And we would emphasize here, for your benefit, that the body *receives* signals as well as it *transmits* them from your mind.

As you go through your normal day, you are abiding in a certain *vibrational field.* That vibrational field requires that you, within some boundary, live in such a way that you can effectively *communicate* and *relate* within that vibrational field. Therefore, the body learns to adapt to where you are placing it, and what you have decided to use the body for. When the soul is desirous of shifting vibrational frequencies, so that it might receive new signals, it is very valuable to *prepare* the body by shifting it out of its normal patterns.

For instance, each time that you eat a certain food, and you eat it daily, daily, daily, daily, month and year on end, the body adapts to that vibrational frequency. It learns how to receive the energy of that substance, to conform to that substance, to abide with that substance, and then utilize the energy of that substance. When you shift away from that substance, there is a *space* that is created. There is a time frame, if you will, in which the body now is no longer receiving the signals that substance brings. And it creates, shall we say, a pause. The very *intelligence* in the cellular structure of the body pauses. And as it pauses, you can begin to send new signals to the cells to be *open,* to be *receptive,* to attune themselves to *new frequencies* which can then be received.

Therefore, it is a very common practice amongst spiritual paths, that when the soul is desirous of deepening its sense of self-awareness, deepening its connection with God, however you wish to view this, that which is called fasting has always been known to help facilitate such a shift, because it puts the body at rest. It takes it out of its normal range of vibrational experience so that it can be open, it can become *attuned to new frequencies*. So the fasting has that purpose, by way of preparation.

But secondly, this also affects the nature of the mind itself, the thinking mind that is linked to the body and to the vibrational field of physicality. Through the process of fasting, the *mind* also slows down. It becomes more *open*. Spaciousness is created within it. And why is that valuable? Because the soul wants to begin sending new signals down through the levels or depths of Mind, through the thinking mind, down into the cells of the body. It's seeking to recreate its perceptions, its structure that your lower self, your egoic mind, the mind that carries you through the day, has been operating from. It's seeking to change this. So fasting is not just a matter of the body, alone. It affects the thinking mechanism of the brain, as well, allowing new electrical signals to pulse through the brain and down through the body. And likewise, it creates a spaciousness so that new frequencies can be received.

It is not unlike living in a house in which you have a certain music playing at a certain volume all of the time, and then, suddenly, decide that perhaps you would like to hear the sound of the birds outside the window. So you reach over to the dial (do you not?) and you turn the volume of the music down. You change the *field* in which you are having experience. And then as the volume decreases, you begin to hear the background—it has always been there—of the singing birds outside the window. And your attention begins to turn from the vibrational field of the music you've been listening to, to the vibrational field of the song of the bird. New images come, new thoughts come, new feelings come through the body.

So fasting serves that purpose. At a deeper level, view fasting as a *deliberate decision* that really has nothing to do—levels of meaning—with just food. It is the decision to *interrupt* patterns that have become habitual. So you fast from sound, you fast from negative thinking. You fast from being busy. You fast from going to bed at the same time every day. You fast from arising at the same time every day, for a day, for two days, for a week, for a month, for forty days and forty nights.

You totally change certain patterns. And just as the effect of releasing the body from habitual use of a certain substance creates a space in which something new can take place, fasting from the simple time frame that you're used to arising in the morning, will create a *spaciousness* in the mind. And you'll become aware of things that you didn't know were going on. You'll receive signals that you hadn't received before.

When I first came to this, my beloved brother, in order to begin to recultivate our communication ability, I often came to him, and then, later, suggested to him, that he take up the practice of arising at 3 o'clock in the morning. That was not his customary time. And yet, by so doing, he *fasted* from his normal habit, which *heightened* his sense of awareness and created, or cultivated, the ability within the brain structure and within the nervous system, to become *attuned* to the *rarefied frequencies* that are always there, but are often drowned out, because you're still asleep. And the rest of the world around you has not yet awakened to fill the vibrational field with all the noise of millions of minds actively running about.

So that is the deeper meaning of *fasting*. It is *doing things in a new way, fasting from old habits, which heightens your sense of awareness, your vigilance to what is present.* Fasting is something that is extremely valuable and should be done by everyone, from time to time. We speak here not just of an occasional fasting of the body, but to begin to look at all of the habits you have, even the ones that are positive. If you go into your meditation room at the same time every day, the body and the mind begins to anticipate what *ought* to happen through learned experience. So go at a different time. If you are used to certain prayers, use different ones, from time to time. If you are used to abiding with certain friends on a regular basis, shift from time to time. If you are used to talking a lot, spend a day in silence.

Begin, then, to look at the habits you have cultivated that are almost continual—so much so that you never think about them. And then, set aside a time deliberately to fast from that habit. If one has the habit of reading the Sunday paper, go for a month in which no paper is read, and observe how this creates space for you to begin to not only perceive things differently, but to receive different impulses.

You'll find new thoughts will come about how to utilize that time differently. Fasting is an art, and one well worth cultivating within yourself.

Now, what did I experience in the desert for forty days and forty nights? Fear, cold, heat, boredom, mental busyness, hunger, joy, ecstasy, delight, freedom, out-of-body experiences, clairvoyance, clairaudience, visitation by angels, visitation by creatures that should have struck fear in me. You would call them snakes, spiders. Hmm.

Beloved friends, such a journey puts you in a position where you can no longer be distracted from all of the "stuff" that is going on in your daily consciousness. It is a time of *purification* . . . purification by having no opportunity to *escape* from truly observing everything that is going on within the field of one's consciousness. There arose within me thoughts of hating God. There arose thoughts within me of deciding to serve Satan instead of God. There arose thoughts within me of wanting to abandon my roots and become a very wealthy merchant surrounded by, what you call, the "dancing ladies" . . . hmm? If you can imagine any thought, positive or negative, rest assured that within that forty-day period, some symbol of that thought also arose within me to be experienced—even cellularly in the body. Self-doubt arose, anger arose. It all arose. The whole field of human consciousness arose within me within those forty days and forty nights.

So that whole time period was a fast. And that was the purpose of removing myself from all communication with anyone, from all comforts that I had become accustomed to. There was only me with myself. And by abiding with myself, I learned that I was never alone. The negative things, as you might describe them, tended to come up after about the fifth day and through approximately the twentieth day. Then it began to shift as I began to notice that I could dis-identify with those things. I didn't have to judge them. I could notice being cold and just accept it.

> *The body's cold. So what?*
> *The body's hungry. So what?*
> *I'm desirous of seeing my friends and dancing and singing. So what?*

I observed things arise. And finally, it was like they knew they had no place to make a home in my mind. And so, they subsided.

And just as when you physically fast, finally the body is empty. And the cellular structures of the body can begin to repair and heal at a deeper level. The nervous system can rest deeply. Likewise, my mind began to rest. And a *spaciousness* was created. And during the twentieth to about the twenty-fifth day, I could feel a transition occurring, as my consciousness began to let go of the world I had known. And everything and everyone became as a distant memory.

And more and more, I noticed that a Light was being birthed or turned on within me. A spaciousness was being created. And out of that spaciousness, I began to tap into levels of consciousness that I had, in fact, experienced before. But now, I had time to really cultivate being with those frequencies in which I could receive communication from other teachers in nonphysical realms.

I began to feel the great Love of God as I'd never felt it before. It came, not just as a thought or an inspiration or a fleeting feeling, but it came to seep down, if you will—and here I speak metaphorically—but a seeping down through my Mind and through the cells of the body and through the nervous system of the body. It came to be grounded, if you will, throughout my whole being. The deep peace, the perfect trust, the recognition that I was not alone, that I had everything I ever needed, because I was One with God.

So there were many states of bliss and of ecstasy, many states of transcending identification with the body and suddenly being transported to other realms and other worlds. Pictures of the rest of my life's path began to emerge, as though coming up out of the soil of the busyness of my mind and all the things—just like you—that I had to do just to take care of daily affairs. None of it was there to disturb me. And the *deeper* purpose began to reveal itself.

And I heard the Voice of my Father speak to me on what you would know as about the thirty-seventh day. And the Voice came clearly from around me and within me, saying unto me,

You are My Beloved Son in whom I am well pleased.

And suddenly, I realized the Truth that is true always:

> *God loves me.*
> *I need do nothing.*
> *I am as my Father created me to be.*

And the opinions of the world dissolved out of my field of awareness, my energy field, if you will. And I began to be fully stabilized in what you might call an *enlightened state of mind.* I no longer identified myself as the son of Joseph. I identified myself as the Son of God.

So that is a synopsis of what I experienced during my pilgrimage and my fasting. The forty days and forty nights, by the way, was a *numerological representation* that was very important in the schools of thought in which I was reared. It represented a time of birthing, experience, and disillusion. It's like a cycle—forty days and forty nights—to be taken more metaphorically than literally. And when I returned, all things had been made new and different. Jeshua ben Joseph had, indeed, journeyed to the desert, but the *Son of God* is who returned. Therefore, beloved friend, occasionally, give yourself permission to fast from the habits you have created.

Question: Please comment on Mary and the messages that are being published recently as coming from her.

Answer: Indeed, beloved friend, do you have volumes for me to fill? Do you have hours to listen to me speak? For in Truth, I could utilize the whole of time to speak with Love of the One that was known as my mother, who remains always an intimate part of myself. For we remain, of course, in perfect communication.

This One, as a soul, chose to allow, to agree to enter into, the drama of my own incarnation into the world. This One was therefore put into a position to bring up within Her everything unlike Love, to look at the very habits of being a mother and to transcend those habits, in order to serve a bigger picture. That incarnation was the one in which She perfected Her own awakening, Her own commitment to what is far beyond each individual's consciousness. That One lives even as I live. And That One has never ceased to follow *The Way of the Heart*—that Way which is perfected when the consciousness knows,

> *I live, yet not I, but That which is the Creation of my Father: The Christed Consciousness, alone, lives through me.*

She is extremely active in what you call your current time frame. She is speaking unto *many*. The appearances that have been recorded by what you call the grand authority of the Church, these appearances are not anyone's imagination. And they will, indeed, *increase*. The messages She is giving, we should say those to whom She is seeking to communicate, require that Her message be given in such a way that is somewhat different than the way in which I'm formulating the message that I'm giving to you through this channel. And why? Because the wise teacher learns the language of the student, the temperament, the space of consciousness in which they are, and then speaks in terms that can be understood.

And so, She speaks of Earth changes. She speaks of the Love of God. She speaks a language to many that you may not prefer, but others do. And yet, there is an art and a skill and a purpose. And Her *entire purpose* is the same as mine: to cultivate within anyone who will listen the realigning of their perceptions so that they can heal their sense of separation from God and return to the Truth of Love, and worthiness, and power, and Grace. To *awaken*, in other words.

There are many who claim to channel Her who do not. And if you pay attention to the vibration you feel, in the books you might read or the tapes you may listen to or what have you, you'll always know Her presence because there will be a *softness*, there will be a *gentleness*, there will be a quality of *perfect mothering*, if you will, in which you feel like you just want to lay your head upon Her breast and dissolve away into the bliss of Love.

Those that are not communicating Her, but would love you to believe they are, you'll always detect some kind of constriction, some sense of egoic energy, some sense of fear over the future:

> *You better do this.*
> *This is going to happen.*
> *There's no way to get around it.*

Those kinds of statements do not come from Her at all.

And, indeed, as I did then, This One I love deeply, and look upon as a radiant example of what consciousness can be.

Lesson Three

Now, we begin.

And, indeed, greetings unto you, beloved and holy friends. If I speak in the language of your world, I cannot find those words that can convey to you the Love which I feel for you. I cannot find the words that can convey unto you the Love I feel, that God has for all of us. If I search the languages of your world, I cannot find a concept, a word, an idea, a philosophy, a dogma that can contain, in Truth, the Mystery that is closer to you than your own breath and awaits your discovery.

If I search throughout all of creation, if I search through the many mansions that exist within the domains of my Father's Creation—and that Creation is infinite—try as I might, I cannot discover anything that can truly describe *you*. I cannot find that which is of greater value than you. In Truth, I cannot discover anything that speaks more eloquently of the Love that God is, than *your very existence*. Therefore, in Truth, I look upon you constantly, and marvel at the Radiance of my Father's Love.

It is, then, through *you* that I come to discover all that God is. And as a man, when I walked upon your plane, I began to realize that the greatest gift that I could ever receive would only come to me as I chose to *surrender* every *perception* that I might conjure up about you, my brother or sister, that would *veil* the Truth that is true about you always.

When I was of nine years of age, I began to awaken to exactly what I am describing to you. And as my father would take me to sit with the elders, and as he would read from the Torah to me, I began to be compelled by something within. Something began to speak to me, that underneath all of the perceptions that I could create of another, there was something Radiant and Shimmering waiting to be discovered. I began to feel very different from my peers. I began to be preoccupied with inner things. And when I listened to the elders speak, I would often feel as though I had drifted far away from where they were. And pictures would come to me, and thoughts would come to me, and feelings would come to me that I didn't understand,

59

that I hadn't assimilated into my being.

But something began to compel me. How might I discover how to see only that Shimmering Radiance? Would it be possible for me to see my brothers and sisters as my Father sees His Children? And, in Truth, I discovered that the way to see with the Eyes of Christ begins with the acceptance that *I*, as a creator, created in the image of God, indeed, literally choose every experience, and call it to me; that *I* create the veils through which I view Creation.

And I began to shift gears slightly. I began, even, to be seen as someone who was rebelling against the teachings of my Essene elders. For I began to move away from *striving* for God, from *striving* for perfection, and began to cultivate within myself the process of *allowing*. I discovered that if I looked upon my perceptions, my feelings, my behavior, exactly as they were, without overshadowing them with my own interpretations—if I could teach myself to embrace things with innocence—veils began to be dissolved from my mind. For when I was nine years old, I had already learned to be *fearful* of thinking, or speaking, or acting, in a way that was not in conformity to the prevailing wisdom of that time, even within the Essene community, which had already become rather rigidified. There was already much dogma. And dogma always leads to bickering.

I began to discover that if I looked with innocence upon all things, a Light began to shine through the things I was looking at. And as I rested more and more in this innocence, more and more, the Light would shine.

And as I grew in age, I began to discover that the old teachers who spoke of the need to "Forgive seventy times seven," knew something quite profound that had even become lost within the tradition, the Jewish and Essene traditions, of my day. For, you see, to *forgive* means "to choose to release another from the perceptions that you've been projecting upon them." It is, therefore, an act of forgiving *one's self* of one's projections. And as we begin to forgive, even unto seventy times seven times, each time you forgive you take yourself deeper into the purity of your own consciousness. You begin to see how *profoundly* you have been coloring, and therefore affecting, relationships, through the simple act of not being aware of of projection.

✳

Therefore, I learned—and learned well—that *forgiveness is an essential key to healing.* The opposite of forgiveness is judgment, and judgment *always* creates separation and guilt. Judgment will evoke a sense of guilt in the one who has been judged, unless, of course, they are perfectly awake. But more than this, each time that you judge anything or anyone, you have literally elicited guilt within *yourself,* because there is a place within you, yet still, that knows the perfect purity of your brother and sister, and sees quite clearly that *all things within the human realm are either the extension of Love, or a cry for help and healing.*

Therefore, beloved friend, when you judge, you have moved out of *alignment* with what is true. You have decreed that the innocent are not innocent. And if you would judge another as being without innocence, you have already declared that this is true about you. Therefore, to practice forgiveness actually cultivates the quality of consciousness in which, finally, you come to *forgive yourself.* And it is, indeed, the forgiven who remember their God.

And so, therefore, in this hour, beloved friends, we would wish to share with you the *power of forgiveness*—how to cultivate it, how to refine it, how to understand the depths of it that can be revealed to you as you forgive seventy times seven times, how to bring up within you that which has not yet been forgiven, but perhaps forgotten. We would speak also, in this hour, of what *perception* is, and what *projection* is.

Beloved friends, these things are of *critical* importance. For anyone who enters into a so-called "spiritual path" must eventually face and deal with their deep need for forgiveness, which is an expression of the soul's deep desire to be forgiven. For there is no one who walks this plane who has not been touched by the *poison of judgment.*

Beloved friends, as we speak of these things, though, let not seriousness enter the mind. For in Truth, all we are really doing is describing for you what you need to do, and can do, in order to release the burden of illusion that seems to cause you to feel a heaviness upon your countenance, a sense of a lack of safety in the world. You could think of it as taking your rheostat and turning it up a bit by *enlightening* you, taking your burden of guilt and judgment from you.

Therefore, in Truth, understand well: *forgiveness is essential.* And what has not been forgiven others, has not been forgiven you—not by a God that sits outside of you, for the Father never judges. What you have not forgiven in another or in the world is but a reflection of what you carry *within* as a burden that you cannot forgive of *yourself.*

You have an interesting saying in your world,

> *It takes one to know one.*

Do you think you would even be able to judge another if there wasn't something within you being elicited that triggers within you the belief that you know exactly what that other one is up to? And that's why you judge them. And sometimes, you judge harshly because you *fear* that energy in yourself, or you remember how hurtful you have been when you have acted from that energy.

But when you have forgiven yourself, rest assured, you will know what it means to walk *in* this world yet be not *of* this world. You will be able to feel the energy or the activities that any other soul may freely choose. And you will discern that energy, you will understand that energy, you will see through it, and still see the Face of Christ before you. You will not *react*, which literally means "to act again, as you did in the past." Instead, even if you are being persecuted (or to speak from personal experience, to be nailed upon a cross), you will have cultivated the ability to love.

And in all situations, no matter what another is doing, your first response will be to enter into the quiet stillness within, and merely ask the Holy Spirit,

> *What would you have me say? What is most appropriate for this other soul in this moment?*

For when forgiveness has purified the mind and the heart and the emotional field of your own beingness, you will discover that you exist only to extend Love.

You are the Savior of the world. And in each situation, your role is to ask the Holy Spirit how you can serve the Atonement, the correction, the healing, that yet needs to be acquired within another soul. So even if one is hating you, you will not respond with defensiveness but with curiosity, with innocent witnessing. And even if your hands have nails going through them, I tell you truthfully, it is possible to still enter the quiet sanctuary of the Heart and to ask of the Holy Spirit,

> *What would you have me say or do that can serve the healing of my brother or sister's heart?*

So, that is where we're going. And all that we will be sharing with you, not just in this hour, but in this year, has as its final goal your complete *Christed Consciousness*, the fulfillment of what your own soul desires: *forgiveness.*

There is, first, nothing you can be aware of in the energy of another that you have not known in yourself. There is nothing another can say or do, or even imagine themselves capable of saying or doing, that you have not also known. Again, it takes one to know one. And when you perceive another acting out of hostility, or fear, or what have you, the only way you can recognize it is because *you have been there.*

The very fact that, in your world, one can murder another's body, and you can react with a knowledge that that is inappropriate behavior, is because, as a soul, you know the energies involved in the attempt to murder another. And, in Truth, if you're honest with yourselves, you can probably come up with at least fifty times in the last year that murderous thoughts have entered your mind. You may not act on them, you may not even dwell on them for more than a split second, but the energy has come into the field of your awareness, and you have known it and recognized it. Who, then, is less than you? Who, then, is worthy of your judgment? No one. Who, then, is equal to you? Everyone. And who, then, is worthy of your love? Everyone.

Forgiveness is the bridge that links you to the soul, the essence of your brother or sister. Forgiveness is that bridge, that when cultivated, will allow you to see clearly not just the energies that another is expressing, but you will literally be able to see what events seemed to cultivate that soul's belief that they must act in that way to survive, to live—what perceptions have led them to feel justified in their inappropriate behaviors. You will see it as clearly as though someone had drawn a picture in front of you. And then you will see skillfully what to say, and what to do to gently help another correct their misperceptions of themselves and learn the path of self-forgiveness. And when that hour comes, rest assured, you will walk in this world, yet you will not be in it. You will be as I became. You will be the Savior of the world.

What is *projection*? Projection occurs when there has first been denial within yourself. Projection is an act in which you psychically try to throw out of your ownership everything that you have judged as being despicable or unworthy of you, something you don't want. And so you will *project* it. You will throw it up and out, and let it land on whomever happens to be near by. Projection is the *effect* of the denial of the first axiom that we have given you. It is the denial of the Truth that nothing you experience has been caused by anything outside of you. Projection then, is the attempt to *insist* that reality is other than the way God made it. That you are not powerful, that you are a victim of circumstances, that you're in a world that can actually do things to you and make you—cause you to make—decisions that you wouldn't have made otherwise. That is always denial. And it is a lie.

Projection is the denial of the first axiom of Truth. And you've mastered it well. When you project onto another, you will then believe that your anger, your hatred is justified. Rest assured, there are many in your legal system . . . in fact, the legal system means merely to take the act of projection and the need to judge and to make it okay socially, so that you need not be concerned with this other as your brother or as your sister, who has been crying out for help. But rather you become justified in punishment. And yet, punishment, itself, is only the insane attempt to convince the punisher that the darkness, the evil—whatever you want to call it—is not in them, it's *out there.*

Imagine, then, a society in which the prevalent legal view is simply that your brother or your sister is an aspect of yourself. And if you would help yourself, you must help them—to meet each cry for help and healing with forgiveness, love, and support. Can you imagine, for a moment, what it would be like to live in such a society? How would it be different than the world you see?

And yet, if you would have these things be different, it must begin with *you*. For the way to heal the world is not by seeking to change what is on the *outside*, but by first changing what is on the *inside*. For when *that* change has occurred, you will become a conduit for an energy that knows how to use your gifts, to place you in just the right situations. And a great Power will work effectively through you—the Power, alone, Which knows how to heal your world. There are many, indeed, that would love to march for peace by angrily attacking those who make war. But if you would create peace in the world, you must be at peace within yourself.

So, projection is an act of trying to get rid of what you don't want to own within. It is the *effect* of the denial of Truth. Projection colors your brother or sister with the very energies that you would judge within yourself. How, then, to begin to break the pattern of projection? How, then, to allow the bridge of forgiveness to be built? It is actually quite simple, but it *will* require your *commitment*.

I have said to you many times, that the world you see is nothing more than the effect of the thoughts you have held within the mind. Therefore, awakening requires the act of *vigilance* and *discipline*—the discipline to cultivate a way of living in which you observe your own thoughts, in which you listen to the words that are coming out of your mouth, in which you observe the feelings that are evoked within your body, the reactivity that seems to own you, and to see these things as *innocent* and simply *self-caused*.

When next, then, something is reflected to you by the world that causes you to become angry, causes you to be in judgment, stop right where you are, and look, not with judgment of your judgment, but with innocence and honesty:

Oh, I see that I am judging someone. That's an interesting cloud passing through the sky of my awareness. I wonder if I might be able to make another choice?

Now, the mind will tell you,

But this person just broke into my house and stole my stereo. Of course I have a right to be in judgment! I have a right to feel angry.

But I say unto you, anger is never justified. It doesn't mean you won't experience it, but stop fooling yourself into believing that there is some validity to it. What if that one who has just broken into your home and taken your stereo equipment, or what-have-you (some other idol that you love .... hmm), what if you understood that you had the power in that moment to remember that all events are neutral? They merely provide you with a chance to choose Love.

What if you literally chose the "insane" way, according to the world, of looking upon that one, who has just done that act, as a brother or sister who is crying out for help and healing, who does not know how to live in this world without being of the world, who does not know the way to self-forgiveness, that does not know the Truth of the Light that lives within them, that does not recognize their great power to create whatever they want in a way that is not hurtful to anyone—to look upon them with compassion rather than reactivity?

It begins in simple ways. And to set the stage, I want you to very much remember that time has been given to you that you might use it *constructively*. That means when you awaken in the morning, realize that you are in school. You don't have to drive anywhere, you're already there. And that the universe is literally helping to assist you into having experiences that will bring things up for you, so that you can choose to look at them differently—thereby discovering the great power within you, the freedom within you, to choose what you want to perceive, to elicit only what you want to feel. So again, that even if nails are being driven through the hands, you finally are liberated in the power to choose Love, and, therefore, to overcome this world.

Having said this, understand then, that each of your days is a blessing and a gift, *if* you use it from the full commitment to awakening. Your day is chock full of a million opportunities to discover a deeper Truth. Therefore, never feel that the purpose of your life must be something other than what you're involved in. For remember what we spoke of earlier: You are literally creating everything you choose, and nothing is forced upon you.

And now we're going to take that thought just a little deeper for a moment, because it literally means that if you have decided you want to awaken, it means you have already called to yourself every experience that can truly best serve your awakening. And the friends and the family, the people you have relationships with, are those who likewise can best gain from the experiences elicited through your relationships. It means that right here, and right now, you're already demonstrating the power that you're seeking—the power to truly choose to awaken, and to command the whole of Creation to serve you in that awakening.

Therefore, when you awaken in each of your mornings, look around. Who's that person sleeping next to you? They are your perfect companion. They are a messenger of God. And just behind all of that, you see, because your mind is resting right next to the Mind of God, when you first said it as a soul, "I want to awaken, I want to go home," the Father answered your prayer and began to send the thought through your spirit and through your soul to your conscious mind,

> *I know how to direct you home. Give up this career and start that one. Move from this location to that location.*

And you began to feel all manner of impulses. You began to read different books. You began to do different things. You met someone and fell in love. All by accident? Hardly!

So, the very thought that you would claim as your own, from which you have created the world of your own personal experience, is also, literally, the *result* of your prayer to awaken. And the Father is creating—assisting you to create—just those experiences as stepping stones that carry you from where you are to where God is. The result is that your ordinary daily life is the most perfect ashram you could ever be within. It is the Holy City to which it is wise to make *pilgrimage* every day, which means to bring awareness and commitment to exactly what you are experiencing, to be thankful for it, to bless it, to embrace it, to be vigilant, to be mindful:

What is this moment teaching me?

Having given that, then, as background and foundation, remember that you do not experience anything that is called an "ordinary moment." In each and every moment, *extraordinary* things are occurring. Extraordinary things are occurring in which the whole of the Universe is *conspiring*—which means to "breathe together"—the Universe is conspiring with you to awaken you, to heal you. Trust it! Love it! That these things are true—and I assure you that they are—it means that *your life*, the very life you are living, is *equal* in power and majesty and effectiveness as any life that has ever been lived. It means that *your very life is equal to the one that I lived*. For it is bringing you home, as my life was my pathway home to God.

And so, to build on what we shared earlier, the third axiom or principle could be encapsulated in this way:

I do not live any ordinary moments. With each breath, my experiences are the stepping stones laid before me of God, to guide me home. Therefore, I will bring awareness to each moment and allow it to teach me how to forgive, how to embrace, how to love and, therefore, how to live fully.

In your ordinary moments, a thousand times each day, you'll be confronted by opportunities to be disturbed. [laughs] Hmm! And in that very same moment, you are being given the blessing of the opportunity to choose peace, to remember to cultivate a perception of your brother or sister that is a perception birthed out of the Christ Mind, not the egoic mind. Forgiveness, then, can be practiced diligently. And you won't need to look too far. You will not need to make a pilgrimage to some far city. You do not need to go sit in a cave in the mountains somewhere to discover the way to God. It is all around you, because you can only be where you have decreed to be. And you have decreed to be there because you, as a soul, truly want nothing more than to awaken. And your life, your life just as it is unfolding moment to moment, is meant for you.

If this is true, and I assure you that it is, the way to God can only be found in your willingness to embrace and live *fully* the very life that is within you, that unfolds through you with each moment. To live without fear, to go forward, to indeed, trust, to embrace the very power and the majesty that is the *seed*, the *soil*, the *ground* from which your life's experience is unfolding. It is precious! It is extraordinary! It is blessed! And it is given you of God! Would you not embrace the blessing of your life, and sanctify it to keep it holy, and to, indeed, draw the line and recognize that your life is worthy of your respect? It doesn't matter what anybody else thinks. It matters what *you* think.

Beloved friends, your life—*your life*—is your way home! If you do not live it fully, how can you ever arrive home? Therefore, fear not your greatness. Fear not the power that comes from embracing your life and claiming its value. Live it *full out* with every bit of *passion* you can muster! Embrace every second of it! Every time you wash your dish and your cup after breakfast, look upon these things and go,

> *My God! This is my life! This is my pathway home! And I am going to live it!*

Indeed, precious friends, in this way, you will come to forgive yourself of the judgments you have made. For who among you has not known the feeling of saying,

> *God, my life just isn't worth very much. I'll never be like so-and-so down the street. And I'll never have enough money. And not enough people are going to know me. And when will my work ever get out as big as that person's work?*

. . . etcetera, etcetera, etcetera.

But I say unto you, every time you've judged yourself, you have *weakened* yourself. Every time you have judged yourself or another, you have slipped down the mountain another notch, when your desire is to be at the summit.

Understanding these things, then, let us look more closely at forgiveness. How does it work? What really occurs when you forgive? *You are a conduit of energy.* To the degree that the conduit is in perfect working order, the energy can flow so radiantly that the conduit actually becomes *transparent.* That is, it no longer blocks. There is no barrier or limit to the Light. When you judge, it is as though you contracted, you made the walls of the conduit smaller, just like building up rust in your pipes. And the flow becomes less and less. As you forgive judgments, it is as though the rust in the pipes were dissolving. It is as though the walls of the pipe, that are carrying the liquid of God's Love, begin to expand and become thinner and thinner and more transparent. Judgment is contraction. Forgiveness is relaxation, and peace, and trust, and faith.

Forgiveness allows the spaciousness within your consciousness to grow. For when you look upon the thief that has broken into your home and say, "I forgive you," you are decreeing the opposite of what you've learned. You are decreeing that nothing can be taken from you of any value. You are decreeing that judgment is the opposite of what you want, and it will cause you to feel the opposite of how you want to feel. You are decreeing your power to perceive differently. You are, therefore, *healing yourself.*

And if you ever want to come home, you're going to have to become very, very *divinely selfish.* You're going to have to become so selfish that *you will not tolerate judgment in yourself*—of anyone or anything. Because you will begin to recognize that every little act catapults you to the other side of the Universe from where you want to be. It causes the very cellular structure (if you could see this, you would never judge again) .. when you judge, even the cells of your body go crazy. They vibrate in a completely dissonant way. And there is contraction. The fluids do not move through the cells. The nutrients do not become transported or delivered to the cells. The waste matter isn't processed properly. Everything gets clogged up, and there is dis-ease.

Therefore, beloved friends, understand well that judgment is not something to take lightly. Should you, then, judge yourself if you've noticed you've been in judgment? No. That's a judgment in itself. Only Love can heal. Therefore, when you know you've judged, go,

Ah, yes! That's that energy. I recognize that cloud that has just passed through the field of my awareness. But, I can choose again.

So, how does this work? If in your "ordinary" daily life—that we now know is not ordinary at all—if you detect that you have been in judgment of someone or some thing, recognize that that judgment is still with you. It's a present thing, even though you may have enacted it five minutes ago, or fifty-five years ago, or ten lifetimes ago. When you notice it, or bring awareness to it, you have made it a very present thing. So it's right there in front of you to be undone. And that's what you need to focus on:

I'm going to choose again.

Know you the experience of looking back in your life, and suddenly seeing a scene in which *now* you know you behaved selfishly from ego; that you were manipulative or cunning or hurtful? Or you recognize,

My God, I was really in judgment of that person. Ah! Ooo! If only I could go back and undo it.

Know you that feeling? I say unto you, you *can,* because everything is *present.* There is no such thing as past and future, there is only *now.* So when you have that thought or that memory, it's coming to you for a *very specific reason.* As a soul, you are learning about forgiveness and how to undo the effects of your previous choices. And so, it is being presented to you, yet again, that you might make a new choice.

So when that old memory comes, stay with it. Look at it. Recognize how judgment worked at that time. And then say to that person and or that event,

I judge you not. I extend forgiveness to myself for what I have created. I embrace you, and I love you. And I free you to be yourself. And I bless you with the Blessing of Christ.

Then see that image or that memory begin to gently dissolve into Light, until there is no trace of it left. And be done with it. And right away the mind says,

Well, yes, but when I kicked that little boy in the shins when I was four years old, just to watch him scream . . . he's not here.

Isn't he? The *body* is not here, but the body is not quite the soul. And all minds are *joined*. It means that where you extend forgiveness within the consciousness, within your emotional field, to another, whether they be physically present or not, you *are* extending to them exactly what you could extend to them if they were physically in front of you. Because, you see, even if they were, they still have to receive it, don't they? They still have *their* choice to make—whether to accept your forgiveness, or to remain in judgment of *you*. And that's their issue, not yours.

Understand then, that you are dealing with *consciousness*. You are not a physical being, you are Spirit. And you are intimately linked with all minds and all times. Therefore, forgiveness of another can occur anytime you decide that it can occur. Anyone you've ever believed has wronged you, can be forgiven by you, in this very moment. Anytime you've judged another and, therefore, been in judgment of yourself, you can undo that in the very present moment, *simply by making a different choice.*

Rest assured, you will continue to project upon others what remains unhealed, unforgiven within yourself. Each time you react to another, you are being given a sign that there's some kind of energy that's been presented to your awareness that you have not forgiven within yourself. If someone is critical, and that pushes your buttons every time they're critical, rest assured, you have not healed that part of your own beingness—that part of your own experience of being critical of others. Whether it's occurring now, or whether it seems to be a pattern that you have interrupted and no longer do, you've still not *forgiven yourself* for having identified with that energy.

Use your ordinary experience, then, in each day to observe what pushes your buttons. And if you will stay with it—and in just a moment we will give you a very simple technique for doing so—if you can stay with it, it will reveal to you the energies that are in need of your forgiveness.

The technique is quite simple.

As you go through your day, observe when you feel as though you are in contraction. Are the muscles of the body tight? Is the breath very shallow? Does your voice become faster or louder when you speak about some energy in someone else? That is a sign that you need to do healing within yourself. When you recognize that these kinds of signs are going on—in other words, life has presented you with an opportunity to be disturbed—that is a sign that there is something that requires healing.

So therefore, count it a blessing if you feel disturbed. Turn your awareness from what you think is causing the disturbance and remember the first axiom:

> *I am the source of my experience. I'm feeling disturbed. What is it in* me *that needs to be healed?*

Begin to breathe deeply with the body and rhythmically. Let the body soften and relax, and ask,

> *What is it within this person's energy that is really pushing my button?*

And you will see it right away:

> *Oh, they're so critical. Criticism pushes my buttons. Where have I been critical of others?*

And it might hit you right away:

> *Well, I'm being critical because they're critical.*

Or memories will come back, distasteful memories, if you're judging them. Let them come back. Continue to breathe and relax. Look upon that energy of being critical. *Honor it. Love it.* For it is a creation. It is your creations coming back to you, that you might *embrace* them and *transform* them. And in that example, just stay with it. Look at it.

> *Ah! Being critical. Yes, I can sure be critical. I've been that way in the past. I know that energy very well.*

Look upon a scene in your memory in which *you* have been the one being critical. Look upon it with deep honesty and sincerity, and say to yourself,

> *I forgive me for being critical. I forgive my judgment of myself. I choose to teach only Love.*

Watch that image disappear from your mind, dissolve from your mind. And bring it back to the present moment and that person that just pushed your button. Again, you don't need to say anything to them at all, although you might. But, within yourself, forgive them for allowing the energy of being critical to temporarily make a home in their mind. And merely ask the Holy Spirit to replace your perception with the Truth. Ask to see the innocent Light within them.

As you cultivate this, you'll become very, very good at it. You'll be able to do it that fast [snaps his fingers]. And once you begin to see the Light in them, you can ask the Holy Spirit,

> *What is this critical energy in them masking? What are they really crying out for?*

And then you will feel compassion. For it will be revealed to you why they are hurting inside. And, lo and behold, instead of being reactionary with them, you just might be compassionate. Your choice of words, your own behavior might turn out to be different than you could have ever imagined. And yet, *through you* will be channeled exactly what serves *them.*

When I was being nailed to the cross, there was, indeed, one who raised the mallet to strike the nail. And as he raised the mallet, his eyes met mine, for just a moment. And I did exactly what I've described to you. I first remembered, and by this time I had mastered this, so that it was done very quickly. I asked,

> *How have I ever wanted to drive a nail through someone else?*

And I remembered my murderous thoughts. I forgave myself and brought my attention back to that one, and asked only to see the Light in him. And I asked,

What is it that this action is mirroring to me*? What is it masking within* him*?*

And I saw that one's soul, and I loved that one's soul. And I felt compassion for that one. And in that moment—mark my words—in that moment of eye contact, that one got it!

Because my energy was different, it created the space in which that soul could make a new choice. And that soul saw suddenly the entirety of its experience, and realized that if it allowed that mallet to fall upon the nail, it would be a decision to choose to continue being nothing more than a doormat for other people's perceptions. And in that very instant, that soul decided to follow a path that would lead to sovereign mastery, and never again to be a pawn of any government, or any group, or any faction, or anyone. He dropped the mallet from his hand—this was a Roman soldier—stood up, and walked away, and disappeared.

That one has gone on to become a Master that is known by literally thousands of beings. He is not in physical form. This one visits many, teaches many. This one, indeed, incarnated perfect mastery, and therefore, transcended the world. And it all began as the result of *my* desire to teach only Love. And now, we have a very good friendship.

So you see, you may not know how powerful your choice for healing is. You may not really see how deeply and profoundly it will affect you, as you go on being a creator—and you go on forever. And you could never possibly know what fruits will be born from that tree in the life of another. But because all minds are joined, when *you* choose healing, through forgiveness, you literally create the space in which the *other* can also heal their life.

Let no moment, then, be wasted. See nothing as ordinary. And see not the perceptions taught to you of the world be justified within yourself. But be you wholly committed to rooting up and out of your beingness *anything* that is unlike the Love of Christ. Think not that I am the only one that can love this way—it is not true. You are here to love as I learned to love. Why? Because you *are* that Love. And everything else is just a smoke screen.

Forgiveness is *necessary*. Forgiveness is a skill and an art that will pay you dividend upon dividend upon dividend upon dividend. It will never cease in paying you. Each moment in which you choose forgiveness, you have literally saved yourself a thousand years of suffering! Whoo! And I mean that about as literally as one can mean it. In short, every act of forgiveness is a miracle that shortens the need for experience in this dimension. And when you find yourself in a situation that you believe is too big, rest assured it is because something big has finally come to the surface to be healed within you, so that more power can shine forth through you, because you've reached the place where you're ready for it. More of Christ can be lived.

It is very, very important to let each day be sufficient unto itself. That is, when you end your day, always truly *end it*. And do not take four hours of ritual. You can do it within one breath. As you take a deep breath, as you rest your head upon the pillow, look upon the whole day, embrace it with your consciousness, and as you let your breath go out, say within your consciousness,

> *I release and forgive this day. It has been perfect. And it is done.*

Let it go, *just let it go*. Why? Because if you don't, you'll just bring it with you. Know you that experience? And for three weeks later you're going,

> *Oh gosh, why did I make that decision three weeks ago? If I only would have made a different decision, this wouldn't have happened, that wouldn't have happened.*

That's probably true. But the point is, now, three weeks later, you're still hitting yourself over the head by bringing the past with you. And you miss the glory of the present. You've all heard that a thousand times, because it's the Truth.

Consciousness is a very subtle and powerful thing. *You cannot help but create.* Remember the goal this year is to learn to *deliberately create* with perfect mastery. Therefore, look upon the things of the day and say,

It is very good. And it is finished.

Let each night, when you rest your head upon the pillow and you know you are about to go off to sleep, be just like God was in the story, your Biblical story of creation, in which it is written that on the seventh day, God rested. God was finished, in a sense, within the story. And have that same quality at the end of each of your days. If you're carrying some kind of emotional reaction because of something someone said or did, or whatever, or something you said or did, *practice forgiveness* before you sleep. Because if you don't, you will keep experiencing the conflicted energies during your dream states. And communication between you and the other one, who has not yet been forgiven, will keep on going on until that forgiveness is complete within you.

I hope that makes sense to you, because it's *very* important. Time should never be taken frivolously. Play with it, yes, but play with it out of *consciousness*, out of *clarity*, out of recognizing that there is no such thing as an *idle thought*. Each thought creates a world of experience for you. And you are worthy of experiencing Heaven.

We will have much more to say about forgiveness as we begin to plummet the depths of what is discovered as you practice forgiveness seventy times seven times. It takes you deeper and deeper into the very mechanics of consciousness itself—the very mechanics of creation. Forgiveness. Put it at the top of your list until you know how perfectly forgiven you are. Be you, therefore, vigilant against denying what is still in need of forgiveness within you. For what you deny, you will project. And each projection is a hurtful act to yourself. Also to the other, of course, but to yourself.

So! We will let that be enough for now. There is much that has been said in this hour that needs to be listened to again, and yet again, so that the awareness begins to truly grasp how *important*, and how *powerful* forgiveness is. You will reach a place where you absolutely *delight* in going through your day expressing forgiveness, like a wave emitting itself from the ocean of your consciousness, even if nobody is doing anything. Forgiveness, itself, becomes a delightful energy to live within.

Therefore, indeed, beloved friends, forgive you well *yourself*, and you have forgiven Christ. And when Christ is forgiven, Christ will arise and make His home in your heart, and in your mind, and even in the cells of your body. And you will know what it means to walk in this world, yet not be of the world. And when you look in the mirror, you will say,

> *Behold, the Savior appears.*

It will not be egoic arrogance that says it, but the recognition of what is true always:

> *I am my Father's Child, and I am sent into this world to bring Light to it.*

So! Be you, therefore, at peace. Practice forgiveness well, until it becomes like taking a breath. And you will discover power that you didn't know could exist, and a freedom whose taste is sweet above honey.

I forgive you [laughs]. Not because I've judged you but because I know the *blessing* that forgiveness brings to *me*. Forgiveness is something I perfected as a man. Perfect it within yourself, as well, and you will know the Glory of Christ.

Be you, therefore, at peace, beloved friends.

Amen.

Lesson Four

Now, we begin.

And once again, greetings unto you, beloved and holy friends. Once again, it is with great joy that we come forth to abide with you in this manner. It is with great joy that I come forth with my friends to abide with you in this hour. It is with great joy that I walk with you on the way that you have chosen. For in Truth, there is not a time that I am not with you. There is not a place to which you can journey where you will not discover my presence.

Only reality can be true. And reality is simple: there is but the simplicity of Love. And from that ocean there is birthed a multitude of forms, a multitude of worlds, a multitude of creations, of which you are one. And like waves arising from the sea, those creations remain linked eternally to their Creator. You are a wave arising from the Infinite Ocean of the Love which is the presence of God. I am a wave that has arisen from the ocean of my Father's Holy Mind. And though two waves seem to appear separated by what is called time—by even two thousand of your years—yet, in Truth, when seen from a much broader perspective, those waves have arisen simultaneously from the Ocean's surface. They arise for the very same purpose: to express the simplicity, and the innocence, and the beauty, the creativity, the truth, and the reality of the Ocean Itself.

And the waves delight in expressing what seems to be a unique individuality. And yet, they carry the common thread of being made of the same substance and are truly governed by the same Laws of Creation. For they know not the moment of their own arising, for only the Depth of the Ocean unseen can know the moment when It chooses to well up and to create the expression of the wave. The power that is not seen, but is hidden in the Depth of the Ocean, rises up through and forms that wave and sustains that wave throughout the duration of its expression. And it is from the Depth of that Ocean that it is decided when that wave shall return to the sea. Does that mean it disappears? Only from one perspective. But in reality, the very substance that was made manifest truly has not known birth and death, but only expression.

What, then, if you were to consider *yourself* as a wave arising from the Holy Mind of God, born of God's infinite desire to expand Himself, to express the infinite nature of Love and creativity? What if you began to realize that all that you have called yourself is the *effect* of Love—that you do not *cause* yourself to come into existence? And yet, as you have arisen from that Ocean of Love, is not the wave made of the same substance as the sea itself? Are you not given infinite and perfect freedom? For just as your Father perceives you, you are given the freedom to perceive yourself, and all of the other waves you might notice, and even the Ocean Itself, in any way that you choose.

The goal, then, of a genuine spirituality is to realign the quality of your perception, to mirror, to resonate with, to be in perfect alignment with the perception of your Creator; to see with God's eyes. Beloved friends, in Truth, you remain as you are created to be. And in each and every moment, you are literally using the power, found in the silent depth of the Ocean of God's Love, that gave rise to your very creation and existence, to *perceive* as you *desire*.

Therefore, in this hour, we will address the very nature of *desire* itself: what it means, what it signifies, how it creates effects, the power of desire, the value of desire, the meaning and purpose of desire, and how to begin to bring that energy (which at times, you know, feels like a team of a thousand wild horses all wanting to go in their own directions), to bring the very Power of Desire under your conscious and deliberate direction, that you might, indeed, create as the Father created you—with perfect, deliberate, infinite Love, with perfect and infinite and deliberate freedom, with perfect and infinite and deliberate joy, and with perfect, *perfect,* freedom.

Desire! When I walked upon your planet as a man, I confronted many different opinions about the nature of creation, the nature of mankind, the nature of consciousness, although the word was not around at the time—what you call consciousness or self-identity. Just as you are now confronted with many schools of thought, so, too, was I. And while that can seem to lead to great confusion, as though one must choose from the smorgasbord, it actually serves not unlike the sand inside the oyster from which the pearl will come. It causes you to grate inside. *You must find your own way to your own truth.* For before each and every one of you lies your pathway and a doorway, an eye of the needle, through which *only you* can fit.

Therefore, in some respects, you are seemingly alone. You must make the decision to *desire, above all things, awakening into perfect remembrance of your union with God*—just as a wave might finally decide that it has been birthed, not to be fearful of being a wave, but to truly claim its individuation, to claim its uniqueness, and to live that fully. And in that fullness, to decide to discover a way to be aware of its infinite union with the ocean itself, to somehow break free of the myopic self-identification as one little piece of wave that arises in a place or a field of time, lasts for but a second and then disappears. To find a way to transcend that limitation, to become re-identified with a consciousness, a living awareness, that you are One with the Depth of the Sea. That you can operate, not from the superficial level of awareness that might be like the foam at the tip of the wave (what you call your conscious or egoic mind), but that you become *in*formed in all that you speak, in all that you do, in all that you create, and all that you perceive, by that which rests in the very Infinite Depth of the Ocean Itself.

Imagine, then, drawing upon a well within you that seems to have no bottom and sides, through which something is pouring forth from places unseen, in which your literal conscious attention, your conscious awareness, seems to be colored with Radiant Light that literally leaves you feeling that you are *not* the body-mind or the personal history with which you had identified before, but that these things are only temporal, or temporary and very impersonal effects of a level of desire, within your soul, which is one and the same thing as the Love of God expressing Itself, for no other reason than that Love *must* be extended.

Imagine transcending your fear of your own survival, because as you look upon your body-mind you are no longer identified as that body-mind; that those things have become tools to be utilized by the Love which rests in the Mind of God; that you live, yet no longer you, but Christ dwells *as* you. *This is a very real experience to be lived*. It is not just a philosophy. It is not just a concept, and it can never be a dogma. There is a *mystical translation* that occurs in the depth of the soul which, in Truth, is merely a *shifting* of where you perceive your sense and source of identity. And the energy, the energy required to take you from myopic self-contraction, in which you have become identified with the little drops of foam out on the tip of the wave, tossed to and fro by a power that seems to be outside of you, to a sense of identify with the Silent Depth of the Ocean, that is everywhere present and seems to know no beginning or no end, the very energy that will carry you from the tip of the wave to the Depth of the Ocean, is the *energy of desire.*

For I say well unto you, that if the Father had not desired to extend Love, you would never have come into existence. Your very sense of awareness of self is the result, the effect, of Love. The very same Love that has birthed the sun and the moon and all of the stars and every dimension upon dimension upon dimension of Creation. That very Love that desired for that Love to be extended is the very Source from which you have been birthed. As you know yourself to be, then, you are the *effect of God's desire to extend Love.*

Therefore, when next someone asks you, "Oh, who are you?", please do not give them a name. Do not say,

> *Well, I was born in a certain town, in a certain part of the planet.*

Don't tell them that you are a Democrat, or a Republican, or a communist, or an atheist, or a Catholic. Tell them the Truth:

> *Who am I? I am the extension of Love in form. I have never been born and I will never taste death. I am infinite and eternal. I shine forth as a sunbeam to the sun. I am the* effect *of God's Love. And I stand before you to love you.*

Now *that* will raise some eyebrows! It will also transform your world. For it is time to stop seeking Christ outside and start choosing to take responsibility for being Christ incarnate. *Desire is everything!*

Take just a moment, right now. Let the body relax, and imagine that you could move back from being the *actor* in the play of your life to being the *director* and the *producer.* And you're sitting in your laboratory, your studio, and you're editing the story of your life. And you're looking at all your little clips of film, from the time you were birthed, the time you went to kindergarten, the time you first fell in love, the time you first decided to go to a movie, the time you went off to college, the time you took a job, or this job or that job, or you moved to another physical location. And look closely and see if it is not true, that for every action you have ever done, for every decision you have ever made, after trying to analyze it all, is there not underneath it the energy of *desire*?

For in Truth, you do not lift the body from your couch to go to the refrigerator without the desire to eat. Something calls you into a field of action, an expression of action. It is desire. No one enters into an intimate relationship without the energy of desire. For who two have ever looked upon one another and said,

> *I don't feel any desire whatsoever, but let's get married, have children, and raise a family.*

Desire! Desire is that energy which brings forth all waves of creation out of the depth of the ocean itself. And yet, who among you has not felt *conflicted* about desire? Who among you has not been taught that desire is evil? Who among you has not been taught not to desire to be great? Who among you has not been taught that the desire for material comfort is some sort of a blot on the spiritual path? Look well within your soul and see if this is not true. Have you not feared, at times, the welling up of desire within you? For well, as I look upon your plane, there are many who become paralyzed with fear just because they desire to have a bowl of ice cream. So afraid are they, that if they give in to that desire, something in the ice cream will cause their body to bloat and their brain to cease functioning. Hmm! Hmm!

And for those of you in intimate relationship—what you call marriage, a commitment of some kind (there seem to be many levels of commitment in your world, each has its own definition)—how many of you have not carried the belief, taught to you by the world, that if you feel an energy of desire welling up within yourself, when you look upon someone who is not your partner, that somehow you have sinned against God? How many of you, then, do not know the experience of trying to reign in the ten thousand horses, so sure that if you gave in to feeling desire, that everything would run amok? And your attempt to keep your life structured and rigid and predictable, would collapse—what you call "all hell breaking loose." Hmm!

And yet, I say unto you, would you exist if God had feared the desire to create and extend love by forming you, at the same time giving you infinite freedom of choice? Without desire, look around, not only would you see nothing, there would be nothing to do the seeing. *Everything* is the *effect* of desire.

Come, then, to see that desire is not evil. It is *not* to be feared. It *is* to be mastered. Mastery is not control. For control, the need to control, is an effect of the energy of fear, and not Love. Mastery of desire comes when you recognize that you are *safe* to feel whatever wave of desire might come up through your consciousness, because *you* decide whether or not you will act on it—you will bring it into the field of manifestation. The *power of choice* is the one power that can never be taken from you. You already have perfect mastery of it, because nothing you ever experience comes to you without your decision to allow it into the field of manifestation.

Come, then, to feel that desire is something welling up from the depth beyond yourself that can be looked at with perfect innocence, and with the wonder of a child. And that that very act of turning to allow and welcome desire is not something that will sidetrack you from the path of awakening, but will, indeed, take you vertically, if you will, into the Heart of God.

For if you are to ever create as God creates, you will need to heal your conflicted perceptions about desire. You will need to transcend that energy of fear.

There are many who call unto me and pray. There is not an hour in your time frame in which there are not many upon your plane, somewhere on your planet, that are praying to me, that want their hearts to be filled with Christ. And yet, at the very same time, they are scared to death of an energy that *wants* to move, because they have been taught to fear, to suppress, desire.

Desire is like the Liquid of Life that moves through the stem of the rose and allows the petals to radiate with glorious color. And when you block the flow of desire, the petals cannot be nourished. Death begins to occur—death of the heart, death of the soul, lifelessness.

If you were to walk down one of your city streets and to truly look into the eyes of everyone you see (and everyone that hears these words has had this experience), would you not recognize that death seems to have already made a home in the minds of many that are living—death of dreams, death of hope, death of worthiness, death of playfulness, death of true power, death of union with their Source and Creator?

Healing requires the willingness to *feel desire*, to see it as good, to see it as holy. Does that not mean that if you feel a desire, that it might not become twisted by the egoic patterns in your mind? Of course not. There's always that possibility that desire will be twisted to meet the needs of egoic mind within you. But rest assured, if it does, who's done it? You! Always within you, you know that desire is good, but you suppressed it. Always, when desire comes forth, those times when you've let it become twisted into serving the goals of the ego, rest assured, you knew perfectly well what you were doing, and you were the decision maker.

You have learned, therefore, to fear desire because that fear is the effect of *fearing yourself.* And that is what cripples you. That is what cuts off the creative flow. That is what leads to everything your world knows as the multitude of psychological diseases—an unwillingness to trust one's self, an unwillingness to love one's self, the belief that the desires that move up through your beingness are something evil and dark. If only you could stamp them out of your being, you could remain in control and everybody would like you because you'd conform to the smallness and the littleness that is worshipped in human consciousness.

Listen well, now, to the next axiom we would give you:

> *The only relationship which holds any value at all is your relationship with God, your creative Source, the depth of the ocean.*

And right away the mind wells up,

> *But what about my mate, what about my parents, what about my children, what about the President of the United States, what about the postmaster?*

Hmm! You will come up with a million examples of relationships that surely have great importance. The *only* one which holds *value* is your relationship with God. For when that is in alignment, all of your creations, your choices for relationships, and how you will be within them, will flow effortlessly from that alignment. Therefore, seek first the Kingdom, and all these things will be added unto you. Do not try to create a rose by starting with the petals. But nourish the roots, and the flower must blossom.

If you are to be in *right relationship* with your Creator, it is absolutely necessary to correct your perception and relationship with the energy of desire. And it begins by releasing your judgment of it in all of its forms. For again, you can only be in Love or fear. You can only be in innocence or judgment. Love and innocence are of the Kingdom. Fear and judgment are of illusion.

Learn then, through simple practice, to *interrupt the patterns* you've learned from this illusory world, so that you release judgment of the energy of desire. This will be different for each and every one, depending on where they begin. But to give you a very simple exercise, when you awaken in the morning, and you've planted your feet firmly on your floor, take pause and ask yourself this question:

> *What do I want right now?*

Right away, the mind will say,

> *Well, I'm too busy to know what I want, I have to go off to work. I have to serve everybody else. I'm here to satisfy the world. I have no time to ask myself what I want.*

Remember that what you decree *is*, and the thought you hold in the mind will be reflected through the nature of your experience.

So take pause and ask,

> *What do I want?*

And then simply give yourself one minute to observe whatever comes up in the mind, or even is felt in the body. Heaven forbid, you might want to have sex! Oh! Then you would know for sure that you are not a "spiritual" being! You might want to take a hot shower. You might want a glass of juice or water. You might want to sing. You might want to stretch or breathe. You might want to turn and look at your lover, your mate, still sleeping in the bed. You might want to arise, and go and sneak into your children's room, and watch them sleep. You might want to sit down and read the morning paper. But the point here is to notice that by asking the question, something will respond within you. And when that response comes, notice that there is a feeling associated with it, a quality that makes your cells sing just a little bit. That is the energy, the elixir of Life, called desire.

In this one minute, you need not rise to act, but to simply observe:

Ah, what do I want? To take a hot shower.

The feeling of the thought, or the thought that emits the feeling in the body, "I want to take a hot shower," is carried on the elixir of desire. And desire is coming from a depth of your beingness that, again, rests right next to the Face of God. And might it not be the case that by following the desire that wells up through your heart, by *feeling* it, by *embracing* it, you might learn and discover what the Ocean is wishing to express through the wave that you are? And if you judge desire, might you not be shutting off the creative flow that the Mind of God wishes to express?

Of course, that's the problem. You've tied the hose in a knot through conflicted judgments. And the idea, now, is to begin—in a simple way—to begin to give yourself permission to *feel desire*, to allow it even into the cells of the body, to observe it, to notice it, to sit with it.

Here is a very common one in your world (be honest with yourself): How many times have you felt the desire to be wealthy? It's not something you're supposed to sit around and talk about or make very public:

Boy, this morning I woke up and I just imagined having so many golden coins that I could buy the entire planet! Oh! "Money is the root of all evil." I can't think that way. Well, I better get busy and get off to my office job, that secretly, inside, I really resent, because they don't pay me what my soul is worth. But I'll pretend like I'm quite fine. Oh, money? No, I'm quite fine. I really have enough, and no, no, I'm really quite fine.

And then as you drive home, and the Mercedes Benz pulls up along side you, you cannot help but turn and go,

God, I wish I could afford one of those. Oh, God! I can't have that thought, so I'll drive my old Volkswagen down the road. But I'm being a very good spiritual person.

Be honest with yourselves: How many times have you felt, welling up within yourself, the desire to be wealthy? What on earth has caused you to *fear* that desire? What has caused you to tie the hose in a knot, so that you try to block that desire from coming into manifestation? Perhaps, when you were a child, you went to one of your cathedrals. And there was someone in a long robe standing upon a platform. And because everything looked so beautiful, surely they must be speaking with authority. And because this cathedral is filled with a whole lot of small little minds that are all living in their own level of fear, when that voice spoke and said, "Money is the root of all evil," you said,

Oh. Well, that is the truth. Oh, yes. That's the truth. Oh, yes. Oh, God! I better fear money.

Hmm!

I say unto you, you have *one Authority*, and it is never held within the office of any church, or any organization, or any one individual. Your Authority is the Voice for God that dwells within your heart and within your mind! God is not limited, and does not require His Children to be limited. For if you would receive all that God would give you, you would decide to rise up and be the grandest wave that you could possibly be. For only in so doing do you *honor* your Creator.

So you could say that God is like a wise gardener who is constantly trying to grow beautiful roses. He knows *exactly* how much moisture to put in the soil. He knows how to make those nutrients rise from the soil through the roots, up through the heart of the stem of the flower to give forth radiant color, so that everyone that looks upon it is touched by the mystery of beauty. And God wonders,

> *Well, it's interesting. These roses that I've created seem to have a mind of their own. As the elixir I tried to give them rises through the stems, they tie themselves in little knots, and only a little bit of the elixir reaches out, and so the petals never quite blossom fully.*

Have you ever had that feeling that you're putting more energy into *staying constricted* than you are into *allowing expansion?*

Desire is creation. Therefore, *what* you desire is of supreme importance. If you will take the little exercise that we have given you and begin to put it into practice, in a very simple way, and in a quiet way, you'll begin to get back in touch with the innocence and beauty of the movement of desire. You can delight in it. When you have a sexual thought, a sexual desire, why not just be with it? Why not notice what it causes to happen in the body? How does your breath change? Does the heart beat faster? Be honest with yourself, isn't it putting a smile on your face? What if you decided to *honestly embrace* that effect as being *perfectly innocent* and *beautiful?* How might your day change if you did not *repress awareness* of sexual desire? You'll notice we're not saying you should walk down the street and grab every body that walks by you. We're talking about allowing yourself the living embrace of exactly what energy is moving through your being.

Why is this important? If you have decided that there are certain energies which are demonic, evil, have the power to distract you from your union with God, you have already decided there is something *beyond* the reach of your power. And that is what disempowers you. And so, you take an innocent energy and turn it into a monster that must be feared at all cost.

Yet I say unto you, the mystical transformation that carries you from feeling yourself to be a disempowered little drop of foam on the edge of a wave, to the sense of freedom and empowered living that flows from the Mind of God, through you, to express only beautiful creations filled with majesty and power and miracles—what takes you from A to B is the willingness to turn to the very energies that move through the mind and the body, and to not fear them, but to look upon them with innocence and wonder. And this is the source of the myths that have been told in all cultures: the knight that slays the dragon, kissing the wild beast on the cheek and it becomes a loving, loving companion. Your monsters are what you fear and repress, because of the judgments you have learned in the world. And the world is only the denial of the Kingdom. It is the exact opposite of Truth.

So you see, if you're sitting in one of your cathedrals and everyone is saying,

> *Oh, yes. Sexuality, very bad! It will keep you from God.*

Right away, you should realize if everyone here is fearing sexuality, it must actually be Divine, and,

> *Perhaps I would do well to embrace it, and love it, and master it, and not fear it.*

If someone says unto you,

> *Money is the root of all evil,*

and then sticks out his hand, and says,

> *Would you please make a donation to our organization? . . .*

is that not an expression of conflict? And yet, such conflict *permeates* the religions and dogmas of your world:

> *Don't desire money. Don't desire wealth. By the way, to keep on this radio station, we really need you to send a donation.*

What are they trying to teach you? What are they in denial of?

Sex and money. Pretty basic things, aren't they? They represent energies that flow from the Mind of God, that would express in unlimited joy and power, and not be willing to settle for limitation of any kind.

When the earth was birthed from God's Holy Mind, and took on its own form, and became an entity just like you, God did not say,

> *Well, this is a pretty beautiful planet, but I can only have a solar system just large enough for the Earth.*

Rather, out of joy, God allowed there to come forth solar system upon solar system upon solar system, the birthing of a thousand suns every moment, as a field in which this beautiful jewel of a planet could spin. *That* is true creation! And what quality of solar system have *you* decided to allow, in which the planet of your own awareness can spin and live and express?

Ah desire! Desire is everything. And again, the simple exercise we've given you will begin to free up the blocks within, and you will rediscover the *innocence of desire*. And then, you can begin to expand upon it, to take a few moments to learn to live deliberately.

> *What do I truly want?*

For you see, because your mind shines forth like a sunbeam to the sun from the Mind of God, when you use your consciousness to relax into the innocence of the question,

> *What do I truly want? What is it in my heart that keeps calling to me, keeps compelling me?*

. . . pictures begin to arise, feelings begin to arise. And I say unto you, they are expressions of—and we'll speak through the symbols that you understand of your world—they are expressions of what God wants to bring forth *through* you,

> *Oh, every time I look in my heart, and every time I allow myself to feel it, what I really want is—I want to put my arms around people. I want to let people know how much I love them.*

Why fear such a desire?

> *It's too overwhelming. I don't know how I'll be accepted.*

93

Who cares how you'll be accepted? What matters is how you accept *yourself*.

What if by feeling that desire, new pictures began to come to you? And suddenly you realized, "What I want to do is join the Peace Corps," as an example. Perhaps it is the case that that very decision to go and put yourself in a solar system where you can spin as your own planet, where you can go and be in the Peace Corps, could be the very pathway through which you learn to receive the great joy of letting your Love out into the world. But if you fear desire, how can you ever know these things?

> *Oh, when I get in touch with my heart, and when I allow myself to feel . . .!*

What comes up by asking that question?

> *I want to have so much wealth. Oh! And I see the thought that says, "Oh, no! Wealth is bad." But what I want to do is, I want to be able to go to every hungry child on the planet and feed them. That's why I want to be wealthy.*

Could it not be that the desire to feed the world is God's desire to speak through you, to use you in a way that effects transformation upon your planet? Can you see, then, that by blocking the feeling of desire you might just be blocking yourself from hearing what you keep praying for, over and over?

> *Father, reveal Thy purpose to me.*

You feel the desire and you go,

> *Oops! First . . . excuse me, Father . . . I have to get rid of this desire.*

Desire in the heart is where you will discover the phone line that links you to the Will of God that would be expressed through you. And if you don't trust desire, you are literally saying that you have decided not to trust your Creator. Hmm . . . not something to just be brushed aside. In healing the conflict around desire, now that you know what it truly is, learn to be *patient* with yourself.

By way of a second exercise, and we would suggest that you create a structure by which this can be practiced that fits into your own life. Again, it need not take more than five, ten, or fifteen minutes, initially, perhaps three or four times a week. Eventually, you'll be doing this all the time, because you'll be creating deliberately. For just ten or fifteen minutes, set aside your world. Remember that you need do nothing, and so the world can wait.

Relax the body and close the eyes. And it can be of great benefit to let the breath become very deep and rhythmic; it relaxes the nervous system and seduces the controller within your mind, the critic that decides what thoughts are okay and which ones aren't. By the way, the critic is never something you created. It is something you let live in your mind that was made up by a lot of other fearful minds, called parents and teachers.

As you relax the body and the mind, ask yourself,

> *What do I truly want?*

And observe the images that come, without judgment. Notice the feelings in the body, and allow this to go for just a minute or two. Then pause, open the eyes, and write down all that you can remember.

> *I saw the image of having forty-seven sexual partners.*
>
> *I saw the image of having golden coins rain down upon me so that I have to have an umbrella over my head.*
>
> *I saw huge bowls of ice cream.*
>
> *I saw myself in a boat on the ocean.*

Whatever it is, write it down.

> *I notice that my stomach got tight.*
>
> *I thought I was going to pee my pants.*

Whatever it is, write it down.

Then, take a deep breath, relax again, and repeat the process. Place the hand so that it rests on the heart. Breathe into it a few times, and then ask,

What do I truly desire?

And again, allow the process to be what it is. Do this over a period of ten or fifteen minutes so that you repeat the process at least six or seven times, writing them down.

Take the piece of paper, perhaps in a journal, as you would call it, and put it aside until the next exercise period, and then again repeat the process. When you have done this seven times, so that you have seven sheets of paper in which you've gone through this process, then, and only then, begin to look back through all the things that came up. And then ask yourself,

What seems to be repeating itself?

You might notice,

Well, three times I wanted a huge bowl of ice cream, but then it seemed to fade away.

Twice I had a desire for forty-seven lovers, but now I notice that I'm really only wanting one.

Whatever it might be, notice the pattern, the thread, that seems to run the most throughout the exercise periods. Then, imagine that thread to be that energetic link that is tied at one end to the piece of foam at the edge of the wave, and the other is anchored to the Depth of the Ocean. And then consider that perhaps if you allowed yourself to move down that thread, to begin to put your energy on that, to begin to clear up the obstacles within your consciousness that block that desire from being consistently lived from, that by so doing, you would carry yourself from the drop of foam at the edge of the wave to the Heart of God. And that along the way, everything unlike Love would come up for you to release it. And that during the process, you would go through a *metamorphosis* that would culminate in your being the *living incarnation of the Power of Christ*—that your soul would *realize the fulfillment* that it has always sought. Hmm! Something to take a big gulp over.

For you see, the reason you have cleverly decided to trick yourself into blocking the energy of desire is that the soul knows that, were it to follow such a thread, *through whole and total commitment*, it will be embarking on the pathway we spoke of in an earlier hour, the pathway set before you by God, that knows how to take you home.

And if you arrive at home, it will mean that you will have had to give up being a *seeker*. And you will have had to become one who is *found*. And you will have to rise above the crowd. You will have to give up all of your identity with smallness. You will have to give up needing the approval of others. You will have left the nest of insanity. You will have arisen and taken up your right place at the right hand of God. Isn't that the deepest fear you carry ... to actually be the Truth of who you are: *Christ Incarnate*?

Now, desire can be much fun. Ideally, once you've practiced this on your own, ask your mate or a close friend (you may even want to show them this talk on your video)—and ask a friend if they would be willing to embark on this process with you, so that, perhaps once a week, you can sit down together, and say,

What did you come up with this week?

Well, here goes... !

It is called *undressing* in front of a friend. It is called becoming *vulnerable* with another. It is called *finding another child to play with in the Kingdom*, so that you can go to the sand box, away from the adult world that says,

Desire is bad. You guys be careful.

And you begin to look at what is true and real from a place of innocence. And you begin to create for yourself a *support group*. And that support group perhaps can grow to three or four friends—or even ten or twenty—in which everyone is involved with getting in touch with what's really in there, by understanding the principle that *desire is the thread that links your soul to the Heart of God*. And God wants only to extend, through you, that which expresses Love in the world. It is called Creation.

Perhaps, a worthwhile project. For when you do not turn to allow the embrace of desire, there is only one alternative. It is to live in *mere survival.* And when you choose the energy of mere survival, the *world* is your master, before which you will be made to bow again and again and again and again and again—lifetime after lifetime after lifetime! You will be a *slave* to the insanity that seems to rule this world. And you will never know *peace.* And you will never know *joy. And you will never come home.* Plain and simple! For you were not created to wither and die on the vine. *You were made to bear forth much good fruit.*

Let the roots be watered by desiring, above all things, to become the fulfillment of what God had in Mind when He breathed into you the Breath of Life. And let that Breath be received in each moment. You will come to see that the only question—the *only* question—you need be preoccupied with is this:

> *How much of God am I willing to receive and allow to be expressed through me?*

It is called the separating of the wheat from the chaff. The chaff are the thinkings of the world that would have you believe in smallness. This can only result in your perpetual suffering. The wheat is the food that gives Life, because it is filled with the Love of God.

Fear not, then, desire. But desire to *embrace* desire. Touch it, feel it, know it, dance with it, sing with it, look at it *innocently. Feel it wholly.* And then learn to discern, through the ways we've given you, what desire is truly: that thread that's shining forth through all of your days. And then decide to let that desire *in*form your choices, so that you create a life that serves the fulfillment of that thread of desire.

You see, I had to do the same. For I began to notice that there was a thread of desire in my heart to create some form of demonstration that would be so overwhelming that *anyone* who turned their attention to it could not help but be reminded that there is something far greater to life than living to survive, and surviving just to live. And even when I was young, I began to get glimpses—at first, they were fleeting. Something was compelling me. But as I learned to trust desire, the pictures became clearer and clearer. And I saw myself standing on hilltops, surrounded by multitudes. And I marveled at the words that came through my mouth in these moments of revelation, when I was still but a teenager. I saw glimpses and pictures of being loved by millions. I saw pictures and things that I couldn't even comprehend, because they were literally pictures of what I'm doing *now.* And how could a teenager, living in Judea two thousand years ago, have any way of comprehending the use of the technologies of your modern world in which to communicate Love? It made no sense to me. But still, I decided to trust it.

A part of that thread was the recognition that death is unreal. And so, therefore, I ought to be able to create a demonstration that would prove it. Now, think about that for a moment. If that thought was born in you, and you tried to share it with the world, wouldn't you be told you were crazy to dare to think a thought so out of line with everything the world believes? But because I followed the *thread of desire,* I began to realize that it kept *speaking* to me, day after day, and week after week. It wanted to grow. It wanted to be nurtured.

So finally, I decided,

> I am going to allow that thread to be nurtured. And I'm going to discover where it takes me, and what it's all about.

And where it took me was into mastery of life and death, mastery of healing, mastery of consciousness. It took me into mastery of myself. It brought me home to my own Christed Beingness.

Because I followed that thread, I can talk with you today. There are many of you that appreciate what I have done, because you see me as a spokesperson for the Truth. Is it not time that *you* followed your *own* thread, and became, likewise, a spokesperson for reality? For just as you have been sent to *me,* there will be many sent to *you,* as you step from being a *seeker* to a *finder.* For as you take up your right place, you become a vehicle through which the Voice for God will creatively touch the lives of countless persons that you may never ever meet physically.

You were birthed to be grand. You were birthed for greatness. You were birthed to shine forth such Light into this world that the world remembers that Light is true, and darkness is illusion. Be you, therefore, that which you are. And *you are the Light of the world.* And

99

I will delight in journeying with you. For if I can join with this, my beloved brother, to create communication, so too, can I join with anyone who chooses to step into their own Christedness. And the thread is the *thread of desire*.

Therefore, begin to turn toward the energy of desire within yourself—to separate the wheat from the chaff—by first learning to feel it, for just a minute, without judging it, and then to *deepen* that process. And I tell you, you will reach the point where, with every breath you breathe, you are in touch with the energy of desire. And that is the only Voice that you will give authority to.

And you won't be able to keep up with the loving creation that wants to express through you. And you will marvel at the friends that come into your life—how your external solar system, in which your planet is spinning, changes. You will marvel and wonder how it's all happening. And you will finally discover that you are not the *maker* and *doer* of your life, that God wants to direct and make Life through you.

And then you will know the Truth that sets you free:

> *Of myself, I do nothing. But my Father, through me, does all things. And it is very good.*

Be you, therefore, at peace. And *desire well*. For when you feel desire, you are watering your roots with the energy of Life itself. *Trust it! Embrace it!* And let the petals of the rose *blossom* within your Holy Being.

We love you, and we are with you. If you could only see how much enlightened help there is surrounding you at any moment, you would never allow the fear of going astray with your desire to be victorious within your mind. And you would step forth with boldness. And all things would be made new again.

How much of God's Love are you willing to receive?

And with that, we close by saying,

Amen.

Lesson Five

Now, we begin.

Beloved friends . . . greetings unto you. We come forth in this hour to continue that pathway which builds the structure, the highway, if you will, by which you may learn to follow and, therefore, master *The Way of the Heart.*

A *way* in life means to have chosen, from all possibilities, that one which will stand out as the way to which you are committed, the way to which you devote the whole of your attention by granting your willingness that the way be followed. And just as when you take a journey upon your Earth, by making the commitment to take the journey, you avail yourselves of experiences that could not come to you in any other way.

When you go to a university to pursue a pathway of a degree, although you begin with a certain idea of what the pathway may hold or bring you, is it not true that the relationships which come along the way, the knowledge that reveals itself to you, and even the end result of the accomplishing of the degree, always seems to be different than, and much richer than, you could have imagined when you began your journey?

Therefore, understand well that *The Way of the Heart* requires the willingness to *commit.* And commitment is nothing more than a deliberate decision that something will be so. And just as with all aspects of experience you've ever known, when all of your beingness is involved in the willingness to make a decision, there is literally nothing that can prevent you from the accomplishment of your goal. Rest assured, then, that whenever you believe you have not succeeded or not completed some decision, fueled by desire, it is because you were simply not *wholly committed*—or it means that you decided to change your mind. And when you *change your mind*, you literally change what you experience in the world, or the solar system in which your *self* spins.

The Way of the Heart, then, does indeed require the decision of commitment. And rest assured, I say unto you, that when you wholly commit to discovering *The Way of the Heart*, you will discover a way of being in the world that is not here. You will discover a way of walking through life in which you experience being uplifted by something that seems to be forever beyond you, yet is within you as the core and the essence of your very beingness. Your way will not be understandable by the world. Your way will not even be comprehensible within yourself. You will be living from mystery—moving from mystery to mystery to mystery—uplifted and carried by something that brings a satisfaction and a fulfillment to the depth of your soul, far beyond anything you can now imagine.

Is it worth it, then, to commit to *The Way of the Heart*? Yes! *The Way of the Heart* culminates with the recognition that you do not live Life at all but, rather, that *Life is living you*. One of its characteristics is the development of the *witness*—a quality of consciousness, a way of being, in which you seem to be witnessing everything that arises and flows through you and around you, from a place of utter stillness.

Stillness does not mean non-activity. It does mean *non-attachment to activity*—whether it be the arising and falling away of cancer in the body, the arising and falling away of relationship, the rising and falling away of a solar system. You will discover that there is a place within you that can look upon all things with perfect equanimity, perfect acceptance, and perfect Love. For in mastery of *The Way of the Heart*, you will discover that *nothing is unacceptable to you*. And only what is accepted can be transcended. You will discover a way of being in which nothing any longer *compels* you—not even the desire to know God *compels* you any longer, for the need of it has been completed.

Then, there arises a way of being in the world that is indeed not here, for you will feel no restlessness, no need to direct your journey. No questions will arise. You will be at peace. And in that peace, the Breath of God will move through you. And you will become as the wind, knowing not where you came from or to where you are going, but you will abide in perfect trust and perfect rest. And the world may not know you, but your Father will know you—and *you* will know your God.

In *The Way of the Heart,* the most primary and fundamental perception which seems to fuel ordinary human consciousness has been finally transcended. The perception of a separate maker and doer has been dissolved, and once again you will understand the depth and the profundity of the simple terms in this sentence:

> *Of myself, I do nothing. But,* through me, *the Father does all things.*

To rest in such a perception means that you have come to realize that the self that you are is merely a conduit through which Mystery lives Itself, through which Love pours forth. You will realize that there is nothing to be gained or lost in this world. You will know what it means to recognize that you literally have nowhere to go and nothing to achieve. You will become empty and spacious.

And yet, paradoxically, while the body lasts, you will appear to be as everyone else. You will arise in the morning and brush your teeth. When the body is hungry, you will feed it. You will laugh with your friends. You will yawn when the body is a bit tired. And yet, through it all, there will be a quality of *awareness*—called the *witness*—that is simply watching it all, waiting to be moved by the wind of Spirit. And though others may not see it, virtually everything you utter will carry the sound of Truth.

You know not how Spirit will work through you, nor will you care. Because, you see, when there is no maker or doer or director, it won't matter to you. That is what it means to live as the wind, for the wind does not concern itself with where it's been or where it's going. It is moved by some mysterious source that cannot be *located* at all. And yet it blows, and as it blows its effects are experienced.

Imagine then, a life in which all that you do is not *for* yourself. Imagine a way of life in which what you do is not *for* anyone else. Imagine a way of life in which creativity, living, flows forth from a Source so deep within you and around you that no language or dogma can contain it—a Force and a Source that knows how to express Itself through you in such a way that it is constantly and only serving the Atonement, the awakening of all of Creation to the Truth of God's presence.

The Way of the Heart, then, does indeed unfold, if you will, along a certain pathway. And in this hour, we will address the stages of that pathway, in a general sense. And then we will speak of the most important characteristic to be cultivated along this path.

First, *desire is everything*, and without it not a thing can arise. Therefore, indeed, *what* you desire is of utmost importance. Desire, then, perfect union with God. Desire, then, to be Christ Incarnate. Desire, then, to be all that your Creator has created you to be, even if you haven't an idea what that might be. For when you hold desire within your beingness, and when you've moved through the process of coming to master the energy of desire (and, again, mastery does not mean control), when you have mastered the energy of desire by grounding it always in the desire to be as you are created to be, then indeed, all of your life and all of the subsequent, or subsidiary, desires will come to serve that grand desire.

When you come into that state of being, *nothing shall be impossible unto you.* And why? Because you're not the one doing it. You are merely a piece of thread in a very cosmic tapestry, being woven by the Creator of all of Creation, Who alone knows how to weave the tapestry of a new age, of a new paradigm, of a healing of this plane and of humanity. And so the first stage is, indeed, the stage of desire. And only by feeling desire, and not by suppressing it, can you truly begin to move toward the stage of mastery in which the energy of desire always serves that Higher Will, which is the Will of God for you. And as we have said to you before, when your will is in alignment with the Will of God, you will discover that God's Will *for you* is that you be genuinely happy, through and through—content, fulfilled, at peace, empowered, capable, responsible.

Desire, in time, is cultivated through *intention*. For you see, you have used time to teach yourself how to be distracted by all of the thoughts and perceptions that make up this cosmic soup called your world. And all of you have known the frustration of having a desire, and then as soon as you walk out the door a friend pulls up and says,

Let's go to the beach.

And you never make it to class, even though your desire is to get the degree. You have cultivated the art of being seduced by distraction. Therefore, it is necessary to utilize time to *cultivate intention*. For without intention, desire cannot become the crystal clear focus, the laser-like focus, that can cut through the dross of this world, that a new creation can flow forth through you.

Intention is not the same as holding a strong egoic, willed, commitment to making something happen. For *The Way of the Heart* recognizes that you have not known how to achieve the fulfillment you seek at the level of the soul, for the simple reason that if you did, you would have already accomplished it. In *The Way of the Heart*, intention doesn't mean putting your nose to the grindstone and not taking "no" for an answer. It means, rather, that you cultivate within your thought processes the art of *remembering* what you are truly here for. You are here to remember that you are the thought of Love in form. You are here to remember that you are One with God. You are here to remember that what I have called *Abba*, the *Father*, though it goes by many names, is the source of your only reality. And you are living in reality only to the degree that That One is living through you.

Therefore, intention in *The Way of the Heart* means to utilize time each day to focus your attention on the *desire* to be Christ Incarnate. Intention is that energy, or that use of the mind, that creates (through consistent practice) the channel, if you will, through which desire begins to move down and re-educate the emotional body, and even the cellular structure of the physical body, and all of the lesser avenues of thinking that occur within the intellect—so that everything involved in your being is integrated, working together, and focused on the fulfillment of that one *grand desire* to accept your function in this world. And your function is healing your sense of separation from God.

How then, to apply intention? Each day then, just as you have used time to teach yourself to be easily distracted, you need only apply one question, to which, you ask yourself daily:

What is it that I most desire?

What am I doing on this planet? What am I committed to?

Those latter are just other forms of the fundamental question. And as you keep practicing asking that question, the answer will become clearer and clearer. For you see, it is the question that influences, stimulates, gives birth to, the answer. For the Universe is always answering your questions. And when you ask unclear questions, you get unclear answers.

Therefore, become *crystal clear* with your intention and remind yourself of it *daily*.

> *My intention is to use time constructively for the relearning of what it means to abide in the Kingdom of Heaven and to fulfill my function. And my function is healing. And healing requires the presence of Christ, for only Christ can express the Love that brings healing into being.*

Desire and *intention*—and in the field of time, these stages unfold as one matures in *The Way of the Heart*. Desire and intention are critical.

The third stage of the process whereby the mind is wholly corrected, and one returns home, is the stage of *allowance*. For the egoic world does not teach you to allow; it teaches you to *strive. You* must be the maker and the doer. *You* must find a way to manipulate or control your environment in order that it conform itself to the image you are holding in your mind. And all of that is well and good, and there are many beings who learn some valuable lessons by following the path of certain teachers that will teach you that you can create whatever you want. And that seems like such a big deal until you realize that's what you're doing all of the time. You are always creating exactly what you decree—and it's no big deal and it's not a secret.

But there will be those that will teach you,

> *Well, just go into your mind, ask yourself what you want, and when you see that picture of that Mercedes, then you simply do all of these little magical tricks and pretty soon you end up with a Mercedes.*

The problem with that, although it can be a useful stage, is that the *intellect*, the worldly part of your mind, can only desire what it has been *programmed* to desire.

The worldly part of your mind says,

Well, I have to transport my body around in this plane. Automobiles do that. The world tells me that a Mercedes is a grand way of doing this, therefore, I will create the desire of wanting a Mercedes.

And when you manifest the Mercedes, you fool yourself into thinking that you've made great progress when, in fact, all you've done is done what you've always done. You have chosen what your experience will be and you have manifested it. There is nothing new about that, although, by so doing, you can begin to regain confidence in your ability to manifest.

But *The Way of the Heart* is about something else. Allowance, in this pathway, means that you begin to view your life differently. It is not a struggle to get out of high school and create a career by which you can create golden coins, by which you can create the proper house in the proper environment so that your ego feels "successful" and, therefore, of being "worth" Love. Be honest with yourself—is not your world built on such premises?

If only I can make my life look successful around me, then I will be accepted, then I can love myself, at least a little. Maybe I can get other people to love me.

That's not it at all. *The Way of the Heart* begins with the recognition that you are *already* loved by the only Source that matters, that you have come for a much higher purpose that can be made manifest *in* the ways of the world, but is not *of* the world.

Allowance, then, is the cultivation of a way of looking at the events of your life, not as obstacles to getting what you want, but as stepping stones, each of which presents you with a blessing of the lessons required to heal the obstacles—not to success, but to the presence of Love as the source and ground of your being. In the stage of allowance, then, we begin to cultivate an acceptance of all things in our experience. We begin to see that because we have made a commitment to awakening and incarnating only Christ, that the Universe is already *conspiring* to bring the people and events into our lives, on a moment to moment basis, that can best provide us with *exactly* what we most need to learn or become aware of.

And so, messengers are sent. That messenger could come in the form of someone whom you fall in love with, and there is something there for you to learn. It could be that you've been blocking yourself from feeling Love for other people, and now someone finally comes that blasts down the door and you can't help but feel that feeling. The messenger could be someone who comes as the grain of sand within the oyster that causes the friction within you that nudges you from your sleep, and you realize that you've been operating out of some very dysfunctional patterns and that you've got to get a better grip, shall we say, upon the Truth of who you are. It may be that you need to learn to express your feelings more. It may be that you need to accept your own creativity more. Something will bring up to you, through your messengers, that which causes you to finally be responsible and be honest about where you are.

For instance, if you think,

> *Well, I never get angry anymore. After all, I'm a very spiritual person. I just got out of seminary and I know it all now. So, ah yes, I'll just live in heavenly bliss.*

And events begin to happen. Perhaps a, um, hmm—we'll use this for an example—perhaps a gay couple moves into your neighborhood and you discover that you have some very deeply seated perceptions that there is something wrong with that sexual orientation. They are messengers, sent to you by the Universe to push you to look more deeply.

Allowance, then, is the cultivation of a quality of awareness in which you rest in the recognition that your *life* is no longer your *own* to dictate and control, but that rather, you've given it over to the Source of your own beingness, to that depth of wisdom in the depth of the ocean that knows best how to bring about what is required to push up the dross from within your consciousness, so that you can release it.

Allowance cultivates trust. Allowance is the way in which intention and desire come to work ever more fully in the third dimension of your experience—the field of time. Allowance is a submission, but not a naive submission. Allowance changes your perception of what you see as the world around you.

You begin to realize that you don't really live in a real world at all. You live in a field of vibrations and energies that is operated by the Law of Attraction, resonance. And you begin to be willing to allow certain things to fall out of your life, even family and friends, *trusting* that because of your desire and intention, what passes out of your life must be okay, for it will be replaced by new vibrational patterns which come in the form of messengers—events, place, persons and things—that can carry you on the upward spiral of awakening.

Allowance means the beginning stages of the cultivation of *humility* and the recognition that you must finally *submit* to something beyond the intellect and the control of the egoic part of the mind—that the maker and doer that's been trying to do it all is finally recognized as being inadequate.

As these three stages mature, you rest into the final stage of *surrender*. And surrender means there is no longer any restlessness. Surrender means you know through every fiber of your being that there's no one here living a life, there is *Life* flowing through the body-mind personality, for as long as it lasts. Here is where the mystical transformation is culminated or completed. It is here that you understand the meaning of the teaching,

> *I live; yet not I, but Christ dwelleth as me.*

Surrender is a stage in which perfect peace is the foundation, not for passivity, not for inactivity, but even *more* activity.

You find yourself, as long as you are in the world, being busier and busier, asked to do more and more. You become even more responsible. And eventually, you come to see that because you *are* Christ, you are responsible for the whole of Creation. And you cannot think a thought without disturbing the farthest of stars. It is that responsibility from which you have shrunk and tried to contain yourself as a tiny myopic piece of foam, all because you've *feared* being responsible for the whole.

But *The Way of the Heart* corrects your perception, in which you come to recognize that your greatest joy, your greatest fulfillment, is in wholly and deliberately accepting responsibility for the whole of Creation. Why? Because you suddenly realize you're not the maker and doer, that you can accept responsibility for anything and everything, because *through you all power under Heaven and Earth is made to flow, to manifest the Love of God.* So, in short, it's in God's hands, not yours. Nevertheless then,

> *Not my will, but Thine be done.*

Does that begin to make sense to you? Do you see how it changes how you've even been taught to interpret my teachings?

Desire, intention, allowance, surrender—but it is a surrender into a way of being that the world can never know. It is surrender into a way of being in which you may never receive—what you call this, in your world—an *Oscar* for your acting. But it is a way of being in which your consciousness becomes totally open to your union with all of Creation. And you will talk with a leaf as it falls from a tree. You will see the soul of the kitten that you pet. And you will talk with angels and masters. You'll be involved in board meetings in the high cosmic conference rooms.

And you will know that the body-mind that you once thought was yours is little more than a temporary teaching device, a *tool* to be picked up and utilized at God's direction, and one to be put aside when its usefulness is done. So that even when it is time to go through the transition that you know as death, nothing will disturb your peace. And as the body *dies*, which means simply that your attention begins to release itself from it—just like the hand of a carpenter is released from the handle of a hammer, and the hammer simply is laid down on the table and the carpenter goes in for dinner, and forgets about it. You'll be able to watch even the process that your world calls death, with total equanimity and joy.

You'll watch your spirit disengage from the body. You'll watch it crumble into lifelessness so that all of your attention becomes focused in a wholly new dimension, a dimension that is so vast that you will be able to look down upon the Earth plane, not unlike the way you might choose to hold a pebble in the palm of your hand, and in one quick glance you see everything about the pebble, and nothing's hidden.

Responsibility. I am one that has chosen to assume the responsibility for the pebble called Earth and all of life that dwells therein. You, too, will know that energy and reality of wrapping your fingers around the entirety of the solar system and becoming, shall we say, the God or the Savior of that dimension. And it *begins* by choosing to take responsibility for your pebble, your domain, your solar system, your personal dimension. And that, again, begins by saying,

> *I, and I alone, am the source of what I experience and perceive. I'm not a victim of the world I see. And everything I experience, I have called to myself, plain and simple—no excuses, no if's, and's, and but's. That's the way it is.*

And gone will be your immaturity, your resistance, to simply being responsible for your experience.

The Way of the Heart, then, cultivates a maturity of desire, intention, allowance, surrender. And no single characteristic is of greater importance than this, and we've already mentioned it. It is called *humility.* Not the feigned humility that is taught in certain world religions, but a *genuine* humility. For humility doesn't mean that you stand in front of a group of people, who stand and give you a standing ovation. And you go,

> *Oh, gosh! You don't have to do that, you know. It's not important.*

So that you can look like you're humble when inwardly you're saying,

> *Oh God, that feels so good! Clap a little louder, clap a little longer. But I won't tell you that.*

Know you that kind of humility? Isn't it the kind of humility you were taught in your schools? Hmm. Don't stand there and beat upon the chest and say,

> *Yes! Thank you! You know, I think I'm really doing this well now.*

You were not taught that that's okay.

Genuine humility flows from the deep-seated recognition that you cannot save yourself, that you are created and not Creator, that you are effect and not cause (in an absolute sense), that something called Life is not yours, that there is *something* beyond your capacity of containment and intellectual understanding. And if that something ever decided to give up loving you [snaps fingers], you would cease to be, that no matter how deep you go into the depth of God, and no matter how deep you achieve an awareness and consciousness of union with God, that what God is, is forever beyond your growing capacity to understand God. It is like an Ocean of Infinite Depth. And when you realize that, strive as you might, you'll never wrap your self, your little self, around that Source, you will rest into humility—*genuine humility.*

And why is this important? Because, and mark these words well, as you progress along the path of *The Way of the Heart*, as you dissolve and loosen the shackles upon the mind, as the interior conflicts are healed and settled, as you begin to accept the abundance that the Father would bestow upon you in all levels of life and all levels of feeling and perception, as you begin to taste of the grandeur and the greatness that would flow through you, you will discover that the "enemies" become more subtle. Every child views, at some stage, its parents as being its enemies, doesn't it?

> *What do you mean I can't have the car tonight? What do you mean I must be home by 10:00 p.m.?*

The parent becomes the enemy.

But that's a very immature and basic and naive level. As you move more and more into mastery, you will be sorely tempted to believe that you're done. You'll be sorely tempted to believe,

> *I can do this. The prayers I used to do when I began, the simple exercises of awareness I used when I started my path, I don't need them anymore. I have mastered that.*

Any time you hear a voice within yourself saying, "I'm done," you may rest assured, you're not. And you stand in danger of losing what you've gained.

114

Humility is the recognition that the more you move into mastery, the more there is the desire for discipline and vigilance. Discipline does not mean doing something hard that you don't like to do. Discipline is like the skill of an artist that cultivates and refines the skill, simply out of the deep desire and delight to create more beautifully, that's all. To discipline a muscle is done by an athlete so that the muscle works even more beautifully than it did the day before, out of the sheer delight to extend greater beauty into the world.

Therefore, the discipline of the mind that is required is to recognize that, while the body lasts and, indeed, while you remain in existence, the creations of consciousness that are unlike Love have created a whole lot of vibratory patterns that would just love to pull you down. It is the recognition that there can be a delight in consciously repeating the decision to teach only Love, and to selectively choose only the vibrational patterns in your consciousness, to be allowed into your consciousness, that reflect the Truth and the beauty and the worthiness of who you are.

Judgment can not reflect such Light. Anger and hatred can not do it. Fear and paranoia, fear of rejection, fear of the opinions of others—such vibrations can never reflect the regalness, the greatness, the grandeur of your Being. Therefore, understand well that humility is *absolutely essential.* For paradoxically, as greatness is expressed through you, the temptation still is to allow egoic energies to make a home in your mind. And the ego's voice will say,

> *Boy, you are really quite a master, you know? You really deserve all this adulation. Why don't you keep ten percent of it for yourself?*

A master accepts the Love offered, the gratitude offered by those whom his or her teachings have touched and gives it all to God, recognizing that of themselves these things could not have been done. I learned, too, to be tempted. And when those would come to me who were sick found healing in my presence, it was very tempting to want to say,

> *Yes, look what I've done. I've really earned this. I spent forty days and forty nights in the desert. I've been to India and Tibet. I've been to England. I've studied with all of the masters of Egypt. Yes, I really*

115

deserve to be seen as a healer and a teacher.

But I learned, through humility, to remember the simplicity that, of myself, I can do nothing. I cultivated within myself the art of always being a *student of Love*, and not the *professor* of Love, who thinks he's done just because he has a lot of letters after his name. So you see that as you progress, and as you allow more of the abundance of God's Love to flow through you, you see you begin to stand up out of the crowd, and you begin to attract those that want the Light. And as that occurs, *you must practice discipline and vigilance by remembering humility always, until you are remembering it with every breath.*

And why? If you are living in this world, and feel that no one looks up to you, no one takes you as authority, there is only one reason. You have resisted the Truth of your being, and through denial have pushed God's Light away out of your fear, your deep-seated fear, that you might appear to be different than everybody else. And the world would teach you to be a doormat so that you fit in, and don't ruffle anybody's feathers. But as you become empowered, one way you'll know that it's occurring is that some people won't like you. You'll push their buttons just by walking into the room, for *darkness abhors Light*. It's that simple.

Humility is absolutely essential. Through the doorway of humility, the Light of Power can be turned on through you, in ever greater voltages. And if that voltage doesn't seem to be flowing through your mind, look well to see if you are remembering humility and giving yourself to it. For the Light of God can only shine through you to the degree that you are willing to take responsibility for it, which involves giving the fruits of it back to its Source, and not claiming it as your own. And when you claim *nothing* for yourself, *all* things can flow through you. And the Holy Spirit can gather millions of beings to come to you in many planes, because it knows you will not distort the Love of God by usurping God's position and putting yourself upon the throne.

Humility is a chief characteristic to cultivate. Therefore, when you pray, indeed ask for greatness. Let the Father know that you are ready for the fullness of Christ to be incarnate and simply hold the promise within that you will always remember that you are not the doer and the maker. You are merely the one who has come to recognize that only the Love of God can fulfill you as a soul. Only the fulfillment of your purpose to be a *channel for Love* can bring you the success that you truly seek. When you are fully committed to that, rather than being committed to wondering about other people's opinions, then that Power can begin to move through you.

When you are willing to let go of the world, Heaven will come to replace it. When you're willing to let go of your need for egoic grandness, true grandeur will begin to pour forth through you. There is a paradox within Spirit. Learn to discern it. Become a master *of* it. And never neglect the need for discipline based on the foundation of humility. You see, this is what has caused you to fear the energy of desire, because in the past (and that can go back a long way), you have decided to find out what it would be like to let all of that power be claimed as your own—to be used to serve the voice of ego. And that is what you are afraid of. But if you cultivate these stages and found them in humility, you will never need to fear the misuse of desire.

Therefore, in your prayers, as often as you can remember to do so, remember that what you decree, *is*. So speak clearly within yourself.

> *Source, Creator, God, Goddess, All That Is, Abba, I am ready to be what You created me to be. I choose to remember that I am effect and not cause. Thy Will be done, knowing that Your Will is my full happiness. Reveal then, that path through which that happiness can be known. For my way has never worked, but Your way always does.*

Then, in each day remember the energy of *appreciation*. It is well and good to appreciate one another. But in the privacy of your own meditation and prayer, appreciate how the power of that Source of Love I've called Abba or God, is living and moving and breathing to bring the people, the books, the teachers, the experiences that are gently unraveling the cocoon of ego around you, awakening you to the Truth, and the beauty, and the majesty, and the grandeur, and the greatness that Life, Itself, is—that wants to breathe through you as magically and powerfully as it breathes through a thunder storm, or the leaf on a tree, or the radiance in a newborn baby's eyes.

That Life is what you are. That Life is the presence of God's Love, the Depth of the Ocean welling up into the Waves of Creation. Let, therefore, that Life alone be your guide in all things, and rest in appreciation before the Infinite Mystery that Life is, and say *yes* to it. Say *yes* to *Life*—that you are willing to let the fullness of it wash through you and carry you into an ever deepening understanding and comprehension of all that God is. And, indeed, if you would well receive it, resting in the awareness of divine humility is the sweetest of experiences that you can ever know.

Many of you look upon me going,

> *Oh! Where Jeshua abides, would I ever love to be there. Think a thought and you're with someone. Think a thought and you're in that universe. You never have to blink an eye because you don't have one.*

I tell you this, where I abide is in a vibrational frequency with many, many other beings whose consciousness *never wavers* for an *instant* from the deep *appreciation* and *humility* before the Mystery of All that God Is—the great delight of knowing that we live, yet not us but our Creator lives *as us*. The only difference between being a master and being a student is that the master has mastered the art of always being a student. Think about that one.

Desire, intention, allowance, surrender—what do you *truly* want? Are you willing to feel it and let that *thread of desire* carry you home? Can you remember to use time constructively, by focusing your intention, by reminding yourself of what you're truly here for? You're not here to survive, you're here to *live* as the Truth of who you are.

Allowance—not a passive acceptance of things as they are, but a recognition that there is something quite beautiful at work. There is an Intelligence, a Love that knows you better than yourself and is presenting you, moment to moment, with jewels and gems and lessons and blessings, that something is weaving the tapestry of your life, and nothing is happening by accident.

Surrender—the cultivation of the recognition that your happiness can be found only in the submission of your will to the Will of God. For your will has been to be in conflict and struggle and limitation.

The Father's Will is that you live without conflict, in peace, and joy, and fulfillment, and happiness. 'Tis called bliss.

Humility—if ever you wonder how to anchor your awareness in humility, stop what you're doing and ask yourself this question:

Did I create myself?

You will know darn well that the answer is:

No, I don't even know when I was created. Something birthed me. What is it?

That will bring you to humility rather quickly. Do you know how to give birth to a star? No! Do you know how to give birth to a leaf on a tree? No! Do you even know how you lift your hand from your lap? No! What then, do you know? Nothing! Allow yourself to understand that you don't know anything. And in that state of *divine ignorance*, you will rest in a humility that finally allows your Creator to move through you and reveal to you all things.

So, beloved friends, *The Way of the Heart* is that way which corrects perception and brings *right-mindedness*, so that you are no longer the maker and the doer and the director. Your opinions will come to mean nothing to you whatsoever. And out of a grand emptiness, you will discover a perfect peace. And Life will bear you on Its wings. And through you, Life will express, in ever greater dimensionality, the exquisite and infinite Love and Power and Creativity that is God, until you swear that God is all there is. And there will be no place to find a trace of you. For if enlightenment is the ending of separation, how can there be a maker and doer? Can the wave direct itself? The ego is the attempt to do so, and it always fails.

Peace then, be with you always. Let peace pervade your being at all times. And know that you are safe in the Love of God that arises from that great source of Mystery, and would move through you with every breath you breathe and every word you speak, until you hear only that impetus of guidance that wells up from the depth of your being as a Gentle Voice that you trust completely. And you will know the freedom that you seek.

And with that, we, indeed, would leave you now. Yet we go nowhere, for you already abide where we are. Trust this. Know this. Rely on this. And explore *The Way of the Heart*. And by such exploration, you will come to know the Truth of Love.

Be you, therefore, at peace, beloved friends.

Amen.

Lesson Six

Now, we begin.

And indeed, once again, greetings unto you, beloved and holy friends. *Indeed, greetings to you, beloved and holy friends.* If you understand the meaning of this greeting, if you comprehend the *depth* of each term used, already you know all there is to know. And you are well prepared to extend the Love of God, forever.

"Indeed" means simply that there are no other options. *"Greetings unto you,"* salutations to that one created of the Father before all things, for I bow down before your radiance. Greetings unto you, *"beloved"* and holy Child of God! Indeed, beloved of God. Indeed, beloved of every molecule in your physical universe. Indeed, loved of your Holy Mother, this precious Earth. Indeed, loved by anything you can imagine that has ever existed or ever could exist, but that has extended itself from the Heart and Mind of God. You are the Beloved, pure and simple. And again, there are no options.

"Holy," because you are whole—not because you have earned that holiness—but because it is that which is the Truth from which you are extended forth forever; because you are made in the image of God; because you spring forth from the Mind of God. You are holiness *itself*, each time you set aside the temptation to dream a useless dream and walk this Earth as Christ.

Beloved and holy *"friend."* A friend is not one lesser than myself. A friend is one who walks in perfect equality, with the grandest of masters, whoever you might conceive such a master to be. A friend—a friend is one who chooses to look upon another and see only the Face of Christ therein. And there is no one present in this room and, indeed, there shall never be anyone present in the hearing of these words, that has not already looked upon *me* and seen the Face of Christ within. And, likewise, I look upon *you* and call you *"friend."*

For when I look upon you, I see not the very momentary dreams that you seem to think are lasting so long. I see only the radiance of that which my Father has extended out of Love. I see only that which has neither beginning or ending. And I see only that which knows neither birth nor death. I see only that which has no limitations. I see only that, the Light of which is already extended throughout all dimensions and all universes.

I see only my brother and my sister. And I see not a trace of inequality between us. And yet I do recognize that, within your dream, it appears to you that I have gone ahead just a little bit. And at times, within your hearts, there is a longing to follow me. And if you would but *heed* that *longing*, if you would make that longing *primary* at all times, your own *desire* will bring you wholly to where I am. And you will laugh when you discover that you haven't moved an inch—that where I am is where you are, and where you are is in eternity, and not in time; that where you are is in the place of your birth: *the Mind of God*. This is the only thing that is true and it is true always. This is the only reality that you genuinely possess. Therefore, indeed, I call you *friend*. For well do I see that you are as I am, and therefore, *indeed, greetings unto you, beloved and holy friends.*

So we can stop now. There is nothing else to be said. And yet the mind races, does it not? And yet it races from the very reality that I have just described about you. The mind races from that source as a sunbeam to the sun. Yet, in reality, it never leaves its Source. And the very power with which you seem to become distracted, by a momentary thought of fear, is the same power by which you *will* awaken to your own call.

In Truth, there is a place within you that already knows the day and the hour. You already know when you are going to decide to live the decision to be awake in God, to be only the presence of Love. *And Love embraces all things, allows all things, trusts all things, transcends all things.* Love is never possessive. Love is never fearful. Love is simply Love. Love cannot shine with specialness upon anyone at any time. For specialness, itself, is a contraction, the attempt to take Love and make it shine only on one object, only on one person, only on one being, only within one universe.

Whenever, therefore, you recognize that you have singled someone or something out and said, "They hold a greater value," you may rest assured that you're not in Love at all, you are in fear. And therefore, if that one were to leave you, where would you be? But if you are *in Love*, as a fish within the sea, all beings can arise and pass away and you will bless them in their journey. And you will remember that you reside where God has placed you. And God has placed you in His Heart. And when you choose to be *only* the presence of Love, even the dream of loss will dissolve from your consciousness as a forest mist before the rising sun.

Indeed, beloved friends, Love does wait upon your welcome. And yet you cannot welcome Love by waiting for it to be brought *to* you by another, not even by *me*. You cannot welcome Love by trying to scurry about to create the environment in which you believe your preferences are being met. You cannot welcome Love when that welcome is attached or linked to any phenomenal thing, anything which has been birthed in time. Love can only be welcomed where Love truly resides. And Love resides within you as the Core and the Source of your very being.

Therefore, if you would know Love, know your *Self*. Embrace the Truth about it and the Truth will set you free. Then, indeed, Love will flow *through* you. And like the great sunlight that comes to nurture this beloved Earth of yours, the Love that flows through you will be *unimpeded*. It will not meet an obstacle. And you will look upon whomever is in front of you and you will know that they are sent unto you of the Father. They have been guided to you by the Holy Spirit because, through you, Love can be given in a way that begins to touch the place of their awakening. That is why you are but the servant of Love. That's all that Life is!

When you choose to surrender, to give up the game, to give up the dream of trying to resist the Truth that is true about you always, you will become a mere channel, a mere conduit. You will become no more a seeker, for you will have decided to have *found*. And surrendering the last vestige of an insane possibility of contracting away from the Truth, when you've given that up, Love will flow through you. But notice that if it flows *through* you, it must first flow *to* you. Therefore, seek always to *receive* in order to *give*. For what can you give another if you have not yet given it to yourself?

How many of you have been taught to try to love, to try to do the "right" thing, the "good" thing? . . . whatever that is supposed to mean. And yet, how many times have you gone within your secret chamber and said, "I am unworthy"? And then you wonder why your attempts to join in Love with others never seems to be quite fulfilling enough, never quite seems to fill the cup, never quite seems to elicit the joy that you believe could be there. For indeed, listen well, your work, if you wish to call it that, is not to seek and find Love, 'tis merely to turn within to discover every obstacle that you have created to its presence, and to offer that obstacle to the great dissolver of dreams, the grace of the Holy Spirit.

I have said unto you many times, that the greatest of gifts you can give is this: to come wholly to the recognition that every attempt you have made to resist being the presence of Christ has *failed you, miserably.* No matter how many times you have tried to convince yourself that you are unworthy, yet does the universe find a way to love you. No matter how many times you have tried to lock yourself into the space and volume of a body, it hasn't succeeded. And at death, you have remembered and been confronted with the *radiance of your unlimitedness.* Therefore, indeed, the greatest of gifts you can give another is to be one who has rescinded the need to insist on the insanity of fear.

Fearlessness is the primary characteristic of mastery. And mastery is not having great power to make things happen. Mastery is only the recognition that what is true is true always and there is no other choice. Free will does not mean that you have the right to believe that you can succeed at being other than what God created you to be. Having free will does not mean that you can elect not to take the only curriculum that Life is offering to you in every moment. It means only that you *do* have the right to put it off yet another day. And each time you put it off, you slumber in your suffering.

But when you elect to take the only curriculum that matters, when you elect to use the power of your free will to say,

> *Now, from this moment on, I will no longer tolerate error in myself. No more games, no more dreams. I am committed to being only the presence*

of Love, for that is the Truth of who I am. It matters not the opinions of others who are yet resisting that decision.

. . . then, indeed, all things under Heaven and Earth move to support you, to guide you to the right person, the right place, the right book, the right sunrise, the right meadow, in order to assist you in dropping the shackles of the obstacles to the presence of Love that you have created as an idol and as a substitute for Love. And that is why, when truly you pray from the depths of your soul, "Father, bring me home," you may rest assured, from that moment on, it's okay to trust every little thing that unfolds. For though you see it not, what you would call the *angels*—friends that simply don't have bodies—are rushing about because you have given the command to say,

> *Yes, I accept your presence in my life. I turn the whole thing over. Now, each moment is dedicated to healing and awakening the illusory sense of separation from God that once I created in error.*

Love! In how many ways have you sought it? Hmm! Can you count the ways? Hmm! Would you dare to try to count each little pebble of sand on the beaches of your planet? For rest assured, each and every soul has already tried to seek out Love in that many ways, if not more. You have sought it in a million forms in which you *already knew* that you *could not find it.* All because you wanted to perpetuate the insane attempt to try to separate yourself from God. And that is as futile as a sunbeam trying to separate itself from the sun.

Indeed, beloved friends, there is only one question you need answer:

> *What am I choosing in this moment?*

> *What have I given mastery over my life unto: what perception, what thought, what feeling? (since feeling merely flows from the thought or the perception you have chosen). What behavior, what action am I choosing in this moment and does it express the reality of my beingness? Am I being busy extending Love, or am I busying myself fearfully trying to grasp at what I* think *can give me Love so that I don't lose it?*

Look well, then, upon your parents, and your siblings, and your mates, and your friends. Not one of them, *not one of them*, holds the power to bring Love to you. So what are you trying to get from them? Why do you ever insist that another ought to be conformed to what you believe you need? It is futile, one hundred percent, absolutely, positively futile to *seek* Love in relationship with anything or anyone.

It is, however, quite appropriate to *extend* Love in each relationship, with everyone and everything. But the extension of that Love requires that you have awakened to the Truth that the *only* relationship that truly holds value is the relationship between you, as the soul, and the Father, or God, as your Creator.

Imagine a light bulb in one of your fixtures, that looks out from its little filaments and says,

> *Hmm! Well I hope the person that just walked in the door is the right one. If I could just reach out and grab them, maybe my own light would come on.*

Hmm. Isn't it a lot easier to simply take the cord and plug it into the right socket? How many times are you going to insist on trying to plug your cord into the wrong socket? Hmm?

> *Well that one didn't work. I'll try this body, I'll try this person, I'll try this career. Hmm. Not getting very much juice from that either. Ah! Well, there was a little juice.*

And then you get angry because it's not giving you enough juice, or it gave you enough juice yesterday but not today, so it must be *its* fault. Hmm!

There is one little tiny socket into which you can plug your cord. It's the only one that it fits in and it's the only socket wired to bring you the Flowing and Living Waters of Grace. And that socket dwells only within your Heart—not the physical heart, but that which is symbolized by the physical heart: *the core of your very being.*

But how many times in each day do you check to see that the cord is still plugged in? How many times do you remember to ask yourself,

> *Is my commitment to Love or is my commitment to fear?*

Fear is the act of disconnecting your cord from the only socket

128

that can truly satisfy you, and running about trying to plug it in to somebody else's or something else's. And I would ask you to consider this one question, as you look upon the whole of your experience: Has it ever worked? Can it ever work?

Imagine trying to hold flowing water in the palm of your hand by squeezing the fingers together. How much are you left with? Doesn't it just run through the fingers, no matter how hard you try? It finds the little holes and it flows away. You open your hand and there is not enough left there to wet the tongue. And yet, each time you have looked upon another—whether parent or sibling or friend or mate or teacher or whatever you have—every time you've looked upon a physical object and tried to plug into that socket to get the juice you believe you need, that's what you're doing. And you literally end up squeezing the life out of the relationship itself.

But in Truth, when you seek first the Kingdom and plug that cord into the socket within your heart, when you remember that you and your Father are One, that only Love is real, that nothing else matters . . . and what you're feeling that might be speaking to you saying, "But . . . but . . . but . . . but . . . " is nothing more than the echo of an old habit. And that habit can not live unless *you* feed it.

Therefore, feed the only habit that matters: the habit of remembering that the Truth is true always, regardless of what is passing before your physical eyes, and, therefore, before your mind. In all comings and goings, in all births and deaths, in all arising and passing away of universe after universe after universe, in the midst of a flat tire or a sudden rainstorm, nothing—*nothing*—holds value except your relationship with your Creator.

When you have experienced, in relationship with anyone or anything, a moment of bliss, a moment of a peace that forever passes all understanding, a moment of fulfillment so sweet and so sublime that no word could touch it, much less express it, what you have experienced is only the flow of the Love of God through you. It was not caused by that person or thing. It was caused because, for just a moment, you stepped out of your drama, you stepped out of your dream, and allowed the Truth to be lived.

Then, of course, you tricked yourself:

> *God, that was so sweet! That was the best thing I've ever tasted. It must have come from you. Get over here! I need you!*

If ever you believe you need anything or anyone, rest assured, in that moment you are living in delusion.

All you need is Love. Love fulfills all things. Love embraces all things. Love heals all things, and Love transforms all things. Therefore, indeed, remember well—you, and only you, can become the cause, if you will, of your fulfillment, of your peace, of your completion of time. And this requires that you do nothing save remember to establish the connection with your Creator.

Is it not true that what you desire most of all is Love? Is it not true that you try, or you at least hope, that each relationship, no matter how short, no matter what its form, that each journey, that each undertaking will allow you the experience of peace? Is it not true that you who find yourselves in and as a body, temporarily in time, is it not true that the grandest of experiences you've known have been those that seem to flood the very cells of the body with Love, with a sublime bliss and a peace?

Accept that Truth, that what you desire beyond all things is *the living experience of Love.* And then remember that nothing you do can bring Love to you. Nothing you do can keep Love for yourself in a form of your choosing. Nothing you do—*nothing you do*—can make Love appear in the form of your insistence.

But releasing the drama, releasing the dream, choosing to remember the Truth that is true always, returning to the Kingdom within, even prior to every breath, and reminding yourself and saying to your Creator,

> *I want only that which is true always. Love is what I want. Love is what You are. Love is what I receive. Love is who I am. I and my Father are One.*

Here, and here alone, do you discover what you seek.

And then you become free to walk this Earth, to be in it, but not of it at all. And though your friends will look upon you, and still see a man or a woman who seems to act much like themselves—and yet, though they see it not, Christ dwells with them. And something in them keeps attracting them to you. They are not sure what it is. The shape of your body? Hmm! The radiance of your eyes? 'Tis not these things. They feel the quality of *Love*.

Can you imagine walking upon this Earth, this very planet upon which you find yourselves, and no matter where you are, feeling as though every wisp of cloud and every blade of grass and all good things under Heaven and Earth were already residing with you, within this sphere of your countenance? Can you imagine walking upon this Earth and sensing that the Light from the farthest of stars that shines during the night is already within you, that the whole of Creation was held in the palms of your hands? Would there be room yet to convince yourself that there is something you lack, something you need, that the restlessness you feel must be valid?

In Truth, you are like one who has been given a perfect treasure, a priceless jewel. And you have placed it into your pocket and forgotten that you possess it. And so you run around trying to look into everybody else's pocket. And you've tried to seduce certain ones to surrender so that you can own the clothing and, therefore, try to possess the jewel that you hope is in their pocket. But the great Truth is that you cannot possess Love until you set it free. You cannot move into holy relationship with anyone or anything until you give up all trace of need to possess it.

When your only desire is Love, you will be willing to set anyone free, to support them in their own journey, no matter what it is or what it takes. And yet, you will never feel your Love waver. And if a twinge of sadness arises because you recognize that two bodies in space are now going to go to separate parts of the planet, as that twinge arises, you'll recognize it as the effect of a mistaken perception. And you will move within, to the place in which all minds are joined. And you will remember that your fulfillment does not rest in *gaining* Love from another but in *giving* Love to everyone.

If, indeed, you would know the Truth that sets you free, heed each and every word that is being shared. And if you would taste the sweet nectar of perfect freedom, be you, therefore, committed to replacing every erroneous perception you've ever made, every thought you've ever held of everyone and everything, to set these things aside and commit the fullness of your energy to the simple but vigilant practice of remembering the Truth—even prior to every breath:

> *I live!—yet not I but Christ dwells in me. Therefore, I submit and surrender to the Truth that is true always. For my fulfillment comes only from allowing Christ to be given to the world.*

And so, you see, the Truth is very simple. It is not complex at all. Get out of the way, let Love live through you. And all of a sudden you will know that, indeed, you are given all good things eternally. You will know that Grace is reality. You will know that effortlessness is the way of Life in the Kingdom. But effortlessness does not mean that you do not feel, for you are in a dimension of feeling. Effortlessness does not mean that you do not discover, that you do not deepen your ability to be the living embodiment of Love. It does not mean that you do not challenge yourself to learn to express Love in a way that can be heard by another. Effortlessness means simply that you abandon the resistance to what Love requires in each moment.

Effortlessness is the way of the Kingdom. In the world, effortlessness means that you let down the wall you have built between yourself and all of Creation. You no longer resist the *lived experience of relationship*, whatever it is—relationship with a cloud, relationship with another person, relationship with a dog or a cat, relationship with—what you call this—your April 15th, when you write your grand government a check. Hmm. Why do you not wrap it with what you call your Christmas paper and your ribbons and send it with much Love? Hmm!

When you've learned to release the barriers, the walls between yourself and whatever is in front of you, when you open the door to what many of you would call your *chakras* and simply allow Love to be lived through you, when you look upon another, or another situation, or another thing, and realize that nothing in this world has the power to hurt you, nothing in this world has the power to take anything from you, *if you remember to extend Love*, then you are free! And you've transcended birth and death. The seeker is no more and only Christ walks this Earth. And if your commitment is, indeed, to look within and discover each and every obstacle you have ever created to the presence of Love, why do you resist *feeling* those things? For well has it been said to you, that on just the other side is the very Love you seek.

Deny then, not, the role of *feeling* in this dimension, for *feeling is everything!* You can't even know the presence of God unless you feel it. You can't *think about* the presence of God. You can't insist on a belief about the presence of God. That doesn't do it, that doesn't fill your cup. Feeling fills your cup. Feeling—*unbridled, unblocked, unobstructed feeling*—is the doorway to that Love that sets you free!

Therefore, when you say, "I don't want to feel this," rest assured of what you're truly saying:

> *Yes, yes. The doorway to the Kingdom of Heaven is right in front of me, but if you think I'm going to open it, you are crazy! It's not worth it anyway. What is worth it, is protecting the substitute I have made.*

And I have called it the ego, the false self, what I once described to you as a gnat shouting at space.

> *That! Oh, that's what I'm committed to. And I'm going to protect this thing. Give up Heaven to protect this useless little thing? Oh, yes! You'd better believe I'd be willing to make that sacrifice! What's Heaven anyway? A bunch of love stuff. Hmm! A bunch of people running around in bliss, some of them without bodies, hanging out in unlimitedness, fearlessness, utter fulfillment. Who needs it? Oh, but this little gnat, this little gnat of mine. Oh! I'm going to make it shine!*

There is much wisdom to look at in your funny little sayings and music and things. How many times have you tried to make that little gnat shine? Hmm!

> *Everybody notice, its shining. Please, notice how great I am. I'm making my gnat shine. Listen to my whining and my complaining and my*

(pardon the expression, what you call the "bitching"), the lamenting, the great sadness. Oh! How grand my gnat is!

Meanwhile, the Love of God flows through a multitude of universes and creates—forever—even new universes. And the Love of God doesn't even notice the gnat at all. No one is paying any attention. Your friends around you don't want to pay attention, although sometimes you corner them and they have no choice. But those of us without bodies—do you really, actually think we waste our precious eternity taking your attempt to make the gnat shine *seriously*? Indeed, because we Love you, we give you the space, and we honor your free will to be as little and as miserable as you wish. And we will wait until you choose to come once again into the greatness in which you truly reside. We never withdraw our Love from you. We simply look through your story line, because what *we* wish to love is the *Christ* that dwells within you.

What calendar day and hour will you decide to *love yourself* as the Father has first loved you? To truly—to *truly*—and once and for all, make the decision to *live*! For until you decide *with*, and *for*, and forever *from* the Mind of Christ, *life has not yet begun!*

> *Oh, my God! That's a bit of a blow, isn't it? Look at all the experiences I've had, Jeshua. How can you tell me I haven't lived? Why, there was this drama, then there was that drama, then there was that drama over there. Don't you remember seventeen lifetimes ago when I did this and then I did that? I struggled through that one, and I've struggled through this one. I have lived.*

No, you've *dreamed*.

Do you awaken in the morning and realize that you've had a whole night of dreams of receiving ribbons and trophies, and what have you, from the world? And then say,

> *That was very real. The trophies must be out sitting on my kitchen table.*

When you awaken and sit up and put your feet on the ground, you go,

> *Ah! Shake my head a little. I was just dreaming.*

While you dreamt, it felt real enough. And that's the quality I'm speaking to here.

And if you wish to take this as an affront, it's perfectly okay It won't disturb my peace at all. Until you fully decide to come into Life as the presence of Christ, as the presence of Love, to *own* each moment of your experience as wholly self-created, for no other reason than that you have chosen it from the perfect and infinite freedom of your Unlimited Beingness, when you look upon all things without judgment, through the eyes of forgiveness, when you decide to embody only the reality of Love, no matter what anybody else is doing, *that is when Life begins!*

As of this date on your calendar, there have only been a handful of beings who have *truly lived Life* upon this plane, a very small handful. There are many of us that would just absolutely be *thrilled* if *you* would join the club! And I'll let you in on a little secret: until you do, you don't get to graduate. You will never leave this plane, filled with conflict and suffering as it seems to be, until you have lived the experience of walking this Earth wholly as *the thought of Love in form,* with no other allegiances but to Love. You will never leave this plane. You will never take up your cross and follow me. You will spin around again and again and again, only to be confronted by the same need to decide *wholly for Love.*

And you'll finally look Heavenward and say:

> *Father, let's get on with it. Enough time has been wasted. Its gone, its okay, it doesn't matter. [claps hands] Now! I am committed to Love. Bring on whatever I must experience to bring up from the depth—the places that I've hid it within me—every obstacle that must yet be dissolved by the Light of the Grace of Perfect Love. And I will do whatever I can, from my side of the fence, to open up those places, to feel those places, to embrace those places, to love those places, to claim those places as wholly self-created.*
>
> *And I will let my parents off the hook, and I will let my siblings off the hook, and I will let my great, great, great, great, great, great grandfather off the hook. And I will let Adam and Eve off the hook, and I will let the government off the hook. And I will love myself enough to heal my*

separation from God.

And I will be humble enough to recognize that if I'm having an experience, because I know I have made the commitment to healing, then You have, indeed, precious Father, brought me all good things. For this moment of experience can be seen through eyes that recognize that it is but a stepping stone to the Perfect Peace that I seek.

My life is no longer mine, for I know not how to correct that one fundamental error. But I can surrender into feeling each moment fully while choosing Love anyway. And Love will dissolve the pain that I have carried, all because I insisted on trying to separate myself from the Source of my being.

This little gnat of mine is being put to rest. For the only thing that can shine is Christ.

For Christ, the Son of God, the offspring of God, is God's only creation. The rest of it is attributed to you. Even space and time is yours. *You*, the Truth of you, is your Creator's only creation. For *you are Love*, and God creates only that which is like unto Himself. And *God is only Love*.

Many of you believe you are on a spiritual path. You will know if that is true by your willingness to *feel* and *experience wholly exactly what is in front of you*, moment to moment. Whoo! So if you have enmity with another, if you have a conflict with another and you sit in your chair and decide to do what you call pray or meditate, in order to change the feeling state within yourself, and you arise later and say, "There, I'm feeling much better now," but the issue has not been solved with another, nothing has changed. Go, therefore, to the other. Open your heart, share, resolve. If you have offended another, ask them their forgiveness. If you have judged another, admit it. Ask for their forgiveness. It is only in such a way that you can truly heal the place of conflict within.

Beloved friends, the essence of this hour's message is quite simple:

Where are you *now*? Are you willing to allow yourself to see everything around you and within you as the doorway to the Kingdom of Heaven, waiting only for you to acknowledge its presence and to open it? Are you willing to truly be right where you are—*wholly, right where you are*? And the mind says,

Well, of course. I'm on a spiritual path.

Rest assured, if you look well into your feelings and find any trace of resistance, you have not yet made the necessary commitment that gives you the *power* to open that door.

Feeling is the message of this hour. For it is only through feeling that you truly awaken. Concepts and ideas can begin to direct the mind to believe that there is something out there that is attractive that might even be better than what you've been doing before. But concepts and ideas do not, in themselves, open the door. They are symbols, and that is all. And a symbol can not quench your thirst. It is only at the level of genuine *feeling* that you can once again know the presence of God Who dwells within you, around you, and through you, even now.

Feel what you have created as a substitute for the Truth. Own it, look upon it, then let it go. Learn that regardless of what choice you may have made in the past, that once you have embraced it, once you have felt it, you remain perfectly innocent and imbued with the power to choose again . . . to *feel,* to learn once again to feel the glorious warmth that permeates the Kingdom of Heaven.

Nothing you do with time can match the importance of what we have shared in this hour. Nothing you do in the field of time holds a candle to the incredible gift that is waiting for you. Therefore, indeed, *use time constructively by deciding to love, that Love may teach you of Itself.* And indeed, beloved and holy friends, when you have done this, you will find yourself translated, if you will, into a form that could never possibly be contained by the space and volume of a physical body.

And you will look upon this entire dimension as a mere temporary learning device. And you will set it aside, as a child sets aside a toy that has been outgrown. But you will do it with *deep appreciation* and *love* for the toy that you've played with for so long. And you will carry with you a deep sense of gratitude for everything this physical dimension has brought to you. There will be not a molecule, if you will, of beingness within you that will feel any resentment, any longing, any anger, any remorse for anything. And all of your experience will have become wholly acceptable to you. For it was by such experience that you were finally driven to want only the Truth. Hmm!

So! From this day forward you will never again be able to truly convince yourself that all of your attempts to stay distracted or conformed to the world are really accomplishing a thing. And you will find that your mind begins to penetrate the unconscious habits you have created in an attempt to hide from what must yet be felt. And you will know perfectly well when you are simply deluding yourself. And you'll start to smile and go,

> *Oh, yes. Hmm, hmm, hmm. There I go again. Might as well set that aside. Plant my feet firmly on the ground and, indeed, live with passion for the Truth of the Kingdom of Heaven!*

Therefore, for now, beloved friends, be you therefore at peace. We said that this year, this *The Way of the Heart,* that we would, indeed, speak ever more directly and even more forcefully to you. For the time comes quickly when this planet will not be willing to tolerate untidy house guests that are not willing to vibrate at the frequency of being to which the planet herself is preparing to move toward. Hmm! Therefore, be not caught by coming home one day and discovering that the landlord has changed the locks and you have not a place to rest your head. Rather, become the living embodiment of Love and journey with your Holy Mother into an entirely new dimension of being. And never forget to sing, laugh, dance and play along the way.

Be you, therefore, at peace, beloved and holy friends.

Peace, then, be with you.

Amen.

Lesson Six
Question and Answer Section

Question: How can I integrate the breath work and techniques that I am learning this week with your lessons in the *Course in Miracles*?

Answer: Beloved friend, the question comes from a quality of mind that would perceive a separation between the two. For only what is perceived as *separate* must be *integrated*. Know well, then, that *A Course in Miracles* is a teaching device aimed at a specific goal or conclusion. That conclusion or goal is the re-establishment of peace. Peace begins to be re-established in the mind when the mind is convinced that there is a way of perceiving, a way of orienting itself to its experience, that brings a greater reward than what has been known before.

A Course in Miracles was given initially to two people who had asked from the depth of their being (although they were not aware of it at the time) to be shown a way to perceive differently. A wise teacher first learns the language of the student. And the two that asked the question carried an orientation in which their primary mechanism for experience was through the level of the mind, or the intellect. Therefore, the teaching tool needed to be conveyed in a way that could be acceptable to them as the student.

Secondarily, of course, as you well know, the essential message that I sought to bring forth through that teaching device is equally applicable to anyone who may be attracted to pursuing the study of it. And yet, the *Course* does not seek to answer every question that a teacher of God will, indeed, come to ask. It is designed only to re-establish the mind at peace, and to cultivate within that mind the willingness to ask of what I've called the *Comforter*, or the Holy Spirit, for guidance, rather than remaining attached to its own devices for decision making. This opens the way for the mind to be guided ever more deeply to what is required to become fully re-established as the embodiment of Love.

What you have called here "breath work" is merely a next stepping stone. Those who would hold that the *Course in Miracles* is a complete teaching device within itself are accurate, *if* they understand that it was given to those who are deeply embedded within the intellectual processes, and that it has a specific goal that is self-contained. Those that would assert that viewing the *Course in Miracles* as a complete teaching tool in itself, if they take this to mean that there is nothing further to explore, nothing further to deepen and become, are inaccurate. View it then, as a *teaching device* with a *specific goal*, given in a way that is acceptable to those who have learned to abide primarily in the level of mind that is engaged in conceptualization.

I answer your question this way because the body, itself, is not outside of the Mind. It arises from within the Mind. And you can, therefore, look upon it and what arises within it, to witness the effects of the thoughts that are actually occurring within the Mind, or have occurred in the past, and have not been corrected or changed. Mind is far reaching. Mind is everything, as the term is used within that teaching device. It should always be spelled with a capital M. Mind also encompasses feeling. Mind encompasses the body itself. For without the Mind's first having chosen the thought, the imagination, there could not even be a physical realm in the first place.

When you choose, therefore, to allow yourself to breathe, recognize that it is from the *power to decide*, that is, the *power of the Mind to choose* that you are creating the effect of allowing the aspect of the Mind, known as the body, to also receive illumination. To integrate *A Course in Miracles* with what you are calling "breath work," and what I have addressed earlier in this hour as the way of feeling, and what, indeed, we have called for the whole of this year *The Way of the Heart*, requires only the continued *little willingness* to surrender any and all limited perceptions of what Life is, and what awakening is, and what Love is, and what healing is, so that the Holy Spirit can guide you into the Truth of all things.

For, indeed, beloved friend, understand well that what was shared earlier deeply pertains to you. Namely this: When, from the depth of your being, you have fully committed to awakening from every last trace of separation from God, when you are truly committed to not seeking for Love, but you are willing to seek for all of the obstacles that have been created within you that block the awareness of Love's presence, then, indeed, what you find yourself attracted to, what you find yourself deciding for, in terms of the experiences that you would call to yourself, these things are the answer to your prayer. For just as my *Course in Miracles* came to your life, as you well know, as the result of your own longing to deepen your relationship with God, so, too, have you found yourself journeying to a tiny speck of dust in the middle of a large body of water—to breathe!

It is an extension and comes from the guidance of the Comforter, the Holy Spirit. Therefore, the integration is simple. Decide not for yourself, but turn decisions over to the Holy Spirit. And then, take what He has guided you toward and make it part of your life. And trust, in faith, that all these things are not without purpose. Ask only that every aspect, every tiny corner of your Mind become so illuminated, so healed, that only Christ abides where even there seems to be the body.

Question: Can you speak about the need, or lack of need, to work directly with the dark side, both on the physical and astral plane?

Answer: Yes, I can do that. [Pause]

Question: Will you?

Answer: That is another matter.

Indeed, beloved friend, first look well and understand the place within that would draw a line and decide what is *light* and what is *dark*. For remember that suffering comes from a split mind, a mind that sees conflict, division, separation. If it is true that only Love heals—and I assure you that it is—can you look upon what you have called darkness and discover the light within it by shining light upon it? Are there dark forces in the realm of experience, within the realm of Creation, as you know it? Yes, but I do not mean by this that there is a force separate from you or separate from the reach of God's Love that holds the power to direct, influence, or control you in any way. Darkness . . . As the journey that you're on begins to end, you will come to see that darkness is nothing more than a part of your own beingness which has been neglected and not loved.

For when you love what you perceive as darkness, you reclaim it as a part of yourself. And by loving it, you transform it. And the power you had given it by separating it from you, returns to you where it truly abides.

Is there a difference between what could be called darkness in the realm in which you live and move and have your being, seemingly as a body in space and time, and that which you call the astral realms? No! Everything exists right where you are. For you abide as fully on those realms as you do sitting on the floor in this moment. An astral realm is made such only because you have withdrawn your awareness of it and sought to constrict it merely into the physical dimension. Therefore, peering out from within a body, it looks like there is another dimension, that you choose to call the astral realm, where things are hidden from your view. They're not hidden at all. They are merely inaccessible if you use the apparatus of the physical eyes. But if you use the eye within, nothing is hidden.

What is astral and what energies abide therein are, therefore, nothing more than that which abides within your own consciousness, your own mind. And what is the way of working and dealing with those dark forces? Where you are in your third-dimensional experience as a body-mind requires only that you look lovingly upon your brother or your sister, that you *touch* them, if you will, with your words, with your smile, with the tips of your fingers, with the words you speak, so that Love is extended and forgiveness given. For those many forces and beings that seem to reside in realms unseen, called by many an astral realm, the strategy, if you will, is perfectly identical. It is one and the same thing, because only Love can heal.

Think well upon what is given unto you in this answer. Contemplate it deeply. Within three weeks' time, given the current momentum of your mind, you will begin to have some rather interesting revelations. You will literally feel the mind, shall we say, being rewired, shifting to a whole new level of perception, understanding, and natural ability. For what seems to be unseen on the astral realms . . . you will then begin to move in the direction of seeing it as clearly as you do the hand before your face. Pleasant journeys!

[*Note: The previous question is not available in the audio version.*]

Question: How can I tell the difference between old ego habits of feeling and feelings which need to be felt to completion?

Answer: First, beloved friend, is there a difference? Your experience is always of and in the present. For what arises is not past, it is now. Is it an old ego pattern? Perhaps. If there is a sense of constriction, a sense of resistance, a sense of judgment of self or another, rest assured, that which has arisen to temporarily dominate your attention is an egoic pattern, since the ego is, by definition, the constriction away from Love. And therefore, the loss of peace is its result.

Look well, then, and simply recognize,

> *What is arising in this moment? Am I willing to look upon it, to feel it, to embrace it?*

And as we would perceive and observe, you're beginning to recognize,

> *Am I willing, yet, to breathe?*

For *to breathe is Life!*

Feel, then, what you are truly feeling. *Observe* what is truly present within the mind. In this way, you take your hands and cup them around whatever that is. And you've done that, then recognize this great Truth:

> *I can choose again. And I can choose peace instead of this.*

Now the "this" is not so much the picture of what you might call a memory or a feeling or something that's coming up. The "this" speaks to your *judgment,* your *perception* of what is arising. *You can choose peace instead of the perception that steals your peace.* And *that* is the place of infinite and perfect power to literally *transform* your life!

Beloved friend, the past does not exist at any moment. If the Mind is causing, bringing forth, a picture or a thought that seems to be reminiscent of the past by your own decree, rest assured that it is arising in *this present moment,* which is the only place creation and

143

experience occur. The past, then, can exist for you only if you re-create it now. This re-creation does not mean that an image or a picture can not arise in the mind, what you call memory, although, it is a very present experience. We are speaking here of the experience you *created* when that same picture appeared in your experience in a different time frame. Your experience is never caused by what arises in your field of awareness. Your experience—listen well—your *experience* is how you have chosen to *react* in the *emotional* and *mental field*, to a *neutral event* that has arisen. All events are *neutral. The reaction to them is what generates experience.*

When nails were driven through my hands, that was an entirely *neutral event*, although, by the way, many friends scurried about. It didn't *appear* to be so neutral. But it was neutral for *me*. Therefore, understand beloved friend, that whatever events have *ever* unfolded in the realm of your experience, *each and every one of them was perfectly neutral, until you responded with the reaction that you were choosing in order to create an experience in the emotional body, in order to create a learning experience about the potentials of your own consciousness.*

Forgiveness, healing, peace, and awakening are equally *potentials* within your own mind. Equal to and, indeed, even greater than, anything that you have experienced heretofore. Therefore, understand, beloved friend: Nothing has been *caused* by anything or anyone outside yourself. What arises is always present experience. Embrace it, look upon it, claim it, own it, feel it, breathe through it, and then recognize that you are free to choose again.

Herein lies the straight and narrow path that leads to *Life!* And you have a friend, currently without a body, who wants nothing more than to witness your *true Living.* And you have countless friends, with bodies, who share the same desire.

Be you, therefore, that which you are! And live from the power given unto you, from the freedom in which you abide always—as the Love that you are!

Lesson Seven

Now, we begin.

Forever, I am with you. *Forever, I am with you.* For long before the stars were birthed, long before the planets arose, long before even a thought of physicality had emerged within the Divine Mind of the Son of God, we were already created together and equally. And yet, that Creation of what alone is real knows no point of birth. Therefore, because the Father is forever, so too, have we abided together, held together, sustained together, in Love. And throughout all time and even unto eternity do we abide together in the reality of Who we are. Therefore, think it not extraordinary when I say unto you,

> *I am with you always, even unto the end of this age.*

What journey have *you* ever taken that is not familiar to *me*? What journey have *I* ever taken that is, in Truth, not familiar to *you*? For when you look upon me and from some deep place of knowingness within, though the words may be different, you say within yourself,

> *Behold! Christ appears before me.*

... when you hold a thought of me in the mind, and the body is flooded with emotion, soft and gentle and light, and you recognize that the holy Son of God was birthed, perfected in your friend, even one Jeshua ben Joseph, what is it within you that *knows* that this is the Truth? What part of your mind, what capacity within your heart can look upon me and recognize the Truth within me, so that you love me? For I say well unto you, it is equal and the same as that part of *my* mind, that part of *my* heart that looks upon you and says,

> *Behold! The holy Child of God is before me. And I love this one.*

That which knows, that which comprehends immediately, is the Mind of Christ, that recognizes Itself in each and every one. That Mind of Christ dwells within you in its fullness *now!* And, therefore, as I have said unto you many times, never fail to remember that it takes one to know one. And if you would look upon me and say, "Beloved friend, thank you," look well upon yourself and say, "Beloved friend, thank you." Indeed, allow the breath to flow.

How many journeys have there been? Hm! How many moments of experience passed under the bridge of your beingness, so to speak, before you first began to reawaken to the Truth that is true always? How many life times, how many worlds, before a Light began to dawn—so imperceptibly at first that it was not recognized? And a tiny voice whispered from a place that seemed so far removed from where you dwelt,

> *Beloved Son, you are with Me now. You remain as I have created you to be. Therefore, be at peace. You are loved.*

And the voice seemed so far away, so faint, that surely, it could not be your own. Surely, it was just a moment's fantasy. And in the midst of some journey, you paused. And as a raindrop fell and hit a leaf, and your eyes looked upon that experience [snaps fingers], you felt and knew that you were one with the leaf and the raindrop, and that, indeed, you *were* those things. How many moments of experience passed by before these kinds of qualities began to emerge in your consciousness, as what seemed to be tiny mad ideas?

> *My God, I just felt myself to be one with all of Creation. Well, better not tell anyone about that.*

Hmm . . . and off you went.

But the moments began to come more often, still perhaps fleetingly, and yet now more familiar—a sense underneath all of the drama, all of the crying, all of the lamenting, all of the resenting, all of the fearing, all of the striving, all of the seeking. The still tiny Voice would come and say,

> *Beloved Son, you remain as I have created you to be. You are loved. You are wholly loving and wholly lovable forever.*

The tiny Voice would still steal through the roar and the din that had seemed to make a home within your mind. And rest assured, you would not be where you appear to be in this moment, if you had not already begun to experience many moments that express the quality that I've just described to you, of truly hearing the still, small Voice of the Comforter within.

Therefore, indeed, each of you knows that there is a longing within you that *cannot* and *will not* any longer be denied. You *know*, from the Christ within you, that Christ has stirred within you, and is rising to take up its rightful place as the Master of your mind and your heart and your body and your breath and your dreams and your passions! And each of you knows that it is absolutely futile to attempt to settle for anything less. And if there be anyone here, in this moment, who actually and truthfully doubts what I've just said, speak up. And so, silence is all the evidence we require.

It does not come because of anything I have ever done *for* you. It comes because it *must* come. It must arise within each created mind, regardless of its journeys, regardless of its attempts to deny what is eternally true. That's called *the illusion of the dream of separation*. It must come and it is inevitable because Christ *will not* be denied. Christ *cannot* be denied because only Christ can express what is absolutely true.

Only Christ can so *in*form the cellular structure of the body that even the simplest of gestures extends Love unto another who beholds it. Only Christ knows how to breathe the breath that releases all trauma, all hurt. Only Christ understands the power of true forgiveness, which is always, by the way, forgiveness of one's self, since no one has wronged you at any time. Only Christ can bring a smile to the lips of a body, such that when another looks upon you and sees that smile, their heart is filled. Only Christ can walk in this world, yet not be of the world. And only Christ can transcend every limited and fearful creation into the beautiful flower that blossoms and gives its sweet fragrance to all of Creation. And is it not that which you long to feel moving through your beingness? Is not that call to awaken alive within you? Oh, beloved friends, you know that it is!

Love you, therefore, one another. And love you, therefore, the Self that has been given unto you of the Father. Learn to hear *only* that Voice, learn to desire *only* that Voice. Learn to follow only that Voice that knows the Truth is true always:

I and my Father are One. And this world is but a passing shimmer and a dream. It holds no value save that which Christ can bring to it. Only Love is real. And anything else is the choice to momentarily believe in illusion.

And, oh rest assured, illusion within an illusory world can seem to hold great power. But all power has been given unto you. All power under Heaven and Earth is given unto the holy Child of God. And that power dwells within you as the Life of your life, the Breath of your breath, the Truth of your truth, the Beingness of your beingness, and the Joy of your joy. And there has never been an illusory creation that has ever, in Truth, threatened it. And no illusion can take reality from you.

The only thing that can occur is that you use that power to believe in loss. And all forms of loss that you perceive through the physical eyes, or through the worldly mind, are nothing more than passing shades of your insistence on believing that loss is possible. All forms of the contraction known as fear are nothing more than temporary modifications of the very power given unto you, a power that you have sought to use to see if it were possible to convince yourself that something besides Love is real.

But the story is over. The dream of separation is ending. The whole of Creation is now experiencing a growing power, if you will, a movement, a momentum that must carry the Mind, from which Creation springs, to a new level, if you will. It's not so much an evolutionary level as a level of *re-cognition*, a level of *re-membrance*, a level of *re-turning*. And that wave of momentum is alive and has already arisen within your heart and mind. You know it. Stop denying it. Stop questioning it. Stop looking for signs from the world around you that it's okay to feel it. *Accept it* as a divine gift from your Creator. For the call has gone out. And though many listen, few hear, and fewer still become wholly devoted to responding.

Therefore, let your prayer be always:

May Christ, alone, dwell within and as this creation that I once thought was myself.

May Christ, alone, inform each thought and each breath and each choice. May Love direct each step.

May Love transform this journey, through time, that in time, I might truly know the reality of eternity, the sanctity of peace, the holiness—the holiness—of intimacy, the joy of the Father's Love, prior to every breath and, indeed, even prior to every thought that arises within the mind.

For when you know that you are Holiness Itself, how could you ever look upon your brother or sister and believe that they have wronged you? How could you ever want to do anything but love them? That is, let the Love of Christ flow through you so deeply and so profoundly that they get that you do not believe their illusion.

For when you give unto another that which alone is true, because all minds are joined, you have offered unto them the only gift that holds value. When you give another the Truth, perhaps even without saying a word, again because all minds are joined, they recognize what has been offered:

The one before me knows the Truth of me and is looking right through every one of my attempts to be less than who I am. Therefore, I see that it's safe to choose again.

And that is when miracles occur.

Do not strive to heal this world. Do not do anything to make a show of how much you love another. Give up the concept of being a busy bee. And simply *be* the presence of Love, simply because you *know* that there is absolutely no value in being anything else, and that, in Truth, you have never succeeded at being anything but the presence of Love.

Each sane moment that you've experienced, each moment of unlimitedness, each moment of genuine intimacy, each moment of grace-filled joy that you've ever known, in whatever form it seems to appear or be bottled before you, has come because you've allowed your mind to slip into the Sea of Peace. And you've merely abided, empty, wanting nothing, seeking nothing, merely the presence of what you are. And when that quality becomes cultivated so that it permeates your consciousness with each breath and with each moment, you will know that Christ has, indeed, arisen this day. And you'll celebrate Easter with each breath.

What, then, could ever possibly arise to obstruct the Truth that is true always? There is an ancient forest somewhere on your planet. A forest, high in a rugged mountain valley, so rugged that no one has ever been there. Unknown to the minds of humanity, life goes on in the forest. Deep within the heart of this forest, this morning, a little tiny blade of grass seemed to be tossed by an unseen wind. And as it was tossed for just a fragment of a moment, so subtle and soft was this wind, that as the sunlight played against this blade of grass, it cast the smallest of conceivable shadows on a stone that lay just a little bit away from the blade of grass.

No one noticed. The shadow had no effect. The rock didn't even notice. No one on the planet noticed. No one in any of the heavens noticed, except me—I needed something to build a story around. That tiny shadow, cast by a little blade of grass momentarily wiggled in a wind in some remote forest, has virtually no effect on the turning of the planets, the creation of new suns, and certainly not one trace of effect on how deeply your Father loves you.

That little shadow is what you have given power to. And it *seems* to be able to obstruct the Truth within you from being lived. For the moment, you gave that little tiny shadow power. And that very moment, fear was born. And fear is always a contraction away from Love. And fear makes you smaller than the blade of grass that momentarily seems to cast a shadow and, therefore, obstructs your recognition of the warmth of the sun that bathes you *always*.

And when you resist healing—when you struggle to do what, as we have been observing you here do, learning to 'speak your truth'—when you resist healing in these ways, you may rest assured, that something has occurred just prior to that. And it is your decision to believe that the shadow is all-powerful, and that if you heal, if you grow, if you change, if you let Christ live in you, that that little blade of grass, and the little tiny shadow it creates for a very temporary moment, will come and punish you and crush you.

152

And if you can truly take this story into your being and recognize the *utter laughability* of such a belief, you will never again *fear* fear. You will never again allow fear to master you and direct the course of your life. You will, indeed, learn what it means to trust what is birthed in the Heart. And you will arise and you will go forth without fear—with no story at all. And you will accomplish whatever creativity wishes to express through you. And the whole while you'll know that of yourself you do nothing, but the Father, through you, can do *anything*. Therefore, indeed, what forms of the shadow of that blade of grass are you allowing to run and own and possess your soul? Hmm! An interesting question.

There are many forms of that shadow, are there not? There are peers and parents and siblings to please. And there are governments to bow down before. There are mates and children that must come first. There are bills to pay. There are desires to check and keep in order. Hmm! There are activities and statements and behaviors, done by others, that require at least seven or eight hours a day for you to analyze and judge them to death:

My, this world is exhausting. But somebody has to do it.

And you thought it was Love that makes the world go around? Trust me, Love does not spin and get nowhere.

Love created you. Love birthed within you as an individual, at least within the dance of time and space, the *power* to choose, the *power* to feel, the *power* to know, the *power* to channel Light and Love, the *power* to know that something exists within and *as you,* that's what Love has done! And has fear ever created anything remotely like that?

So what do you want—creation or mimicry, peace or the ability to simply drug yourself with triviality? All power under Heaven and Earth flowing through you with every breath so that your consciousness witnesses not what you do as the maker or doer, but that which the Divine is doing through you in each moment—so that you get to marvel at the creativity of Love, the very same Love that moves the sun and the moon and other stars. Now *that's* a delightful pastime!

And when your life, this one Life (and you only have one Life. You might have many bodies but you will have one Life), when you give that one Life wholly (what is this called here—"with the lock, the stock and the barrel"), when you give it all to being only the presence of Love . . . And if there are any cobwebs in the way of that, lets get on with it and get them swept out of the way:

> *I've got better things to do because the whole of Creation is waiting to move through me, and I want to be aware of it. I want my experience, my lived consciousness, to be blissfully absorbed in observing the flow of Love through this mystery . . .*

. . . you call the body and dare to call *your* body, as if you have some right to possess it. Give the body to God. God knows how to use it, you don't. When you are in that place, Heaven and Earth will move to become your servant . . . not until. Send a conflicted message, nobody shows up for the dance. And when you move into that place, for no other reason than besides that *you want it*, you will know, because you will *be* the Truth that sets all things free.

So now you know what the shadow is. Perhaps sometimes you enjoy dancing with it. The great question is: Are you going to let the shadow lead or are you going to lead? When your life becomes that—I'm not speaking of perfection as you would consider this—when your life becomes that motivation, that attitude, that declaration, and that devotion, then perfection will be witnessed through you. For perfection is miracle-mindedness in which that which saves time occurs. And when your life becomes that, when you no longer have any conflicted—what is this word?—*commitment*, when you no longer have any conflicted commitment in your beingness, you will know exactly what the result of *my* life was for me, because you will *be* that.

Yes, I know what you're worried about:

> *Does that mean that when I get really close, I'm going to have to go through my final initiation of crucifixion? And if I have to do it, will you promise that they at least sterilize the nails? Could I choose the day or the hour? I don't like to get up too early.*

Hmm! You already know what crucifixion is all about. You've done it to yourself a million times in ways far worse than a mere nail driven through the hand that creates a little twinge of pain. Hell is nothing more than the state of being rutted, or stuck, in the process of crucifying one's Self, which is nothing more than the attempt to murder and destroy what God has created out of Love.

Stop wasting your energy trying to love God. That won't do it for you. Stop wasting so much energy trying to learn how to love another. That won't do it for you. And for *God's* sake, please refrain from all attempts to get anyone to believe that you love them. Hmm!

Put the whole of your attention on giving up the patterns of belief from which you have attempted to crucify the Self that God made and placed within you as your very *awareness* of your existence. Learn to *love* that Self beyond all created things. Learn to *nurture* that Self. Learn to *cultivate* within that Self only that which speaks of joy and Truth, so that your words and your actions and your very presence always uplifts another, so that when another walks into the room in which you are sitting or standing or moving, they feel like a breath of fresh air just hit them, even if you haven't lifted a finger.

As long as there is a trace of energy within you in which you are striving to get from any perceived thing or object around you what you are sure you lack inside yourself, you can not know the love of Self. And you can not experience freedom. *Happiness is an inside job.* Hmm!

So then, what happens? You finally get it right and you decide,

> *Okay. What's that little shadow been doing? . . . little blade of grass . . . hmm! Well, let's take care of that one and that one and that one and that one. How many blades of grass and how many shadows are there within this beingness that seems to be overlaid over the Self?*

Does it matter? You're busy birthing Christ!

What happens when that really occurs? First, and listen well, *nothing will be unacceptable to you.*

155

Well, but well, but, does that mean if somebody is not a vegetarian that they're still loved? Hmm!

Does that mean if somebody votes for (what is this one—uhh, the man named after the bird—Quayle), if someone were to vote for Quayle, does that mean that they're not insane, that I can love them? Hmm!

Does that mean that someone who seeks power and, therefore, creates a war and kills five thousand women and children, that I can still look upon them and not have my Love be disturbed?

Does it mean that whatever arises within this temporary world is really, truly, literally, not a problem for me any longer, that nothing is unacceptable?

Yes. It doesn't mean you condone it. It means it's no longer unacceptable. For what you can not accept, you will *judge*. And every judgment is the attempt to *murder* what you have decided has no right to be.

Judgment is the opposite of forgiveness. It lives on the side of the fence with fear. Forgiveness lives on the side of the fence with Love, and only Love can heal this world. Imagine, then, living in a state of beingness in which, literally, nothing was unacceptable to you, because you knew that the Source of your true beingness was far beyond the limitations of anything created in space and time—that even death, which has been created out of the contraction known as fear, that not even death is unacceptable.

When I spoke many months ago to this, my beloved brother, who allows me to blend with his mind, and said to him, "If you will choose to trust me, I will show you the way to peace," I had to wait for his reply. I could do nothing to take from him the freedom required to become wholly committed to allowing Christ to be birthed where once a useless illusion had reigned. And when I said to him (in your understanding of time) quite some time ago, "I will show you how to become the being out of which all of Creation is arising so that you will know the Truth that sets you free," it raised up within him the most root or fundamental of fears possible. What is that? It is the last to be overcome: the *fear of death*. For when you are confronted by the Truth, you know that everything you have sought to create as a substitute for the Truth must die. That is why it is said, "The last to be overcome shall be death"—fear of death. Death is *allowed* that Christ might live.

There is no one in this room—listen carefully—there is *no one* in this room, and *there shall not at any time be anyone who hears these words*, to whom I have not spoken that promise unto. I will show you the way to the Truth that is true always and sets you free. But *only you* can make the decision to bring the *whole of your being* to that journey. And all it requires is *this much willingness*—what you call a "smidgen" in your world.

A smidgen of willingness is all it takes. I know the way home because I have completed the journey, and I will show you that way. With every word that I utter, in this form as well as in other forms, my one intent is to reveal the place within you to yourself that is the presence of Love that you seek.

What if you chose to actually commit yourself to considering and hearing what I'm sharing, and return to the innocence of a child, as you contemplated what it would mean in your life? Rest assured when the journey *to* the Kingdom is completed, the journey *within* it begins anew. And the bliss and the wisdom and the creativity and the laughter and the friendships, the family, the joy, the serenity, the peace, that has been, for the most part, as what could only be seen as, surely, an impossible dream—these things will become your most ordinary state of being. And yet, none of it can occur through any power that can move through *me*.

I can guide you, and I can show you the way. And I can walk beside you on the way that you've chosen. And, at times, I can give you my strength until yours is as certain as mine, by carrying you. But ultimately, you must *demand* that I put you down so that *your feet* touch the soil of the Kingdom of Heaven and *you* walk, under *your* strength, under *your* certainty, beside me. And you will, indeed, find in that day and hour that I will as often ask you, "How do you think we could do this? What would you like to create with me?" as you ask it of me. And then, indeed, we are as brother and brother, sister and brother, friends, dancing and playing in the Kingdom prepared for us of our Father.

One little shadow cast by a tiny blade of grass is all that seems to prevent you from coming wholly to where I am. And if you tarry yet a little longer, it's okay. You see, you can not prevent me from knowing the Truth about you and loving you. And when you are *in Love*, when you are so immersed in simply loving, isn't it true that you have no sense of time at all? There's no sense of effect disturbing your peace. You're just, what you call, "swaying to the music." You are loving, and your wholeness grows even more holy.

Therefore, indeed, *love one another as I have loved you.* For the Father has first loved me that I might show you the Truth of what Love is and the reality of your beingness. And I will not cease in doing this, regardless of how long you choose to tarry. For Love is, indeed, patient and kind. Love is not deluded, and Love does not allow delusion. Love embraces all things, trusts all things, allows all things and knows perfectly well where it's going, and never ceases in that journey until every blade of grass is released from casting shadows, and the whole of Creation is returned to the Heart of God.

Learn to love your Self and cry out to this world:

> *I and my Father are One! Ahh! That is the soil from which I move and live and have my beingness. So be it!*

And always remember that the Father looked upon His only Creation and said,

> *Behold, it is very good!*

And that goodness has a name and it's your name, and your name, and your name, and your name, and your name, and your name, and your name and my name. And behold, it is *very good! That Light deserves to shine!*

And so, with that, the message of this hour is given. I believe you can discern what it is. And yet before you stands the doorway. Will you open it through the *power* of your choice? For what you experience will reveal to you what choice you have made this day.

And with that, beloved and holy friends, may peace be with you always. And may the Truth that is true always shine within your hearts and minds throughout all ages. And remember, there's a perfectly good reason why I keep saying, time and again, I am with you always.

Peace, then, be unto you always.

Amen.

Lesson Seven
Question and Answer Section

Question: If God wants only me to be happy and doesn't require any specific action of me, what does it mean to be the servant of God? Is there a divine plan for action God would have us follow, or are the actions given us based wholly upon our momentary self-perceptions? Do we have to do things here in a particular way?

Answer: First, beloved friend, that is not one question. That is a host of questions. I have said unto you many times that the Father asks only that you be happy. And if, indeed, you are not asked to do anything, what then, could it possibly mean to be a *servant of God*?

When you serve another, you act, you are in such a way that they receive the joy of knowing that your full attention has been with them. To be a *servant of the Father*, then, means that you have finally chosen to set aside anything else that would distract your attention, and to place the *fullness* of your attention, which is the fullness of your being, on the Reality of the Love the Father would extend unto you. You serve God by *receiving unceasingly* what God would offer to you.

Imagine going to work for someone who makes chocolate ice cream. And you say unto your employer,

> *What would you have me do?*

And the employer smiles and says,

> *I love this ice cream that I make so much that all you need to do is eat it. I will pay you very well, if you would just fulfill that function.*

And you look at this one and you go,

> *Well, I happen to like chocolate ice cream, too. And if that's all I need to do, you can rest assured, you're going to have the most loyal employee you could ever possibly imagine.*

To serve God is not to work in the world in order to fulfill some conception that the mind has conjured up about what it means to serve God. It means only to drink so deeply that your cup is always *overflowing*. There is no sense of lack and, therefore, no need to reach *outside* one's self to have the cup filled. And when your attention is so devoted to the Reality of the Love that dwells within you, your cup does begin to overflow. And as it overflows, it will seek its own way, that is, like a river that has overflowed its banks will begin to cut new grooves, will it not? And you can never tell, you could never bet on which direction the new streams are going to go in. But it will bring the sustenance of Life and of Love to all that it touches.

But those new streams will cease flowing if the main river ever forgets its source. Therefore, you need do nothing but receive the Reality of God's Love for you. And, again, as you do that, it may seem in the course of your life that you are asked to embrace some phenomenon that is passing by, whether it be healing the shadow of one little blade of grass within what you think is *your* conscious mind, as opposed to everybody else's conscious mind, to doing something that seems to be involved with relationship in the world, whether it be feeding a hungry child, bringing the nurturance to another through touch or through song, planting a seed in the ground, delivering a piece of mail. It doesn't really matter.

As I've said many times, when you *truly understand* that you need do nothing but receive the Love of God unceasingly, you will have become that perfect servant. And then, if it arises that you're going to be a street sweeper, you will simply sweep the street. And you will not have anything else in mind, save that your cup is overflowing. And others will pass you by and they'll say,

> *This person is just a simple street sweeper, but I find myself wanting to walk this way to work, just to say hello. It seems to make my day.*

And perhaps you'll be asked to be the savior of the world. Only the voice for ego would see a difference of being the savior of the world and a street sweeper.

Therefore, strive not to know what you should do in the forms of this world, but be you wholly dedicated to being in loving devotion, in order to receive all that God would shower upon you: Love so grand that the Mind can not even conceive of being without Love. And, indeed, your cup will overflow.

Herein is the essence of the many questions disguised as the one.

Question: What is the difference between a twin flame and soul mate? Please describe the importance of bringing two whole people to a relationship and maintaining uniqueness while creating synergy.

Answer: It would not be appropriate to say that you can *create* synergy. Nor would it be appropriate to say that you can *create* genuine individuality. What you can create and cultivate is the willingness to be wholly committed to *allowing* every last trace or obstacle to the presence of Love to be dissolved from within you. Synergy and genuine individuality arise from your devotion to being unceasingly open and receptive to the Love of God. Like a flower bursts forth from a seed well planted, both individuality and synergy in a *holy relationship*, which is where only synergy can be found ... these things arise from the *receiving* of Love, the *allowing* of Love, the *remembrance* of that Love.

What is the difference between what are called twin flames and soul mates? First, the only difference is a matter of definition. The concept of twin flame was given by a friend of mine as a way of assisting minds to see that there is an aspect of them that is uniquely and profoundly linked to something that is as much them as the self they think they are is, that has become fragmented, that what was whole became apparently fragmented, and, therefore, mind becomes imbalanced.

The idea was to create a story line in which the mind, so attuned to seeking for fulfillment outside of itself, would, at least, begin to desire that which symbolizes the movement into wholeness, the linking together of the male and female energies within the consciousness. At the risk, of course, that some minds would actually believe that to discover and find one's twin flame requires finding another personality in a body. And yet, because in Reality that fragmentation has never occurred, you need not go any further, in Truth, than your own awareness, your own beingness, to discover that that one is still within you. And you can not be separate from that one at all.

It may be that in the field of time, you, as a consciousness, will need to have the experience of attracting one who seems to be in another body, so that you can come together. But that is more the fruit of *your* belief that you *are* the body than of some objective reality. For in Reality, the Truth is one. Separation does not exist. Period.

And for soul mates? Same story. It can be appropriate to use those terms to describe to some minds what they're experiencing, as a way of giving and understanding that allows them to relax and get on with it. It is also true that within the drama of the dream of separation, there are souls—fragments of awareness, if you will—that have danced together and played together and have never lost the sense of union or love with, and for, one another. And therefore, over a period of *time* and the creation of *specialness*, those seeming two souls spark something within one another. They recognize the Truth in the core of the other, because they never really lost it, as they may have successfully lost it in other relationships. And, therefore, it is . . . hmm-m . . . it occasionally happens when two such that are on the path of awakening require coming back together, in space and time, to spark, to re-spark the commitment necessary to heal the sense of separation and to awaken from the delusion that a separate self has ever existed.

This means that you are not in need of *anyone* to be whole. It also means that when you discover that wholeness within yourself, you will be free, if you wish, to enter into relationship with anyone you might choose, and who would choose you. Hopefully, it will come from a place of holiness and freedom, and not fear and specialness. For the latter leads to pain that must yet be healed. The former leads to ongoing creativity and enjoyment.

It is only when two who are whole come together, having looked within and *truly understood* that *there is no lack* and, therefore, *no need*, that the power of creativity can flow through that entity. And any such committed relationship creates another entity, and gives birth to that which reflects the Truth, so that it can be seen by others who abide in space and time.

Do not attach *specialness* to the concept of twin flame or soul mate. If anything, remember that your *soul mate* is your Creator. Everybody else is your *friend*.

Question: How can we bring to light unconscious blocks that keep us from manifesting our heart's desire?

Answer: The answer is not as difficult as it may seem, for these blocks are merely various forms of the *decision against peace.* Therefore, look well and notice how you *truly feel* in any given moment, not necessarily what you're telling yourself. Is peace present? If it is, and something seems to be coming into your attention, you may rest assured that the Holy Spirit is asking you to bring the Light of Love to something that requires healing—without asking you to identify it as your own. We spoke of that the other evening.

You can not bring to Light what needs to be healed, since you do not know what healing truly is. Learn to know what true healing is, and what requires healing will present itself to you. And *true healing* is the *decision for peace*—not the denial of *feeling*. For peace is like an ocean that embraces all waves that may appear. One simple thing is all you need do:

Am I truly at peace in this moment?

If the answer is no, you need only ask,

What is in need of healing that peace might be restored?

It will not be hidden from you. Willing to put that into practice?

Response: Absolutely!

Jeshua: Now when you make such a statement, there are those of us who say,

Oh, well! I'll bring you some of my "case load."

When there were stories written about me that said I *took on* the sins of the world, and when you hear of masters or teachers who transmute the sins of their students, just think of that as "karmic case loads." And when one says unto us,

I'm willing to do all of this. I'm going to put this into practice—absolutely!

Ah, well! We've found a possible "employee." You'll never be given more than you are capable of transmuting. And, of course, you can always quit and look for another line of work!

Does the answer make sense to you?

Response: Yes, it does. Thank you.

Jeshua: Thank you for asking. It signals the desire for the answer.

Question: What is the interplay between playing out strong attachments, habits, compulsions, addictions, in order to let them go with gentleness and understanding, or using discipline and self control to end these attachments?

Answer: Discipline is not a rigidity or resistance *against.* Genuine discipline is merely a product, if you will, of the Mind. *Genuine discipline* requires only that you bring your attention to precisely what is true in any given moment of your experience, without judgment. Discipline is the vigilance of awareness and the decision to *be* the presence of Love.

The answer seems simple and short and to the point, but if you will contemplate it, even if you will sit in your meditation and write the answer out slowly, so that you watch the letters of the words appear on your plain white paper, and as you give yourself permission to be patient, not in a hurry, more will be revealed to you. And yet, the essence has, indeed, been given. Enjoy the discipline of contemplating the answer.

Question: There are two religious movements dear to me that I've seen growing over the past twenty years. These are the Christian Pentecostal and the New Age. How have you been an influence in their growth and development, and how do you feel about them now? If you had the opportunity to address these groups, what message would you desire to communicate to them?

Answer: First, I've been instrumental because I subsidize their marketing. [Laughter] And you laugh, but I mean that quite literally.

Hmm! There were many, there are many even in this room that would say,

> *Those are two movements dear to your heart that seem rather wide apart.*

And this is important because the form is always secondary. The healing of the separation from God, melting into genuine forgiveness, the willingness to merely let Love live where once there was a little tiny gnat, insisting on its own ideas—this is what matters. In this way, then, a pathway that genuinely seems to carry one to the recognition of the Truth and, therefore, sets them free, is equal to any other path, regardless of the "external decorations" that come with such paths. Indeed, beloved friend, enjoy what you do of each of these paths. Appreciate them. And walk on.

If I were to assemble everyone that represents each of the groups you've recognized and stated, what would I say unto them? The same thing:

Only Love is Real.

God is but Love.

You are God's Creation. Therefore, *your Reality is Love.*

Now go and live from your Self, that your Self might give Love to this world.

Don't look ahead to tomorrow. For the time spoken of is *now* for any mind that decides that this is so.

Look not for a savior to come from the clouds. For I am with you always. And I dwell within your heart, where, in fact, you dwell as well, hanging out in your living room as friends having a cup of tea.

I would say unto each of them:

See not difference in one another, but see merely the distinctiveness of a pathway through Life, in which Love can be remembered and lived.

And if that would not be sufficient for them, I would suggest that they seek yet another path.

Lesson Eight

Now, we begin.

And as always, once again, greetings unto you, beloved and holy friends. As always, I come forth as your equal—to abide with you, to walk with you, to communicate with you—from that Mind and that Heart which we eternally share as One, that Mind which is alone the reality of our *shared* Sonship, our shared existence. As always, I come forth in joy and also with humility. For I cannot join with anyone unless they provide the space within their consciousness and bid me enter therein.

Therefore, understand well that when I come to abide with you, I come with a humility born of the recognition of the Great Mystery that has given you your existence. And that Mystery I have called *Abba,* Father. And why? You have not come forth from some mechanical, unthinking force. You have come forth from Pure Intelligence. You have come forth from Pure Love. You have come forth from a Source beyond all comprehension. You have come forth from the Radiance of a Light so bright that the world cannot see it nor contain it. You have come forth from That which, alone, is eternally real. And because you have come forth from It, you are One with It, always.

This means that you abide in a relationship—created to Creator, offspring or child to parent—that is *so intimate,* a bond *so deep,* that it cannot be broken at any time. As a wave that arises from an ocean cannot be separated from the ocean itself, so too, in each and every moment in your experience, do you abide in a union so *powerful,* so *mysterious,* so *intimate* and *immediate* that the mind cannot comprehend it.

This union, then, connects you, as the created, with the Mystery beyond comprehension that contains every drop of wisdom and intelligence necessary to create consciousness itself. And consciousness, awareness, the power to be aware, the power to choose—this is what you truly are. And if this Source, this Mystery, can birth this most fundamental aspect of Creation, does it not deserve to be called *Abba* or Father, That which creates like unto Itself? Can you, then, begin to feel, to know, not just as an intellectual idea but as a *lived reality*, a *knowingness,* that if you are aware, in this moment, it is because you are One with the Source of all Creation and cannot be separated from It in any way or at any time?

Fear (and we have spoken of this many times) is like a contraction. And, again, if you were to imagine a wave arising from the ocean and then going into contraction because it thinks it is separated from its source, that contraction literally squeezes the life, the very flowing waters, out of that wave. And could that wave possibly continue when its very life force has been squeezed from it? Does it not then become mere drops of water fading from view, only to dissolve back into the ocean itself? And its radiance has been lost, never to be seen again. If it were possible for the wave of your consciousness to truly have its life force squeezed out of it, you, too, would fade away as droplets returning to the ocean, to never be remembered, to never be seen again.

But listen, and listen well: *that* would be death. But in reality, you are *alive, always.* And even when you have identified yourself with the great constriction that fear is, your fears have *never* been able to squeeze out of you the great life force, the great reality, the great gift, of awareness. You have, therefore, never ceased to be. There has never been a time that you have not existed and there will never be a time when you will cease to be.

You are, therefore, very much like a wave that has begun to arise out of an unseen ocean. And as that wave gains its momentum and moves across the surface of a planet, so to speak, you are like a wave that is in continual movement. Moving where?—into a forever extension of your awareness, itself. Into a forever extension of whatever you choose to pick up along the way and make a part of your Self; into a forever extension that will carry you into the experience or the fruits of the very thoughts you have held onto as your own.

Therefore, understand well: Right now, in this very lived moment, wherever you are, whatever you are experiencing, all that you see, all that you feel, all that you know, all that you seek to avoid, all the things you value and devalue, all things are contained *within* your awareness. For if they are not found there, they do not exist for you.

Therefore, look upon that which resides within your awareness, within your consciousness. What are the things that you *know* that you know? What are the things that you would avoid? What are the feelings that you have not explored? What are the objects, the people, the places, the values that you strive for, that seem to thrill even the cells of the body? What is the body, itself, if not that which arises within your awareness?

Look at the planet around you. Look at every object in your room. Look at every thought you choose to think. Look at the perceptions and ideas that you defend so vociferously. Look at the thoughts, the feelings of others, that make you cringe or wish to withdraw from. These things abide within you like the very power or life force of the wave that has arisen from the ocean. All of these things you have picked up along the way. And the way has been very long and varied indeed! For if you can imagine never ceasing to exist, it means that you have been as a *wave of awareness*, passing through, so it were, every time frame, every planetary system, every dimension of creation.

And along the way, one thing has remained constant. You have been in *constant relationship* with *all* of Creation. Oh yes, you may select out a few people, a few objects, a planet, a dimension, and focus all of your attention. And attention is nothing more than the decision what you are going to use the power of your awareness to focus on. And it seems that you have excluded everything else. That is like an *optical delusion* of consciousness. While it is very true that you have *selected out* aspects of Creation to focus your attention on, yet underneath—in the depth of the wave that is unseen by the physical eye, unseen by what you call your conscious awareness, your day-to-day mind—you have remained in perfect communion with *all* of Creation.

You are, therefore, *in relationship* with all created things, and there is a communication that occurs without ceasing. Imagine being able to look into the air of your planet and to literally see the radio waves, the TV waves, all of the electrical waves that keep, again, without ceasing, bouncing back and forth across your planet. This is what you swim in daily. Your consciousness pervades this field of vibrations. And *you* are the one who selects out what you are going to be aware of, what you are therefore calling into your lived experience. And, therefore, you select what is going to make an *imprint* upon you.

Imagine, then, a pool of clear, still water. And into it you drop a solitary pebble. And from the pebble there radiate waves. This is what is occurring *constantly* in the field of your wave of awareness. And as you have attracted to yourselves certain persons, places, things, objects and, above all, thoughts, beliefs, perceptions, you have dropped them like little pebbles into the still clear pool of your vast and eternal awareness. And what you experience are the effects, or the *ripples,* of those pebbles. They literally join with the other ripples that you've created. And as these ripples move out and touch one another and come back to you, that is the *field of creation* that makes up your physical, third-dimensional reality.

You are, therefore, never experiencing anything except what *you* have chosen to create through your selection of the pebbles that you have dropped into the field of your awareness. You literally never experience a solitary thing. You do not experience objects. What you experience is the *effect* of a thought or a belief in objects. You never experience another person, for they, themselves, are made up of a whole web of vibrations.

You could say that each person and each object (to use your language) is really a field of relationships themselves—unique and seemingly different from you, but a web of relationships nonetheless. For what child can be separated from their parents, from their cultural background, from the unique experiences that they have had as they have interacted with the webs of relationship that have been around them since the moment of their conception? What kitten can be separated and singled out from the matrix of its mother and father? What leaf on a tree is separate from the temperature of the air, the quality of water and nutrients that come to it from the very soil of the Earth? *Everything is a web of relationship.* And all webs are in relationship with all other webs and they become grander and grander and grander on *ad infinitum.*

You are, then, a web of relationships, out of which you have selected *certain* pebbles—whether they be thoughts or perceptions or experiences—and you have dropped them into the still clear pool of your awareness in order to create even more ripples. And then you have chosen which ones will have the greatest value for you. These you *lock in* to your being and they become your *emotional field*. The emotional field is the first level of crystallization of the body.

From the emotional field, a further crystallization creates the appearance of a *physical form*. And it is that which you push around the planet in your very temporary third-dimensional form of attention, while all around you, and just beneath the level of your conscious daily awareness, you remain in communication with all webs of relationship throughout all dimensions of creation. It is for this reason that an inspiring thought can come suddenly to you and penetrate your daily awareness. And you wonder,

Where did that thought come from?

Or suddenly a picture appears in your mind. It could be of anything—a man and a woman making love, a man and a man making love, a child playing in a park, a dolphin, a picture of conflict or war. Where did it come from? Because you live in perfect communion, and you are like a grand field of energy in which all webs of relationship are reverberating constantly, you actually have access to the complete entirety of Creation. And this entirety is not limited to what's occurring *now*, as you understand time. You have available to yourself everything of which you would call the *past* and the *future*.

These things are available to you at all times. And there is not one of you who has not experienced this for yourself. Perhaps you suddenly thought of a friend, and then the telephone rang, and you knew it was them. It makes no sense in your causal third-dimensional plane, but because underneath—even though your conscious mind was busy making breakfast and wondering about which stocks to buy and sell, or which perfume to put on the body—underneath you remain in perfect communion. It is why, when there is a deep resonance between friends, separated by thousands of miles, all of a sudden you know they need *you* to call *them.* You feel a sense of concern. Maybe they just stubbed their toe, but you pick up the vibration.

You all live this. You all know this. There is no secret about it. What I would seek, then, to attract your attention to is this . . .

One of the pebbles that has been dropped into the field of your awareness (and this is generally true for virtually everyone involved in the third-dimensional experience called physicality), one of those pebbles is this: Imagine a sentence being dropped from a vast height, picking up speed until it strikes the still pool of your awareness and sends a ripple out, creates a vibration through you. And the sentence is simply this:

> *It is not possible for me to have complete mastery over which pebbles are dropped into my awareness. I am at the mercy of the vibrational field set up by the ripples of all of the thoughts and webs of relationship in which I swim constantly.*

That perception is *absolutely true* . . . as long as you choose to believe it. That perception or belief is *absolutely laughable* and *powerless* as soon as you choose to acknowledge that this is so. What's the point of that? It is simply this: If you would choose to awaken wholly, if you would choose not just to be a wave that has mysteriously arisen from the ocean, if you would choose to be more than just another soul that has arisen from the Mind of God and is, somehow, crashing about through the universe, it is *absolutely necessary* to own, as your own, the pebble that drops into the still, clear pool of your awareness with the thought,

> *I am the one who chooses the effects I experience. I, alone, interpret all neutral relationships or experiences. I, alone, place the value upon objects, things, thoughts, belief systems. I, alone, am the literal creator of my moment-to-moment experience.*

This, as you can see, changes everything. For never again can you allow yourself to feel as though you are merely a victim of unconscious forces. Never again can you look out beyond yourself and *find fault* with another. Never again can the energy of blame be projected from you to be *dumped* upon another. Never again can the energy of *judgment* hold sway in your Holy Mind. This thought, this one singular pebble, dropped into the still pool of your awareness, is *absolutely essential* if you would decide to *awaken wholly*. And that is what this hour is about.

For though you would hear the Word many times—that is, that which carries the vibration of Truth—it can be denied as many times as it is heard. It can be allowed not, or, I should say, you can choose to not allow it to settle deep into that pool of awareness, so that it affects every drop of water that makes up the wave that you are. You can hold on to the hope that you are still a victim of the world that you see, that events hold some value in themselves that does not come from what you place upon it. And as long as you *choose* to deny the Word, you cannot be set free.

For the mind that chooses, in even a small part, to perceive itself as a *victim* of its world of experience, remains power-less, remains in a state that generates frustration, weakness, fear, self-doubt, unworthiness, suffering, pain, emotional pain of aloneness or separation from others, lack of fulfillment, and ultimately, the echo of the belief that you have been squeezed so tightly by fear that you are literally separated from the Ocean of the Mind of God. *Awareness is all that you have and all that you are.* Out of your use of it comes all that you choose to experience.

And out of *that* comes your decision of *how* you will experience what you have called to yourself. In Truth—and please listen well—no experience you have ever had has defined you or identified you. No experience you have ever chosen to create, to call to your self, and then to value as you valued it, has *ever* made you higher than or less than any one else—not even me—though there are many who still need to believe that I am far beyond them. No experience you have ever had has proven your unworthiness to be supported, to be loved, by your Creator.

And, therefore, you remain as you are created to be, a wave filled with the very selfsame Power as the Ocean Itself, a wave, a soul, a web of relationship arising from the Holy Mind of God with the momentum to flow on forever—with the freedom to create by deciding which vibrations you will allow to settle in and become a part of you, which thoughts you will defend, which perceptions you will cleave unto.

You are, then, eternally a creator. And this is the one thing that you have no free will about. You can never decide to be a non-participant in the very mystery of Creation's extension. Because when you hold the thought, "I refuse to participate in God's Creation," you have literally created the perception, and therefore the experience, of yourself as being outside or separate from Creation itself. You've created the insane emotion of trying to separate the wave from the Ocean Itself. And you *will* create the perception of separation even though nothing, in reality, has been affected.

Why is this important? Because you see, the process of healing is not difficult. It requires only your *willingness to accept* that you are the *effect* of the Creator's desire to create like unto Itself, as a wave is the effect of the Ocean's desire to express Itself in a new way, a new form, and to bring a uniqueness to every wave that arises from its Mysterious Depths.

Surrender, then, is the process in which you finally relent, you give up resisting the fact of your very existence. You stop whining about it. You stop lamenting it. You stop worrying about it. You make the decision to *get on with being alive!* And what is alive about you is going to be alive forever. And there is no place to hide and nowhere to go.

When you have dropped that pebble into the mind,

> *I am not a victim of the world I see. I am a ceaseless creator, made and of one substance with, my Creator Itself.*

Then, indeed, the questions begin to take a different shape. You begin to use the power of your awareness to deliberately and selectively choose which vibrations, which webs of relationships, you're going to pull into your field of awareness—which ones you're going to resonate with and which ones you're going to let dissolve from your mind, from your awareness.

And if you have held onto a thought of smallness, a thought of lack, a thought of powerlessness, now you begin to see that it's perfectly neutral, perfectly safe to look upon everything you've ever created and experienced and say,

> *'Tis very good, and now I'm done with it. What's next? What pebbles can I drop into my Holy Mind in this very moment? Can I look upon the current experience I'm having and see that it's nothing but the effect, the ripple, of a pebble or a thought that I dropped into my mind so long ago, so long ago that I don't even remember it? Can I look upon those events that are unfolding around me (and if they're unfolding in your body, trust me, that is still around you, for you are much more than just the body), can I begin now, and am I willing now, to drop a different pebble into the still and infinite clarity of the pool of awareness that is what is alive about me always? Dare I think a different thought? Dare I drop such a pebble into my consciousness?*

And so what pebbles could they be?

> *Hmm, I think I'll become a world savior, a Christ. What would that be like? What vibrations would I need to let go out of my life and which ones would I need to open to? What would it feel like? What would I see as I look out through the field of my awareness at Creation? Hmm. I think I'll allow myself to be able to commune with any web of relationship, any soul, any being, that exists on any plane of Creation. Why, perhaps I'll even allow myself to know that I can be in communication with Jeshua ben Joseph. How wealthy can I become in this third-dimensional reality? How many golden coins could I possibly create in order to give them away to others? How many places on the planet could I take a body and plop it down upon, in the span of one short physical life? How many beings could I say "I love you" to? How big can I make my heart be? How deep can I experience peace?*

The realm of possibilities is as infinite as you are. And the ones you select and choose are the ones that will create the web of relationships that you will call your life, your experience, even right down to the quality of how you will experience the *transition*, mistakenly called death, in your world. Would you call it a death when you leave one room and close the door behind you and step into another room? Of course not. You just say,

> *I was there; now I am here.*

That is all that truly occurs when the molecules you've called to yourself are unglued because you release your value of them, and their constituents, their parts, dissolve back into the dust or the energy field of the planet. You merely leave one room and step into another.

What I call you to in this hour is this: to be willing to allow the pebble to be dropped into your field, or *pool of awareness,* that carries the energy of the thought,

> *From this moment forward, I elect to birth a* Christ, *and thereby learn what Christ is!*

And your experience becomes the unfolding learning of what Christ is. And when that learning completes itself, you discover that what you have learned is what you are created to be. And you have returned full circle. The prodigal son, journeying through the field of all possibilities, has returned as the Awakened Christ, and has taken up his or her rightful place at the right hand of the Creator.

What does all that symbology mean? It just means you finally think only with your *right-mindedness.* You think as God thinks, and God thinks lovingly. God thinks infinitely, timelessly, patiently, certainly, and above all, God thinks *play-fully*—full of play! When you feel, welling up within you, such Love and such joy that you can hardly contain it, don't you start dancing and moving the body about, going,

> *Oh, my gosh! What am I going to do about all this energy?*

And you call your friends and say,

> *Let's have a party, let's go to a movie, let's create a delicious feast. Who could I write a letter to? Oh, who could I send flowers to?*

Don't you become caught up in the desire to let some energy expand out of you, to touch all parts of your creation?

Well, imagine being God—infinite, vast, without a top or bottom or a left or a right, filled with nothing but pure, unconditional, radiant Love! Can you imagine being able to contain yourself and say,

Oh, well, I think I'll just sit here in this and not let anybody notice it.

No! God said,

Let there be light!

And it was very good! And He looked upon all of Creation, which literally means not just this planet but all of an infinite number of creations of dimension upon dimension upon dimension, and all little webs of relationships called souls that He brought into existence in one split second and said,

Lo, it is very good! This is My play! And My joy and My Love and My aliveness has poured forth and overflowed My Grand Being and brought forth into manifest creation—you!

You, each and every you of you, made of the very substance of that overwhelming Love and playfulness, the power to create infinitely, and thereby to extend Creation Itself! That is who you are! And that is where you find yourself, *now*, and now forever. And you will never escape it.

Mastery comes when fear has been completely dissolved. And fear is dissolved, not by fearing it, not by hating it, not by judging it, but by being looked upon with perfect innocence, embraced in the same way that as a scientist would watch the ripples of a little pebble that's been dropped into a pool of water to see how they've created other ripples, and other temporary disturbances in the field or the surface of the water.

As you look within and notice the things you've become afraid of and how fear has constricted your creativity, your joy, your playfulness, and your unlimitedness, you merely look with innocence and wonder and say,

Oh, I see how that ripple has affected the creation that I call my life. Hmm, Do I like it? Not any more. Good! I think I'll be rid of that. What can I replace it with?

Mastery is a state in which you have embraced yourself as a ceaseless creator and assumed complete responsibility for everything which comes into the field of your awareness, *without judging it*, so that you can simply decide whether it's going to stay or be dissolved in its effects. *Mastery* is *fear-less-ness* . . . no longer fearing the infinite, creative power of your perfect union with God. *"I and my Father are One!"* is one expression of mastery.

And if I, who uttered those words once, so long ago, in your experience of time, can demonstrate to anyone who will look, that consciousness transcends the limited beliefs about the body and life and death that the world seems so determined to defend at all costs—if I can demonstrate that only Love is real, if I can demonstrate the power to communicate with minds across Creation, if I can bring forth creations by joining with other minds who may temporarily think they are just a body, such that written words fall upon a page and the page becomes part of book that becomes part of something sitting on your shelf, such that your heart is touched at just the right time—if I can do these things, so, too, can you. And indeed, greater things than these *shall* you do!

Beloved friends, is it not time to assume complete responsibility for the *grand freedom* that has been imparted to you by *Abba*—Father, Creator, Source of your being? Is it not time to begin spending time *disengaging* from your entangled view that holds you to believe that what you feel and what you think is the *effect* of all of the energies and things that are coming *at* you, from around you, and begin to use time to decide which pebbles you will drop into the *field of your awareness* consistently, day by day, hour by hour, and even breath by breath?

For these things create your tomorrows, and you cannot ever escape the reality that you are and always will be in the process of creating your tomorrows. Death will never separate you from it; denial does not change it. And you are free to decide what your tomorrows will be through the act of seeking first the Kingdom, which means to rest into that inner silence in which you *know* that you are a wave having arisen with perfect momentum out of the depth of the Ocean of God's Holy Mind, and that what you carry with you is the result of the thoughts and the beliefs and the perceptions—like pebbles that you have dropped into the wave of your awareness.

This very process is what created you, and this very process is how you have always created. If you've ever received an education, how did you end up with your body in a classroom? Did somebody kidnap you and sit you down and say, "Here, you must learn these things"? No. You first held a thought, a picture, and you placed a value upon it, and you attracted the means that carried you into the lived experience of receiving the education that *you* had decided upon.

What relationship have you ever entered out of lack of awareness? None. You dropped the pebble into the mind that said,

> *I want relationship with another being, another body, another place upon the physical planet.*

You've always been doing it, and you have always experienced the fruit or the effect of the quality of vibration of the pebble that has created the ripples that have become your experiences. In reality, then, your experience, that is, your awareness, what is true about you, is no different than what is true about me.

The only difference has been that I learned to train myself, hour by hour, to drop only *unlimited pebbles*, that send out vibrations of unconditional acceptance and Love and forgiveness, and unconditional and unbridled vision, and revelation, while *you* have selected to do that a *few* times, but then you rush back and pick up the pebbles of unworthiness, or limitation, or lack, or fear, or smallness, and you drop ten or twelve quick ones in. Then you go back to the other cupboard and go,

> *Hmm, the pebble that says, "I and my Father are One" . . . oops, had enough of that!*

And back you go again. So, while I stay on this side of the fence going,

> *I and my Father are One! I and my Father are One! I am Unlimited Beingness forever! How many universes can I be the Savior of today?*

you have gone,

That sounds very good. I and my Father are One. Oh, here is a pebble that says my car needs to break down today.

Hmm.

This is all there is! Which side of the fence are you going to sit on and drop the pebbles in? Which *tree* will you eat the fruit thereof? The tree of knowledge of good and evil? Hmm. Use that symbology well, for when you drop the pebble in the pond it is like saying,

> *Well, I think I will take a bite of this piece of fruit. Oh, but it's so sweet, it's so good and so perfect, I'd better have a bite of a rotten one, too, to balance it out.*

The tree of good and evil, positive and negative, unlimitedness/limitation, forgiveness/judgment, love/fear—it's like holding a beautiful flower and seeing the petals and going,

> *Oh, it's so beautiful. I can't quite take it, so I think I'll prick my finger on the thorn and bring myself back down.*

No one ever told you, and your Creator never insisted, that you eat of the tree of good and evil. For all *good fruit* has been given you freely. And you are always free to choose *which* fruit you will eat thereof.

> *I and my Father are One! Mmm, what a blessed Creation. I've been having so much fun as this wave. Yes, I see what I have carried along with me. Well, it was fun. I gained a few things. Now, what's next? Unlimitedness (kerplunk!), perfect love (kerplunk!), wealth (kerplunk!), the ability to heal (kerplunk kerplunk kerplunk!), oh, yes, I see that little pebble over there sitting on the shore that I've picked up a million times: unworthiness (kerplunk!) But no more! Be done with you! I and my Father are One! I and my Father are One! Father, create through me the* good, *the* holy, *and the* beautiful, *for this is the reason for my beingness! How big of a wave can I become? How powerful can I become? How radiant can I become? How much of You can I express through me? (kerplunk!)*

For remember well, that *you are creating your tomorrows NOW!* And what you experience never comes to you from outside your Self.

If you worry over lack of golden coins, kerplunk! And you begin to attract the vibrational ripples that will *seem* to picture back to you, reflect back to you, the truth that you have chosen to believe:

> *I live in lack and I can't get out* (kerplunk!). *I can't possibly talk to Jeshua. I'm not worthy. Maybe Jon Marc, perhaps he is worthy enough, but then, he's special* (kerplunk!).

And the vibrational waves that come to you are that static that restricts your ability to transcend the third dimension and plug into others. So that even if I yell and shout,

> *Hey, I'm talking to you. Listen!*

the mind says,

> *That's not possible, because I've dropped a rock in* (kerplunk!) *that says, "It's not possible." And therefore, I do not hear a thing.*

Do you begin to get the picture? Do you begin to *feel*, in the core of you beingness, the essence of this hour's message? *You cannot escape being what you are created to be.* And in each and every moment you are, literally, using that *ceaseless* and *unlimited power* to create. And you remain perfectly free at any time to create anew. And what you will experience in your tomorrows is only the effect of which pebbles you are choosing to drop into the field of your awareness as thoughts *now*.

So the only question is (and with this question we will complete this short message, but a very important message upon which we will be building) the question is this:

> *Am I, as a creative being, made in the image of God, willing to deliberately, consciously, and actively choose being responsible for which thoughts, which pebbles, are dropped into my mind in each moment? And if the answer is yes, what do I want the new pebbles to be? What vibrational qualities will I call to myself and thereby create my tomorrows?*

Any time you react to what you believe is outside of yourself, you may be absolutely *positive* of this: You have elected to pick up that old pebble that said,

> *I'm a victim of the world I see. What I experience is caused by forces outside of me. The fault really is in my mother, my brother, my father, my child. The fault really is in the government, and the planet, and the quality of air. The fault really is from a source outside of me, and I have no choice but to react to it.*

To which I can only say,

> *Would you rather be right, or happy?*

Therefore, indeed, beloved friends, consider well the essence of the message of this hour. For, upon this, we will begin to build as we move toward the ending of this year of *The Way of the Heart*, which is but a foundation from which those that are willing can spring forth into a grander dimension, a grander experience of living as a deliberate co-creator with God.

But it all begins with a need to be responsible for *owning* the Truth of the message of this hour. For without that, there can be no change in your consciousness, and therefore, in what you will experience in your tomorrows. So if there is something in your present that makes you shudder, just think what's waiting for you if you once again deny choosing this responsibility and the power that comes with it.

And with that, indeed, beloved and holy friends, remember that I come not to bring peace to the world, but to shake it up so that those beings who make up the world can discover where true peace is truly hidden: *within themselves*. And where Heaven abides: *within themselves*. And where Christ lives: *within themselves*.

Peace, then, be unto you always.

Amen.

Lesson Eight
Question and Answer Section

Question: During a period of higher consciousness, I was aware of a presence that encompassed individuals. It was plain to me that it performed a function of guiding the person into appropriate experiences. I'm not clear if this is what you call The Holy Spirit. It seemed to be like an Oversoul of the person. Would you please clarify this presence and the Holy Spirit?

Answer: Beloved friend, the answer to be given fully would require some complexity and a great expanse of your time. For there are many qualities or nuances of experience within consciousness, what you would call "higher consciousness," though personally, I know of no such higher or lower. There is merely *awareness of,* which is what consciousness is.

What I have called as the *Holy Spirit* is not an *entity.* It is a *form of energy.* I've called it before *right-mindedness,* which merely means Mind that is operating in alignment with unlimitedness, aligned with the Mind of God. Therefore, what is required, by way of guidance or knowledge, simply flows in an unimpeded way. The Holy Spirit is that aspect of one's own Mind that is, indeed, and has always remained aligned with the Mind of God. Therefore, it would be very appropriate to say that The Holy Spirit is as your Oversoul, if you will. It is an aspect of your own beingness given and shared equally by all. The Comforter, The Holy Spirit, is right-mindedness, correct seeing, right alignment.

In the experience that you had, it was a very valid experience. You weren't coloring what you were experiencing at all. You were just witnessing it. It would be very appropriate to say that you were, indeed, seeing, perceiving, feeling, what you can call the Oversoul, an aspect of one's soul. And yet, at the same time, it was and is, remains the presence of the Holy Spirit, that part of the Spirit of that being that has remained whole always. Often what is called guidance, those little intuitive nudges, the clear pictures and visions, the feelings throughout the body, emanate from that part of your own right-mindedness. It seems to be speaking to you from another place only because you have not yet cultivated the quality of understanding that that is more you than the you that you thought was you.

Higher consciousness—there is no such thing. There is only the remembrance and the recognition of what is true always. Yes, you can constrict yourself into what you call lower consciousness, but what's present? Consciousness, the free will choice and the use of unlimited power to generate experience for yourself. That doesn't sound very low to me at all. It is infinite. It's just that perhaps tomorrow, you might not make that same choice again. But it does not make it lower. Lower and higher are a judgment.

There is Love and fear, but I've never said that fear is *lower* than Love. It is merely a choice. And *from choice comes experience.* And you are free to gather to yourself whatever form of experience you wish—that which expresses Love or fear. But underneath each of them, the power to choose remains one and the same—infinite forever, unstoppable forever—given to you freely by a Creator Who loves you, Who loves you so much that you are given perfect freedom.

Question: What is the difference between that which needs to be healed and just being the perfect being we are?

Answer: There is no difference. When you are, in Truth, being the perfect being that you are, you will find that there is an absence of resistance. The mind that seeks to try to understand what must be healed, or the mind that says,

> *Well, this is coming up and I really don't think that's who and what I am anyway, so why don't I just abide in some spiritual realm?*

That mind is in *resistance.* It has lost its humility. It has lost its perfect trust that the Father of all things knows how to guide you home. And home is merely back to a place where you become willing to allow something to be extended through you.

Let me share with all of you something that's rather important that has not truly been brought out as clearly as it needs to be. Often, when something comes up for healing, it is an energy—listen well—although you seem to associate it with some memory or experience that you think is within your very private realm of experience, what is actually coming up to be healed is an energy that is involved and is controlling the life of another soul. It's being presented to *your consciousness* because *you* are at a place where you have the *power* and the *clarity* to *understand* that it *can be healed*.

And that is why when you choose healing, when you don't resist what comes up, when you realize that Love trusts all things, embraces all things, allows all things and transcends all things, when you realize that you are merely the bringer of Love, then it doesn't matter what comes up!

Oh! This needs healing.

And you heal it from an *impersonal level.* You don't identify with it, even if you think it's linked somehow to something you are quite certain has been part of your past experience.

Sometimes you can't even remember where you put your car keys. How do you know for sure it's from your past? Just heal it. Because when you do that, you are being the perfection of the beingness you are. You are being Christ that is saying,

Come and lay your sins upon the altar of my Heart, and I will heal it for you.

It doesn't matter where it came from. It doesn't matter who caused it. All that matters is the healing. If it comes up and you recognize there's an obstacle, something that requires healing from the perfection of your being, wrap the Love of Christ around it and heal it. And when you do that, you uplift a brother or sister who you may never physically meet.

If your commitment is to Christ, your commitment is to the healing of anything that is unlike Love. It's mere entertainment to try to figure out whether its your stuff or somebody else's. Does it matter? And is there a separation between you and all of your brothers and sisters? To assist another to heal is to heal yourself. To heal yourself is to uplift another. There is only Love and fear. Ultimately, you are really just healing fear by bringing Love to it.

There seem to be many minds and individuals through which Love and fear seem to battle for ascendancy. That is like the waves on top of the ocean. In this realm of experience, you believe that there are many separate minds. Ultimately you are all but an aspect of one another. And there is only one Child of God that exists.

Heal what is presented to your consciousness, and stop identifying it as yours. There is Love. There is fear. There is the need to heal, which is the bridge between the two. Will you choose to identify as fear and, therefore, deny Love? Or will you identify yourself as Love and get on with it? If you are abiding in the perfection of your being, I believe the answer becomes self-evident.

So! There are so many that come and ask me questions, but I never get to ask one. So I'm going to ask a question.

Will you, you who hear these words, will you be willing to be the Light that lights this world, by fully becoming committed, in each moment and with each breath, to the choice for healing through Love and forgiveness?

Just something to think about from time to time. Peace be with you, then.

And those of you that are listening to this tape, or hearing these words and are near the time when you are to lay the body down and get the precious "beauty sleep" you need, will you rest your head upon the pillow this evening and give me just a moment of your time by acknowledging that you know that there is no distance between us at all, save the width of a thought you would choose to think? Think, therefore, and know that I am with you. And we will, indeed, journey together while the body slumbers.

Peace be with you always.

Amen.

Lesson Nine

Now, we begin.

And indeed, once again, greetings unto you, beloved and holy Children of Light Divine. Again I come forth to abide with you, as your brother, and as your friend, who looks upon you and sees naught but the Face of Christ within you. And Christ is the firstborn of the Father, that is, it is That which is begotten, and not made. Christ is God's creation. Christ is the Holy Child of God. Christ is as a sunbeam to the sun, radiating forever from the Holy Mind of what I have called *Abba*.

Therefore, I come forth to abide with you in perfect joy, and in perfect freedom, and in perfect reality. I come forth to join with that part of you that abides always in perfect knowledge, perfect peace, perfect knowing-ness, and in perfect union with your Creator. I come not to speak of things that you do not know. I come not to use words which do not already abide within you. I come not with the wisdom that you do not already contain. I come not with a Love grander than that which already flowers within the silent places of your own heart. I come *not* to place myself above you. I come only to walk as an equal beside you.

I come because I love you. I come because I am your friend. And of all the things that I could possibly choose to do with the unlimited power of consciousness, given equally unto me of my Father as it was given unto you, of all of the places and dimensions and worlds in which I could reside in this moment, in Truth, I come to abide *with you,* in this manner, as together we utilize a creation device, a communication device—you would call it a body—in order to bridge the gap that seems to yet separate you from me.

In reality, all dimensions of Creation reside in a space far smaller than the tip of a pin. In reality, all dimensions of Creation are so vast that you could never measure them. In reality, there is no gap between where you are and I am. And this is why I can be no further from you than the width of a thought. But, oh indeed, beloved friends, the power of a thought is the power to create universes, and within universes to create yet more universes, and within those universes to create world upon world upon world upon world upon world.

And your lived experience is that, momentarily, your attention seems to be focused on your unique world, which shares some things in common with many other beings. You have what is called in your world a *consensus reality*—we would say a *consensus experience*, born out of a *universal reality*. Beloved friends, even as you abide in your awareness in this moment, you are the creator of the world you experience. And you do this in so many ordinary ways.

When you stand face to face with anyone, and for just a split second, you alter the position of the body through which you gaze upon them—you take up a new stance, a new perspective—and in that very split second, you have created a new experience for yourself. When you look upon that friend and the mind moves from neutrality (which is where you begin every experience) into the thought,

> *Oh, that is my friend, Mary. That is my friend, St. Germain. Oh, that is my friend, Peter. That is my friend, Joanna. That is my friend, Nathaniel.*

Whatever the name may be, when you hold that thought, already do you begin to change the experience.

You are a literal creator in that moment. For when you name anything, you define it according to the factors that you have built into the name that you use. When you look upon a field of energy arising from the mystery of your planet Earth and you say the word "tree"—[snaps fingers] that fast—you have brought forth, into your manifest experience, everything you have ever decided on that is associated with the field of energy that you have called "tree." And in this way, your experience is entirely unique. It has never been before; it will never be. Nothing can repeat it. And this is why Creation is forever new.

Yes, you can stand with your friend and look upon a tree and nod your head and say,

> *Well yes, of course, that's a tree.*

Yes, I see the branches, I see the leaves.

But as soon as you have named it, you have brought forth with yourself all of the associations you have called to yourself, your experience, of that field of energy that you have called "tree." Rest assured, those in your world called environmentalists and those in your world that you have labeled loggers, definitely see a different experience though they use the word "tree."

Which is right, then, and which is wrong? This does not apply. And in this hour, we want to address for you another of the important *pebbles* that you must drop into the clear, still pool of your awareness. It is simply this: All webs of relationship, all energy fields, are *absolutely neutral.* What creates experience is how you decide you will view that web of relationship, that field of energy. The *effect* of that decision is also completely neutral.

But how can that be? For when a logger sees a tree and sees only the profit to be made, forests disappear. And when an environmentalist looks at a tree, the tree remains and the mighty owls and the birds have a place to make their home. Surely, are we not to perpetuate the same reality, the same experience that all human beings have had? Is there not loss when the forest disappears? Listen well and carefully: *All events are neutral. You* are the one that places the value upon it.

Now, does that mean that one should become cold-hearted, unconscious, and blind to their actions? Of course not, for part of awakening means to realize one's interconnection with the web of all relationships. It means awakening a reverence for the mystery that is Life. But it also means to release judgment of another who would view the tree differently. For you see, the body that you have crystallized, out of a field of infinite energy, has but one purpose. It is a communication device.

Therefore, let your primary perception, your primary guiding light in your third-dimensional experience, be this:

What do I choose to communicate to the world, with every gesture, with every breath, with every word spoken, with every decision made?

For ceaselessly, while the body lasts, you are engaged in the process of communicating to the world, making manifest to the world, what you have chosen to value, what you have called into your experience and imbued with value. This means that ceaselessly you are engaged in teaching the world what you believe holds the greatest truth, the greatest value.

And when an environmentalist looks upon a logger and becomes exasperated, and judges that logger, or vice versa, the body is being used to communicate the value of judgment. That creates fear and contraction. And the result you see in your world of many, many minds choosing to value the right to judge is the effect you call your *world*, in which everything seems to be expressing conflict, struggle, what you call the "butting of heads"—the conflict, the Armageddon of opposite ideas running into each other. And just beneath it all, all events remain completely neutral.

And even if the forests of your planet were completely taken away, that would be a neutral event. And why? Because if all of the trees were gone, if the very physical planet you call Earth died, dissolved from view, *Life* would continue. Life would merely create new worlds. It does it all the time. *You* do it all the time.

The events, then, that you experience are always neutral. And what you see occurring in the world around you remains neutral until *you* make the decision what it will be—*for you*. You will name it and, therefore, you will define it. And when you define it, you call all of the associations of that to your self. This is why once I taught it is very wise to forgive seventy times seven times—for a very selfish reason. For if one wrongs you, and you spend your energy convincing them that they have wronged you, that, therefore, you have a right to be angry, to be attacking in any way, you call to yourself, even into the cells of the body, the energy of conflict, judgment, war, death, disease, unhappiness, and separation—that fast!

But if you forgive seventy times seven, then in each of those moments of forgiveness, you call into your field of energy what reminds you of unconditional Love, perfect peace, a power that transcends anything that arises in the world. You call to yourself the reality of Christ. And all of it hinges on nothing more than the pebbles that you drop into your mind.

Where, then, have you drawn the line? Where have you said,

> *Well, I will allow neutrality to all events in this sphere, but not in that sphere. If my friends divorce or separate, well, okay, I'll see that as neutral. But if my spouse leaves me, that is not neutral. If my friend's father leaves three million dollars to his children, well, that's fine. That's a neutral event. But if my father leaves his three million dollars to charity and leaves me out of the picture, that is not a neutral event.*

If the streams in a country on the other side of the world from where you are become polluted because the consciousness of a community allowed a factory to be built without safeguards,

> *Well, it's on the other side of the world: neutral event. But if they build it in my backyard, it is no longer neutral.*

It is always wise to look lovingly to see where you have drawn the line, to see what you will look upon as neutral and what you cling to as being filled with meaning and value that is unquestionable. For there you will find what requires forgiveness within you. We have shared with you that mastery is a state of fearlessness. When you place a value upon something, and then become adamant that that value exists in the event or the object outside of you, you have but secured your place in fear. And fearlessness is as far from you as the east is from the west.

Look well, then, to see where you have placed a value, and insisted that that value be unshakable. How many times in each of your days, do you say,

> *Oh, boy! If my dog ever died I would not be able to take it. That would just be the end of me,*

or,

> *If the banks collapse . . . oh, God! I wouldn't be able to take that!*

Be careful what you decree. Look to see where you are emotionally enmeshed with the value you have placed upon anything or anyone,

197

any relationship whatsoever, whether it be the relationship with your spouse, the relationship with your government, the relationship with your body, the relationship with your cat or your dog, the relationship with your bank account—all of your relationships.

For you have made them what they are. And where can freedom be experienced, save within a consciousness that has learned how to transcend the contraction of fear? And fear is the result of your attachment to the values you have placed upon the events you experience, which are made up of events, persons, places, things—all of these are actually just events. Every web of relationship comes to you perfectly neutral. You decree it by naming it and defining it. When one comes to you in anger and you react, recognize that you first decided that they are angry, and you have brought forth with it all of the associations you have ever decided to value concerning what anger means.

And yet, in that very moment, you hold the power to witness this field of energy circulating through the body and mind and the speech of another, and to see it as a dance of energy, a mystery arising from some unseen source, some unseen web of relationships. And you could look upon it with curiosity and with wonder, if you defined it *differently*. This is true for all things that arise. Even that which is called the great diseases of the body, that seem to threaten the life of the body in your world, can be looked at with complete neutrality. But if you define them in a specific way, you will call to yourself the fear of that event, which comes with all of the associations you have learned from the world, from your own experiences.

The message of this hour, then, is simple, but it is very important. And it builds on all that we have shared previously with you. You are a creator, and you cannot help but create. The question, then, is: *What will you create in each moment?* Far beyond the great thrill of the magic of creating events or objects in third-dimensional reality are the *qualities* that you create, such as peace, unlimitedness, forgiveness, compassion, wisdom. These, too, are creations.

Compassion doesn't exist floating about in the universe until you *manifest it* and *cultivate it within your own consciousness.* Christed

Consciousness cannot be said to truly exist, for *you, until you create it within yourself.* Your union with God doesn't even exist, for *you, until you decide to open to the lived experience of it,* much as a food you have never tasted might as well not exist for you until you journey to that country, purchase it, and place it in the body. Or in your day and age I would say that you must go to your grocery store and find the gourmet international section. Hmm!

Nothing can be said to exist—for *you*—until you have tasted the *lived experience* of it. So when you hear talk about enlightenment, when you hear talk about union with God, when you hear talk about unconditional Love, stop nodding your head, thinking you know what these things are, and turn your attention within. Do you abide in a *lived experience* of these things? That fast you'll know what the answer is.

If the answer is,

> *No. I hear talk about enlightenment and I get little glimpses, but I don't really know what it is because I'm not feeling it completely in my lived experience.*

Right away you will know that there must be something that you have valued *other than* enlightenment, that you are insisting remain in place in your consciousness.

What is it? Search it out, find it, and decide whether you still want it. We would perceive that there are many in your world who like to walk around *as if* they are in a state of peace, with the smiles upon the faces. Perhaps they carry the Holy Bible in their hand, or some other such text. They wear some religious icon upon their body so as to create the appearance of one who is at peace. But inwardly, when they turn on their television and they watch how the logger has felled yet another tree, inwardly they respond by calling that one "ignorant" or "stupid" or "limited." In that moment, they have spoken to the universe the truth that they are choosing to live:

> *I am not one who wants to know what peace is. I am not one interested in forgiveness. I am not one interested in wisdom. I am interested in judgment and the "high" that I feel in my body through the act of judging another as being less than myself.*

In short, it is time to give up the pretense. It is time to begin viewing yourself from the perspective of an absolute, ceaseless creator; to begin looking at exactly what you are creating in each moment of your experience; to bring the quality of childlike innocence to what you *actually* experience, not what you tell everybody else you are experiencing. It is time to become honest with the effects of the ripples of the rocks or the pebbles you have dropped into the field of the awareness, as a great form of play.

For you see, a creator who understands their infinite power to create, who understands that it's going on ceaselessly, that effects are being generated moment to moment to moment to moment, that will indeed be making up their tomorrows, *gladly* gives up the energy of denial and turns to look upon every moment of their experience, that they might discern what choice they must have made to bring about the effects they're currently experiencing.

When a bill comes, and your body shakes and you go into contraction and worry because there are not enough golden coins in the checkbook to pay for it, the creator *stops* and looks upon all that is being experienced in the field of the body, in the emotional body, the thoughts being held in the mind. They begin to notice how they are viewing the objects around themselves, the world around them, in order to begin to wonder,

> *What thought must I have dropped into the pool of my mind to create the* effect *of lacking golden coins? And is that a thought I wish to drop into my mind so that I create similar effects in my tomorrows?*

Here is the doorway of wisdom: *Do not create unconsciously* and then just walk away. But learn ceaselessly from your creation. For in this way you begin the process of dissolving the creation of an un-enlightened being and you begin to build the creation of a Christ here, and now, in this moment. Never, never believe that your *thoughts* are neutral. I said earlier events are neutral, but your thoughts are not. For your thoughts literally are imbued with the power of creation. They do not create neutrally. That is, every thought reverberates a quality of vibration that spreads out from you, touches the shores of manifested reality, and comes back to you. That is what you experience as the positive and negative events of your life.

Now, it is very true—please listen carefully to this—that at any moment as you go along in your experience, as you experience the reverberation, the coming back of the ripples you've sent out, in that very moment you are not a victim of what you have created. Because in each such moment you remain as perfectly free as you were when you first dropped the pebble into the pond that even created the ripple in the first place. You are free to choose how you will experience the effect of that ripple. And if you experience it with unconditional freedom, with unconditional acceptance and Love, forgiveness, neutrality, innocence, you literally defuse the effects of that ripple upon the pool of your consciousness. And then, in that moment, you become instantly free to begin creating, in a new way, the ripples that you will experience in the future. And this is why you are never a victim of anyone's creation, especially your own.

It's not that life is so complex that you've created all these momentums and now you're stuck with them. In any moment that you *get it,* and you stop reacting as if you were a victim, and looked merely at the ripples that are coming back to you that you've sent out from yourself and said,

> *This has come into my field of experience as an awesome mystery. And this means that I am an awesomely powerful being! Therefore, I will look lovingly upon this ripple. Yes, I know it needs to play itself out, but as it does so, I'm going to be wise enough to see the transparency of it, to see the lack of effect that it really has. It doesn't change who I am. It doesn't add anything to my life. It doesn't take anything from it. It merely is an experience, called Life, passing through the field of my awareness. If I look lovingly upon it, if I embrace it, I can transmute it, and, therefore, already be engaged in the process of creating a whole different kind of vibrational ripple that will create my tomorrows.*

That means that while the power of your thoughts are not neutral, the events called the *effects* of those thoughts can be either neutral or not neutral, depending on how you use the very primary power of awareness. We're seeking, then, to share with you how infinitely *free* you are.

There are many in your world that teach this illusory doctrine of what is called the *karma*, that what you send out now you *must* experience sooner or later, and how you experience it is directly related to the quality of the ripple you send out. *That is not true.* That would make you a *victim.* And if you are made in the image of God, and I assure you that you are, *you are not a victim of the world you see.* You cannot, in reality, be victimized by anyone or anything at any time, because your reality is that you are made in the image of God. And if you could truly be victimized, it would mean that God creates *unlike Himself.* Does a salmon come from an oak tree? Does a nebula come out of the womb of a woman? Does a raspberry grow on a grocery store shelf? No. *Like begets like.*

Therefore, why would you ever believe that from God, Who is but Love and Unlimited Creativity and Power, could ever beget something that is small and little and powerless? It doesn't happen. God cannot be victimized. Therefore, God's creation remains victimless. All events remain neutral, and all that the environmentalist and the logger are doing is using the power of consciousness to momentarily create the belief that they are this and not that. They place a value, of their own choosing, upon an event of energy that they call a "tree." And by what value they place upon it, they call the quality of experience that they will have into their field of awareness. That's all that's happening.

The energy that makes up the tree is eternal forever. It may change form, but Life remains. Therefore, lament not the passing away of a species, but trust the Grand Intelligence that gave rise to it in the first place, for it is still busy creating even greater universes. This is why loss does not exist.

How does all of this relate to your daily experience? We want to suggest (and this is very important as we move into the following year) it's going to become *very* crucial that you have a foundation upon which to build, if you are ready to completely assume responsibility for having been created in the image of God, and that therefore you are an eternal creator. Begin *now* to utilize some time each day, without letting a day go by, in which you *sit with yourself*—not with your mate, not with your parents, not with the television, not with your favorite sport team, not with your favorite actor or actress, not with your favorite religion, not with your favorite god or master or savior (not even me)—*sit with you* and start *by acknowledging that you are One with God*.

Understand that the very body that seems to have a heart within it, that is beating life for you—this itself is the effect of decisions and choices you have made—that the very chair that you are sitting on is the result of your attracting a web of relationships that's quite unique into your field of awareness, called the physical universe. And in that moment you are having an experience you've never had before: *you are sitting in the chair now*! And the event is completely neutral. And nothing that you are experiencing in your consciousness exists or is sourced by anything outside yourself.

Give yourself five minutes to choose, to practice choosing, how you will experience sitting in a chair, with a mind full of worry, or a mind full of peace? A mind thinking of all the things it could be doing, or a mind *marveling* at how the weight of a body feels pressed against the seat of a chair? A mind that creates tension in the way the breath flows through the body, or a mind that creates ease and comfort?

Five minutes of practice sitting in a chair as an infinite creator of exactly what you are experiencing in your emotional field. Just that. You might even want to play with what it would feel like to sit in a chair *as a Christ*. What would that feel like? I'll let you choose whether or not you would like to experience it. Five minutes each day. Do it without fail! Be with yourself, and decide how you will experience yourself *now*!

For you see, the you that sat down into the chair, with whatever was going on in your consciousness, whatever feelings you were having throughout the body, whatever was going on in your primary relationships, how the food was digested in the body, all of it, the whole realm of your experience, was the effect of how you have been a million times when you've sat down to be with yourself in a thousand different chairs. Utilize the very process of sitting down in a chair as a symbol of preparing the mind for the dropping of a pebble into it, out of which will reverberate the vibrations, or ripples, that will come back to you.

You see, it's much easier to send out ripples, which you'll be doing anyway, and experience them, when they come back, in a blissful way, a way that brings you peace and joy and fun and laughter and play and unlimitedness, instead of having to constantly butt your head against something that you'd rather transmute, or run away from. But it begins with five minutes, in which you acknowledge that you can create whatever experience you want, as a feeling that floods through your awareness, as a quality of thought that you allow to keep repeating in the mind.

You can sit in a chair as an Awakened Christ, *now*!

> *I and my Father are One! It's a beautiful day! I've manifested a physical form sitting in a chair in a corner of one little tiny dimension of Creation. How amazing this moment is! I think I'll just sit here and feel the heart beating in the body, the breath flowing through it. Ah, there's the sound of a bird. I'm glad I called that to myself. I like the way that sandwich is digesting in this body. What beautiful thoughts can I think right now? Who can I send Love to without lifting a finger? I am unlimited forever! I am free! I am free! I am free!*

Do you think you would like to have that experience for five minutes? Why not begin today? For so many of you upon your physical plane keep searching for some form of magic that will bring the Kingdom of Heaven to you. You can't bring it *to you*. You can only become aware of how you are using it to create the ripples that you send out *from yourself*. Do you know the saying in your world, "Wherever you go, there you are"? You *are* God's creation. You're in Heaven now. Heaven is not a place. *It is a state of unlimited and infinite creative power*, because it is the reflection of God's Holy Mind.

Why not be one who practices being the presence of Heaven? And if that seems too awesome, or too far beyond you, then just play with it for five minutes a day. And trust me, I will love you no less if, for the other twenty-three hours and fifty-five minutes, you decide to play at pretending and feeling that you are little, unworthy, unloved, unloving, unlovable, that you are the scourge of the Earth, that life is constantly victimizing you—go right ahead. I would never interfere with your free choice. I may not come and knock at your door, except for those five minutes. But you remain free to utilize time any way you wish.

But for just five minutes, experience yourself as Christ, crystallizing a body as a temporary teaching and learning communication device, plopping itself into a chair in a totally neutral corner of Creation, because *you* want to have the experience of sitting blissfully at peace in your perfect knowledge of your union with God, in this moment. You might even find yourself daring to have thoughts such as this:

> *Well, since I'm an infinite creator, what would I like to create for my tomorrows?*

And if, during that five minutes, there's a knock upon the door and it's the bill collector, who cares? That's *that* soul's experience of thinking they're a bill collector and you're some bad person they must corral. Let them have their experience. Sit calmly, hear the knocking on the door, and allow yourself to be entertained by the beautiful worlds you are creating for your tomorrows. Here is the straight and narrow path that leads unto Life; here the eye of the needle through which you must pass.

For it is not enough to just embrace the idea that,

> *I am the creator of all that I experience.*

You must then choose to *actively* put it into practice. It begins with the practice of five minutes a day—that's all. And when you feel that you can fulfill that for five minutes, then you can make it ten, and then twelve, and then fifteen, and then twenty, and it sounds like such a little piece.

> *You mean, for twenty minutes hang out as though I am Christ Incarnate, totally in union with God, totally free to begin creating different ripples than I've ever experienced before, knowing that they will come back to me and become my manifested experience? No doubt about it! But twenty minutes? Even if I could achieve that, that's such a small fraction of the time of a day.*

Beloved friends, if you had faith as a tiny, tiny, tiny little seed, you would know that you, from that little tiny faith, will create the mighty oak tree, whose branches will shelter you from the blistering sun and give comfort unto many. Twenty minutes is an eternity when it comes to creating your tomorrows!

And if you believe that the other twenty-three hours must be taken up by experiencing the effects of what you created a long time ago, the ripples that are coming back, so be it. Play with it. Let yourself transmute those moments.

> *Oh, here I am answering the door. Yes, bill collector. Hi. Come on in. Have a glass of water. You know, you're absolutely right, I didn't pay that bill. Did you want to know why? Silly me, I've actually decided to create the experience that I'm someone who can only create lack. That's why I have no golden coins in my checkbook. It's just the darnedest thing, isn't it?! Oh, very good, so you're going to turn my name over to the authorities, and now I'll have no credit with anybody on the planet. Well, go ahead if it makes your day. I have other things to do. I'm busy creating a new tomorrow. And I know that all around me is going to be taken from me anyway, since everything birthed in time ends in time. My house will be gone, my car will be gone, my clothes will be gone, my friends will be gone. Everything I've experienced in time is changing anyway, so go ahead, take it from me now. It'll just speed up the process.*

I do not speak of this tongue-in-cheek. I speak from the perspective of one who *is* an Awakened Christ, who already *knows* how to birth universes to create that which is holy, good, and beautiful. I *know* that this is the way. It's the *only* way. Release the value you've attached to your experiences, even the bill collector, and spend your time, instead, deciding which pebbles you're going to drop into the field of your mind. For you will create as the result of what you choose to think today. And what you value today will show itself to you tomorrow.

I learned to value unlimitedness. I learned to value Love. I learned to value fearlessness. Yes, my method for doing that was rather unique, and I would not recommend that you follow in my footsteps. Unless, of course, you like the drama of being nailed to a cross, and then stood up in front of all of your friends, in order to learn to transcend fear in your mind! I learned to value unbroken communication with every soul in every dimension of Creation. I learned to value only my loving thoughts. And I birthed or grew a Christ out of the very seed of awareness that exists equally within each of you.

Therefore, where you are in this moment, look around. Look at the objects that you see. Look at the people that you see around you, if there are any. Whatever sounds may be coming into your field of awareness, whatever pictures or ideas you may hold of what you are or what the world is, these are all fleeting and temporary illusions. They will pass away, and began passing away, the moment they were created.

Therefore, indeed, beloved friends, *look at all that is around you, and decide what value it holds for you.* Will you see it as something that you *must* have in your existence? Or will you choose to see it as something you've playfully drawn to yourself, you appreciate it, and it can be gone tomorrow, and your peace will not be disturbed? Which way will you view the world?

Five minutes, one for each finger and thumb on a hand; one minute in which you choose to sit as Christ in the midst of your kingdom, your creation, and *you* decide which thoughts you will hold and, therefore, determine how you see all that is in the field of your awareness, and which thoughts *you* will allow to begin to generate the ripples that you will send out that *will*—there is no way to escape it—that *will* return to you.

For once, indeed, there was a farmer who went out to plant the seed in his ground. But before he went to plant the seed, he selected the seed *very carefully.* And while other farmers rushed out, because they thought,

> *Oh, look, it is the time for the plant to begin. Everything is perfect. The conditions are just right. We must make haste and plant.*

And they bought whatever seeds they could get and went out and spread them across the ground, and began their busy work of doing what they had to do. Rest assured, they will have their harvest.

But the wise farmer waited, and while he was laughed at by his colleagues, he carefully selected every seed. He waited until he could hold it in his hand and say,

Oh, I like the vibration of this seed. This feels very good. Oh yes! I can just see this beautiful plant that is going to arise from this. The fruit of it will be the sweetest in the valley.

And he gathered his seeds. He paid no attention to the passing of the dates on a calendar. He paid no attention to the changing weather conditions.

He knew that when the time was right the seed would be planted, and from it would burst forth the flower of those seeds. He *knew* it! He gave no thought to the opinions of his colleagues. He enjoyed the process of loving the seeds that he was making his own. And then, the farmer went out and he cast the seed upon the soil of his farm, which is likened unto the soil of your own awareness. And he planted the seeds, and he tamped them down, and he nurtured them, and he watered them, and he cultivated them with a smile upon his face.

And yes, the neighbors' seemed to be already sprouting up through the ground. He couldn't have cared less, for he knew that *these* seeds would bring him an *eternal* harvest, that they would not just burst forth once from the soil, and then throw out some mediocre fruit, and then die. For he had selected seeds that would constantly bring forth, in each season, the *best* of fruits. And he loved them, and he nurtured them, and he cultivated them. And long after the other farmers had grown weary and tired and had experienced drought, and seeds that brought forth fruit where insects would come and destroy them, that would not be purchased and bought by the people in the market place, this one farmer became the greatest of farmers in the entire valley.

And people would come from all over the world to bite, to take a little nibble, out of the fruit that came from his garden. And yet, the farmer merely delighted in continually loving and nurturing these seeds, and cultivating the soil in which they were planted daily. He never took his consciousness away from his perfect union with those seeds. He never once forgot that *he* was the one that created his farm as a direct result of his careful selection of which seeds he would plant in his soil. And while others marveled at his good fortune, and while others were jealous of his good luck, the farmer always knew that no magic was involved.

He merely followed in the footsteps of the wisdom given to him by God:

> *Take My Fruit and plant It in your consciousness. Know that you are One with Me, and that Fruit you experience is the result of the seeds you plant in your own consciousness, that you cannot help but experience the result, the fruit, of the seeds you plant. Nothing bursts forth on the vine of your experience by accident. Therefore, create with Me, My Child. Create like unto Myself, by knowing, KNOWING that you are a creator, a farmer, a planter. And you will, indeed, harvest the quality of the seeds that you plant, just as you, Beloved Child, are the harvest of the seed I once planted, when first I held the thought of you in My Holy Mind. And in that moment, you arose as a sunbeam from the sun, made in My image. I held you as the thought of Love in form. And I bestowed you with all good things.*

> *Therefore, see yourself as I see you. Embrace yourself as I embrace you. Accept yourself as you are—a creator, creating without ceasing.*

> *And just as I sat upon My throne (so said the God of all Creation, which really means sitting in the center of All That Is), and beheld you as a loving thought, so too, choose only to allow loving thoughts to enter into your consciousness. Choose to only allow loving thoughts to be expressed with your words. Choose only to allow loving thoughts to be translated into your gestures, your choices, your actions, and thereby, create as I created you—that which extends joy forever; that which extends the holy, the beautiful, and the good, forever. For that is what you are. And that is how I thought of you when I created you. And that is what you remain eternally.*

> *Therefore, join with Me, by extending your creation, as I have extended you. And since you have manifested a physical body, accept My Son's teaching, and let that body be placed in a chair, that you might think like the Mind of Christ for five minutes. And you will beget an eternity that reflects the Radiance of Heaven, just as you reflect My Radiance when I look upon the Unlimited Soul that you are.*

Indeed, in all of the valley there was but one farmer that was wise. Will *you* elect to join the union comprised of all of the hasty farmers? Or will you choose to take up residence as the *one* farmer who knows how to create wisely, and, in faith, rests on perfect certainty, and merely sits back to wait for the ripples of Heaven to come and replace the ripples of hell, that once you created unwittingly?

Everyone, you see, is a minister. You cannot help but minister to the world in each moment. Therefore, begin your ministry of Enlightened Consciousness *now!* And I promise you this, absolutely, irrevocably: *You will experience all that I have known, and more!* You will experience complete victory over death. You will experience complete unlimitedness and abundance. You will experience perfect peace, perfect miracle-mindedness, perfect unbroken communion in bliss with all of Creation!

Once, when I was a man, I was taught to sit at the base of a tree for five minutes a day and to imagine myself to be the creator of all that I could think, all that I could see, all that I could feel. Five minutes taken out of the hours of play of a child. You are a child at play in your own kingdom. Will you give yourself five minutes to learn to be a Christ that creates in unlimited perfection in alignment with the Mind of God, whose experience is always radiantly blissful and free of limitation and fear? You *will* experience your creation. What that creation is, and how you experience it, is entirely up to you.

This, then, will be the fulfillment of the message of this hour. And, as you can see, it's very much built upon the last. But it begins to translate the Truth into an action—very simple, very practical—so simple and so practical that you'll be hard-pressed to find a reason against it, an excuse. For those of you so busy trying to take care of dealing with all the things life *throws* at you, even *you* know that you can find five minutes. And that five minutes can be the beginning of birthing a whole new universe for yourself.

Hmm—happy sitting! And with that, indeed, beloved friends, peace be unto you always, by making the decision to choose to receive peace, as a Christ. Herein lies the secret of much of what will be coming in what you call your future months. For that which I specifically seek to do in this specific work, that you know and call as Shanti Christo, is the birthing of a multitude of Christs that dwell upon your planet Earth at the same time. It has never been done before!

Imagine a world with *ten million awakened Children of God,* fully awake, not just as a belief or an idea, but who have mastered fear, who no longer live in doubt, whatsoever, and are busy creating universes that mirror perfectly the Kingdom of Heaven. Imagine it—if you dare!

It begins *now.* Peace then, be unto you always. Practice well for your next thirty days or your month period before we meet again. If not, you'll find yourself having to go back and start anyway, before you can receive the next phase or the next stage, what will be shared. The choice is yours.

Peace, then, be unto you always.

Amen.

Lesson Nine
Question and Answer Section

Question: Is it necessary, Jeshua, to go to the other aspects of ourselves and ask forgiveness for errors that we feel we have made?

Answer: This is a very, very good question. I am glad you have asked it. In fact, I want to make a suggestion to you that you transcribe that question and the answer that I am to give you and send it to this, my beloved brother and his mate, and mention to them that I have suggested that it would be most appropriate to include this question and answer in their next communication with their friends.

Now, is it necessary to go to those aspects of ourselves and ask forgiveness, those voices within the mind? Is it necessary to go to them in order to bring about some form of healing? Now listen very carefully. There is, in Truth, nothing which is *necessary* in itself. There's not something etched in stone that must be achieved in order for healing to occur, except complete and unconditional *self-acceptance.* The way in which each mind arrives at that goal will be unique and somewhat different. And why is this so? Because each mind uses its freedom of power, its freedom of consciousness, to create a spiral that took it seemingly away from its deep sense of perfect union with God.

If you could imagine many strands of thread suddenly unraveling from a central ball of thread, and they all seemed to go off in their own way and their own direction, that would be like the many minds which have split apart from the One Mind of the Son of God. And therefore, they find themselves seemingly at the end of that thread, somewhere out there in the vast space of Mind wanting to come home. And then, they begin to create their pathway back to God.

As the mind does that, it is actually using the very thing which *is* the Kingdom of Heaven, which is your union with God. You are using the power of consciousness to create perceptions of yourself, and all that you see around you, to make the journey home. An idea comes into the mind and you move in that direction. And it seems to work for a while. And then, you have to go to a different idea, a deeper idea. Everyone is doing that. And so, they are literally creating their pathway home, not quite recognizing that what they are seeking is the very power to create, with which they are creating their pathway home.

So, at any time, there can be the miracle of miracles, the quantum leap, that transcends time, because the mind can suddenly understand and get all that it needs to do and understand is to accept itself, and it is already home. Generally, there are glimmers of that. And so there are little quantum leaps, little accelerations in which old ideas and perceptions are discarded as self-acceptance deepens.

Again, for you, as well as for many, there seemed to be stages at which accessing the different voices that you have made, in your attempt to fragment yourself from God, can then be perfectly appropriate, perfectly empowering—and even, it will seem to appear, *necessary* from where you are, as you come up that strand of thread on your way back to perfect union.

So, for each mind, then, it is necessary to go within and truly be honest.

What am I feeling?

I keep sensing that I haven't forgiven myself, or this thing, or that thing.

I feel this voice keeps calling to me that says, "You're not good enough. You're not good enough."

If those voices keep calling, something keeps calling for your attention. Then that can be best accepted as your way home. It may be different from someone else, but that's irrelevant, since comparison and contrast is a tendency of the egoic mind and not the Mind of Christ.

Merely observe what is occurring for you. And then allow yourself to take whatever action is necessary to help bring about that healing that keeps calling to you. Ultimately, all healing is the healing of the perception of illusions. So yes, the voice that is calling to you is an illusion, a chimera. It's an echo of an old something that never really

213

happened. But within the great dream of separation itself, it is rather senseless to be in denial about it.

Therefore, beloved friend, for you we would say, yes. Because these voices call you and because you have a feeling, even in your body, that you haven't totally come to self-forgiveness, then, by turning your attention—playfully and innocently—and listening to those voices that are echoing to you (the very places within yourself to which you have not extended forgiveness), this will bring those voices to the surface. Then, have a dialogue with them as if they were a separate entity.

And then, learn to wrap your arms of forgiveness around those parts. This is an important aspect of your unique pathway home to the ball of thread sitting in the middle of the Heart of God. This is true for everyone. There cannot be denial. There cannot be comparison, analysis, judgment. There can only be acceptance, allowance, embracing, trusting, feeling—until that One Mind finds its way to bring the ship into the harbor. No one can do it for you. However, you can have many friends, such as me, who will assist you in the way that you have chosen.

Does all of that make sense for you?

Response: I will send it to Jon Marc and Anastasia.

Jeshua: Indeed. I would appreciate this, as it serves in the bigger picture of the thread that is being interwoven now between many who have been called, and many who will be called, to join in this adventure which is called the energy of the Shanti Christo. Think of it this way: As the One Mind fragmented into many points of Light, in one corner of the Universe there were a few hundred thousand points of Light that said,

Well, we spun out together, we might as well spin back together!

Response: That's precious. I've wanted to ask you that question for a long time.

Jeshua: Yes, I know. Did you know that the question that seems to be resisted in the mind is exactly the doorway being presented by the

214

soul to the conscious mind through which one takes its next leap up the thread back to the Heart of God? That is why the questions that come up from the depth of the Mind are of utmost importance. And you can train the Mind to observe the question itself and go,

> *Ah! This is a doorway coming up for me. I wonder what it is that is within the question? What does the question that is coming up from the depth of my being reveal to me? What does it conceal from me? What energy is beginning to shift in me now?*

The question always reflects what's coming up from the depth of the Mind itself, to be learned, to be integrated, to be transcended.

There! Now you have something to consider from time to time.

[*Note: The previous question is not available in the audio version.*]

Lesson Ten

Now, we begin.

And indeed, once again, greetings unto you, beloved and holy Children of Light and of Love Divine. As always, I come forth to abide with you in perfect trust, in perfect acceptance, and in perfect peace. As always, I come forth to abide with you from that place which we share eternally as the one and only begotten Son of God. I am, therefore, that Mind which whispers to you in each moment of your inspiration. I am, indeed then, that Mind that sneaks into your mind in the space between two fearful thoughts and reminds you of the Truth that sets you free.

Once, I was a man—that is, just like you. I once turned my attention and became identified with a unique being that was birthed in time and faded away from time. And I walked upon your plane as all men and women do. But as I walked upon your planet, I began to ponder the meaning of Creation, the purpose of my very existence. And while others seemed to be gleefully caught up in, or at least surrendered to, the ways of the world, seeking out their momentary distractions, their attempts to gain and control as much wealth as they could, and all of the rest, I would often wander off alone, to sit beneath the trees beside a flowing stream, to try to unlock the mystery that shows forth itself as the beauty of a flower, to try to see the power that revealed itself as the wind that would dance across the grasses, to count the sparkling diamonds shimmering across the surface of a lake as the morning sun arose to shine its light upon it.

And I began to learn to ask of that Source, that Mystery,

> *Father, One that has birthed me,* why *am I?*
> Where *am I?*
> Who *am I?*

My desire, then, increasingly became to know the Truth that could set all mankind free. And I discovered that unless that freedom became fully manifest in *me,* it made no sense to talk about it with others. And so I sought out the greatest of minds, the best of teachers.

And yes, I was blessed by a family structure already dedicated to understanding the mysteries of what they knew as God. And they led me to many such teachers.

And as my own wisdom began to evolve, the teachers would look at me and go,

Hmm, something interesting is occurring here.

But there were already those who knew more about me than I knew yet about myself—prophets, seers, astrologers, the wise ones of many cultures, who knew already that into the framework of the *consensus mind* of mankind, which you would call your *collective consciousness,* there was to be dropped a pebble, into that still clear pool, that would create ripples that would begin to change how the consciousness of mankind perceived itself. I did not yet know these things for myself, for the very birth into this world was yet veiled in mystery for me, just as your birth was veiled in mystery for you, as you took on being human.

And as I grew, I began to have revealed to me, in the depth of my silent prayer, and in the depth of my very silent meditation, glimmers, insights, recognitions, remembrances of other dimensions. I began to develop the ability to be in communication with masters of my lineage who had long since left the planet. I began to understand that consciousness is not limited to the space and volume of a body, at all. And as I watched the people in their busy work, I began to see that the vast majority of beings totally confused *themselves* with the *body.* They lived as if they dwelt within the body and, therefore, were imprisoned in some strange way. They lived as if what occurred to the body occurred to them. They lived as if they did not know that they could transcend the body at any moment, that they could taste the vast expanse of consciousness, that they could journey to other times and places with little more than a surrendering of attention to the world they had made.

At first, I did not understand these things and I perceived myself to be *quite odd.* And within me, there were conflicts, as the *fears* in my consciousness arose, the fears that are part of the human consensus reality, the conflict.

Shall I remain like everyone else? Perhaps I should return to my father's carpentry shop and simply accept that I am destined to just be a carpenter.

But there were other voices that spoke to me and called me, that would come often in the night. And as I developed my ability to discern these other realities, these other dimensions, by shifting my attention from the world of the body to the world of inner vision, often they would come in the night and stand beside my bed. And I came to know who they were. I came to recognize the masters and teachers of a very ancient lineage of which I was a part. And they would come and whisper to me,

Forget not the purpose for which you are sent forth from the Mind of God, for through you there shall be birthed the beginning of an ancient remembrance. And your life shall become that which demonstrates to many the Truth that only Love is real.

The point of all of this is simple. I want to convey to you, yet again, that the life I lived as a man was not unlike your very own. I began veiled in mystery, a child among children, a human being, struggling to make sense of his world. Yes, there was within me something calling, a longing to know something that the world did not seem to teach. But is it not true that many of you have felt that same call, that same longing—to touch what is invisible, to see what cannot be seen, to hear what ears have never heard, to embrace what arms cannot reach, to abide in perfect peace and perfect trust?

Beloved friends, understand well, then, and I say to you yet again, that I come only as your brother and your friend; one who has walked as you walk, one who has breathed as you breathe, one who has cried as you cry, one who has laughed as you laugh. *I am as you are.* And if there be anything that I can give unto you, it is simply this: As you look upon your life, and every event that unfolds within it, every time you feel that you have failed, every time that you become conflicted, every time you're sure that you'll never be able to transcend all of these ups and downs and emotional waves that seem to come with living in your world, remember, *I have overcome the world.* And because I have done it, *it is done for you, already.*

And why? Because we share the same Infinite Field of Mind that far transcends all levels, dimensions, of manifestation. You can tap into what has already occurred. You need only look upon me as your brother and friend, and *acknowledge* that the world has been overcome, and then accept the *freedom*, which is the effect of its overcoming, *as your own.*

So that you learn to sit in your chair, after your five minutes of abiding as Christ, in which you say to yourself,

> *Here, I am free. Heaven is now. The past is passed away, and I choose anew. And, this day, I commit myself to teaching only Love by sharing only loving thoughts. This one day, I will look upon each one that comes into my experience and I will first breathe deeply the presence of the Holy Spirit. And I will look out through eyes transformed by the simple acknowledgment of the Truth: All minds are joined, and I see not a stranger before me, but one who walks as I walk, who feels as I feel, who longs as I long, who is humbled as I am humbled, who prays for peace as I have prayed. And therefore, I will give them what they seek. And in that giving, I receive it.*

The way is *so simple* and *so easy* that the mind of the world overlooks it—"It simply cannot be." But that which is simple seems impossible to that which insists on complexity. And a mind that insists on conflict simply cannot accept that there *is* another way. And yet what waits before you, then, is simply this: In the end of all of your struggles, in the end of all of your doubts, and in the end of all of the moments of your unconscious *conforming* to the mind of the world, there yet remains the simple choice to be made, the choice to acknowledge the Truth that has *already* set you free.

> *I and my Father are One. It has been that way forever. 'Twas accomplished in the being of Jeshua ben Joseph, who revealed to me the Truth of myself, because he loved me. And if he can do it, I can do it. And even in this moment, I accept my destiny to walk this Earth awake and at peace, in mastery and not in fear. And I begin my ministry now.*

For who can you seek that can heal you? Who can you discover that can bring some form of magic to you that can overcome your resistance to the Truth? Look high and low and you will not find them. Seek forever, and you will remain a seeker forever. For the Truth is set within your heart and all power under Heaven and Earth is given unto you. It is *that* power that changes the momentum of the mind and heals every wounded perception.

In the end, then, of all seeking, you must look into the mirror and decide to *be the one who heals* himself/herself. *You* are the one who decides, from infinite freedom, how to use the power of your mind in each moment. Therefore, the only question that a seeker of Truth really truly need ask himself/herself is this:

> *Would I know conflict or peace? Would I be right or happy? Would I see the complete neutrality of all events in this world as wisps of a dream, being birthed and passing away? Would I see myself whole and complete? For as I look upon the world, I have judged myself. And as I look upon myself, I judge the world.*

This was the simple secret that I once discovered when I walked upon your planet—that it wasn't about achieving some grand mystical state of consciousness. It wasn't about acquiring great powers that could attract the attention of thousands. It wasn't even about being able to manifest, although these powers may indeed often express themselves through the mind as it awakens. It is about accepting the Truth that is true always, and being determined to allow that Truth to be the foundation from which you *enjoin* each and every moment of your experience.

> *I am awake. I am safe. I am at peace. What do I truly want this moment to be for? For as I decree it, so shall it be.*

Beloved friends, the way *is* easy and without effort. You exist to extend your treasure. And your treasure is that which is laid up in Heaven through the decision to remember only your loving thoughts, to extend only loving thoughts, to allow your actions to express or to manifest, in the field of time, the good, the beautiful, and the holy. And *never* is your freedom taken from you. Never in any circumstance do you lose the innocent freedom to teach only Love, to be the presence of peace, to recognize that the world can give you nothing, just as the world can take nothing from you.

When a child goes through a shift of awareness—you call it the maturation process—there comes a point, not by struggle, not by design, not by much processing, not by any manner of strategies. The child merely, in an instant, looks at the toys that he has been playing with and simply transcends them. And the parents come home and the child has taken the toy truck and put it away in the closet. Hmm. The doll is put on the window sill and a book is picked up instead. Who makes the change? No one outside that child.

And when you put aside any negative habit, as you would perceive it to be, when you have given up placing value in something that no longer serves you, you merely transcend it, and it is done with—no big deal, no one does it for you, you simply decide. You pull back the *value* you had placed on it, and the objects that were the symbols of what you were *valuing* merely drop out of your life.

In just this way, unenlightenment can be put away as though it were a toy that you have outgrown by merely looking at all of the effects of unenlightenment, and then to ask the question,

> *Is this what I wish to have continue as my experience? Or am I willing to put the doll on the window sill, and pick up a book instead?*

A book that speaks of Life, a book that is filled with wisdom, a book that teaches you how to step lightly in the world, to be in the world but not of it. And *that book* is the depth of your consciousness in which all things are already written. And that *depth* finds its source in your heart. And you enter it, therein, through forgiveness, through the process of *relinquishing* the world. Not hating the world, not despising the world, but simply relinquishing it. You *allow* your time to serve you in the process of relinquishing what does not serve you any longer, and what only disturbs your peace.

And as you cultivate that practice you will find that the peace that is already within you, that you've touched a thousand times in a million different ways, begins to grow more constant—like the rays of the sun beginning to filter through the fog that has settled into the mountain valley, obscuring the clarity of all things. Your peace descends gently, like a dove, descending, as some would say, through the crown, down through the brain-mind, and down even to the heart, the abdomen, and throughout the cells of the body, while the body lasts.

Gently relinquishing the world rests on your decision to choose to teach only Love, because you have realized that when you don't, the effect that you know immediately is painful, it is conflicted, it is unfulfilling, and that that is what you want no longer. Here, you have begun to transcend the world that you have made and to reclaim the world made for you, a world that rests in perfect union, in the union of Father and Son, God and Offspring, Creator/Created. The way *is* easy and without effort.

What value have you ever placed upon the world that has restored to you the peace that you seek?

> *Oh, this automobile will do it; this relationship will do it; this new career will do it. If only I can take a trip to the far corners of the world, then I will be at peace.*

And so peace never quite comes.

A creator, abiding in enlightenment, knows that all events are neutral, so neutral that they have no effect, except for those who choose to be caught up in illusions. The creator, awakened, merely creates out of devotion to the Mystery of That which has created him or her. The mind of an enlightened creator does not arise in the morning and say,

> *How can I survive yet another day in this world?*

In the morning, when an enlightened creator arises, the question is,

> *How, this day, might I extend the treasure of the good, the holy and the beautiful? How can I, right where I am, experience these treasures, even within the space and volume of this body? How can I look lovingly upon what my physical eyes show me, so that I discern or extract the good, the holy, and the beautiful, and therefore give them to myself?*

The mind of an enlightened creator *knows* that *of themselves they do nothing.* But in each moment of decision, they can *allow* the great power and mystery of Love to direct their course. And they can

225

begin to utilize time to *refine* their ability to hear *only* the Voice for Love—moment by moment, breath by breath, day by day, until time is translated into eternity. And the mind rests, reclines, in its perfect union with God.

Events still occur. The world is still what the world will choose to be, unaware that there walks in its midst one who is *awake*, who needs to make no show. They merely *are* the presence of wakefulness—knowing that each moment they will now be *in*formed by the guidance of the Comforter, the guidance of right-mindedness, the guidance of enlightenment, so that they are no longer attached to fearing,

> *What should I say? What should I do? How will this person take it? How will that person take it?*

The world is no longer a concern.

And they experience their very life as an ongoing flowing mystery, as though *something else* were living through them. And this is the meaning of my friend's words, "Let that Mind be in you which was in our Lord, Christ Jesus," as you would read in your bible. That Mind is the mind of perfect freedom. It doesn't belong to anyone, but it can be cultivated to flow through you. But only, *only,* if every fiber of your beingness is *wholly committed to holiness.* You can't leave a finger outside and get to Heaven. *All* of your mind, *all* of your energy, *all* of your gifts, *all* of your very awareness must become committed to being the presence of Peace. And *this* is what no one can do for you. Sitting at the feet of enlightened teachers, listening to me on your tape or your video, will not do it *for* you.

And the wisest of students are those that hear the word and put it into practice, diligently, *for themselves.* Not for their mother, not for their father, not for their spouse, not for their brother, not for their sister, not for the sake of the planet, not for the sake of the universe, not for the sake of the new dawn that is coming, not for the sake of anything but *themselves.* For their Self is what God created. And that Self calls out to you to *honor it,* by separating your Self from the illusions that you have allowed to make a home in your mind, and being *wholly committed to teaching only Love.*

226

There is no other way. Yes, you can learn to sit in meditation and allow the mind and body to float free, to relax. Yes, you can learn rituals that help to focus your attention so that you remember what you are committed to, and the distractions of the world don't seem to quite catch you or hook you as much. There are many strategies that you can enjoy and experience. But in the end, it is only this: a quiet choice within, that no one recognizes, that no one sees, that no one hears. This is why I once shouted at the Pharisees,

> *Oh yes, well, you indeed get your reward standing on the street corners letting everybody know that you're fasting and praying, when, indeed, you should go into your own closet to pray.*

That is, to be in your own privacy, making not a show, but simply using each moment to reaffirm your commitment to learning all that Love is by teaching it. And by the word, *teach*, I mean simply that you choose to *express* only Love in each moment.

Forgiveness is an act through which you learn what Love is, that carries you into a transcendence of the world. Sharing only loving thoughts—supporting thoughts—as you look gently upon the Christ in another, is a way that takes you into the transcendence of the world. Looking upon all things of this world and seeing their perfect harmlessness, their lack of ability to constrain you or imprison you, is a way that takes you beyond the world.

And yet all of these things rest on the practice of "seeking first the Kingdom," which means not to believe in me, not to have some theological notion about what God is, not to adhere to a certain religion, or a certain church doctrine. *The Kingdom of Heaven is within you.* It *is* the very power of choice. Which pebble will you drop into the pool of your consciousness?

Imagine reaching a point where, just prior to every action that you engage, without ritual, without difficulty, without the grand shows and displays, the burning of the much incense and the lighting of the forty million candles, hmm, and all of the Gregorian chants or the rock and roll, or whatever you choose—without *any* of it—in the silent temple of your heart, you make a simple choice:

In this moment, I am going to discover what it means to teach only Love.

It might be a simple smile. It might be to let your eyes gaze at the beauty of a flower, and go,

Aah, it is very good.

It might be to eat your breakfast and actually *be* there while you are eating it, instead of letting your mind be running about to the office.

Here, beloved friends, is the way to the Truth that sets you free. *You must absolutely become wholly committed to being awake for no other reason than that you have realized you have no other choice* (you have already made them all and they've only led to pain), that your Self is calling out to be recognized for what it is—an awakened master, the presence of Christ in you, that would inform every step, inform every decision, inform the quality of your perception, inform the very nature of your forever-expanding, transparent consciousness. For it is your consciousness, alone, that can reach out and embrace all created things, until you literally realize that *all things have arisen from within you!*

That's how *big* you are! That's how *grand* you are! And why? Because that's *all* you are! You are the ocean from which waves and waves of dimensions and worlds have arisen. That Mind is what you are required to let be in you, even as once it was within me, as I walked upon your Earth. Do not make it difficult.

And whenever you hear of a teacher teaching this, or a teacher teaching that, ask yourself this:

Do they offer me simplicity or complexity? Do they offer an ordinary peace, or must I have several trappings around me? Do they give me complex meditations and prayers and things to do, or do they simply remind me of the Truth and ask me to rest in it? Will they tell me that I need to go on a thousand pilgrimages? Or do they remind me that when I make my cup of tea in the morning, Heaven is present, if I will remember who is making the tea?

Christ is.

Be you, therefore, not distracted. For in the end of this Age there is coming forth a whole smorgasbord of those who profess to be teachers of enlightenment, who will guide you into all knowledge. Look carefully and see, do they demand of you that you follow them? Do they demand of you that you give up your own discernment? Or do they egg you on to look deeper within:

> *What are you feeling? What do you think? What do you want to do? Are you willing to accept responsibility for the effect? What do you believe? What do you want? You are free. I am equal to you. I'm just in the role as a temporary guide for you and someday you'll be far beyond me.*

How do they speak? What do they teach? Is their fear filtering into their words? Do they believe that they must teach you to control the forces of nature, the forces of the mind? Do they teach you to protect yourself against evil? There are many, and there will be many more. And when you hear these things coming from them, turn and flee from their presence! For you do not need them. You are already beyond them.

Ask only,

> *How can I extend my treasure this day?*

And lay up treasures where moth and dust cannot corrupt, that is, where time and materiality and the body and the world cannot "hook you," but rather lay up treasures which are in Heaven: forgiveness, peace, unlimitedness, recognition of your unlimited power, that which brings you joy and puts a smile upon your countenance. Lay up for yourself these treasures and all things shall be added unto you.

For there is a way of being in the world that requires no planning or striving, though to enter it does require the relinquishing of fear. To enter it requires a commitment to teaching only Love, until the mind is again whole and undivided. There is a way of being in the world that isn't here at all. The body still abides. Yes, you still act just like everybody thinks you act. That is, they know your name, they know where you live. You know which car you're supposed to drive, you know who you go home to at night. But, through it all, there is pervaded in your consciousness a *transparency* as you look upon all things.

And whatever feelings arise, come and go. But somehow you begin to recognize that you are much larger than the things that come and go, that you are watching a dance of shadows, a dream, gently passing by, that is gone in a cosmic split second. This does not become a way in which you *deny* your experience, but it gives you the freedom to *embrace* it and *live* it, *totally*, with *passion*, with *purpose*, with *power*, and *in perfect freedom*—no anxiety, no pressure, just the willingness to dance in the world of dreams, while remaining *awake*. Hmm.

For those of you that are hearing this message in a consecutive manner, if, indeed, you've been putting your five minutes into practice, you are already carrying yourself closer and closer or, perhaps, more and more deeply, into the transparency I'm describing for you. And that transparency grows to a point, you might think of it as a critical mass, when *suddenly* you as a *beingness* can no longer even hold the thought of yourself as a body in space and time. And then the body simply dissolves away. And your consciousness will never experience the limitations of the body again. But you will bring the joys that bodily experience taught you of with you. For they are imprinted in your consciousness forever. This Earth is a beautiful place, but it is a pale reflection, only, of the radiant, transcendent beauty of the good and the holy that pervades my Father's Creation. Love it, embrace it, thank it, but do not cling to it.

Learn, then, to teach only Love. And now, by way of building on what you've been doing, we would simply ask you to add this very simple practice. When you sit in your chair for five minutes abiding as Christ, remembering the Truth that has set you free, begin to ask yourself the simple question,

> *This day, how can I extend my treasure? How can I add to that which I am storing up in the Heaven of my consciousness?*

Immediately, you'll begin to get pictures—an old friend who needs a phone call, someone to write a letter to. It could be something as simple as picking up your cat, placing it upon your lap, and seeing all of infinity in that living being, and feeling the joy that comes as you run your hand along its fur. It could be something as grand as going to your Washington, DC in order to send a blessing to your President. It doesn't matter what it is, because that Voice of Love will be guiding your actions. It may be as simple as turning to your spouse and saying, "You know, I appreciate you." That's all. Whatever it is, let that day not fade away until that action is accomplished, or at least set into motion.

So, you see, the great question is,

> *Am I willing to trust the flow from my Father's Mind, through my own, as that which empowers me to extend my treasure?*

Yes, it does mean living unlike the way the world lives. Yes, it does mean going against the grain. And you may seem to need to apply more energy to it at first, as you get the momentum of your mind to turn in another direction, to shake loose all of the sludge that has settled into your consciousness.

But I can promise you, if you will take up such a path—simply, joyfully, gently, patiently—*the end of your journey is certain.* If you choose a path filled with magic and many complex strategies, the end is not so certain. The way is easy and without effort.

> *I am already That which I seek. I need only allow It to guide me. And while this body lasts, I will allow it to be a communication device that extends the treasure of perfect Love, perfect safety, and perfect peace to all who enter my house.*

And your "house" is your field of energy, the expanse of your presence.

And lastly, we would suggest that you do this, especially those who will be engaging this process in a consecutive monthly manner, to do this until the time of what you call your Christmas celebration. Toward the end of your five minutes, look at yourself from within your mind's eye, as though, from the last Christmas until this, you have journeyed around a circle. You've journeyed through many astrological houses, many influences of energy. You have engaged yourself in relationship with countless brothers and sisters. You've had thousands of visions and dreams and revelations come to your consciousness. You have had umpteen million opportunities to be disturbed and lose your peace.

You have been like a sojourner, the prodigal son who has gone out through the realms of human consciousness and *now* you see yourself completing the circle. From the time you first hear this, count the days until what you call your twenty-fifth of December. And let each day be seen as a step, a pilgrimage, a completion of a very ancient circle. Let each day be one in which you reaffirm your commitment to releasing everything unlike Love in yourself, so that as you come to your December twenty-fifth, you will dedicate yourself to being prepared for it.

And on December twenty-fourth you will go to bed early enough, and in quiet and in prayer, so that you can awaken before the first rays of the new day come to caress the Earth. And you will take yourself out of your doors, even if you must bundle up the body, and you will make haste to a place of vision, a place where you can look out over wherever you live, and let that represent your ability to look out over all of Creation. There, turn to face the direction of the arising sun, and go into a simple prayer. Close your eyes. Realize that you see nothing through the physical eyes anyway. Stand with the arms at the sides and the palms open. Breathe deeply into the body, relax the mind, and begin simply to say within yourself:

> *Death has occurred, and now the birth of Christ is at hand.*
>
> *Father, I accept fully Your Will for me.*
>
> *And Your Will is only that I be happy and use time to extend my treasure.*
>
> *And now, I receive the warmth of Your Light and Your Love.*

And then merely stand, and wait, and receive the warmth of the Light. For rest assured, even if the skies are cloudy, as the sun arises, there is a change in the energy of the air. And if you're quiet, you can feel how it begins to affect the energy sphere of your awareness and of your body. Drink that solar energy in through every cell of your body. Drink it in until you feel your very spinal column warmed.

And when the whole body—from the crown of the head to the tips of the toes and down through each finger—is filled with Light, then gently open the *Eyes of Christ,* and let yourself see *a new world, a new creation, a new beginning.* Now the journey *to* the Kingdom is over, and the journey *within it* can begin. Graduate school is just around the corner.

So, your instruction is given. And to those of you that may hear these words in some distant time frame, the same Truth applies. Listen well to what has been given, for we have been stepping into some very simple but very powerful initiations, that were once given to me as I, too, awakened to the Reality that *only Christ dwells within me.*

And with that, beloved friends, we will bring this hour to a close. Listen *well* to all that has been shared. Do not take it, shall we say, "lightly," although it is only filled with Light. Consider well each phrase, each sentence, and even the pauses between the words. For in those silent pauses, revelations can come. *It is time to birth fully the presence of the peaceful Christ within you!*

And when you journey back down to your home on that December twenty-fifth morning, do something that celebrates *your* birthday. Not mine, yours. I can handle taking care of my own celebration. And then be joyous and celebrate in whatever way you wish. And know that the New Age, the New Day, has dawned. And never again will you ever be able to convince yourself that there is an excuse for believing in anything that is less than an *Enlightened Christed Consciousness.*

Peace, then, be unto you always. And *always* am I with you.

Amen.

Lesson Ten
Question and Answer Section

Question: Can you elaborate on the importance of our natal charts and the different influences and energies that transits in astrology bring?

Answer: As I have shared with you before, it is appropriate to say that the soul chooses to enter into a field of energy that has a certain *flavor* to it. And that flavor is the *matrix of vibrations* that makes up the energy field of creation in the dimension that you're entering at the time of your birth.

Nothing arises by accident. And those children that delay their birth, or speed it up, are simply trying to, shall we say, get to the "train station" before it leaves. They don't want to be too late or too early, because they've already decided which "car" they're going to be sitting in. And why? Because when they do so, they create for themselves a certain flavor, a certain sphere of energy, a certain creative matrix, certain fields of energies that set up the learning situations within their own consciousness. They then attract the situations, the friends, the relationships that can express—what would you call this—the *flushing up* of those energies that the soul is choosing to explore, and play with, and master.

It's really not all that complex. It's very, very simple. The danger comes when the mind looks upon its intellectual understanding of those matrices, those fields of energy, those certain flavors, and believes that the *power* is in *them*. That is like a carpenter suddenly becoming deluded and looking at the hammer and saw on the table, and then, sitting back and waiting for the hammer and saw to build the house.

Take up the tools, take up the qualities that make up your beingness, that even influence how the genes of the body generate energy, how they digest foods, all of the preferences and likes and dislikes. And begin to see these things as symbolic:

What energies am I choosing to experience?

Why do I hate the country so much and love the city?

Why do I hate the city so much and love the country?

Why do I love the snow and hate the sun?

Why I do love the sun and hate the snow?

These are energies, matrices, fields, sandboxes in which you are playing. But your role, your goal, is to *transcend* and *master* those energies, not to be mastered *by* them, not to wait for *them* to dictate to *you* what choices you will make.

To come into this world and master this world means to embrace all of the matrices, the fields of energy, that dance and play amongst themselves and create the interwebbing of relationships we have spoken of prior. And to learn of these things, to cultivate an awareness of how they work, so that you can master and direct *them*, rather than the other way around.

And ultimately, mastery is achieved when you have perfected the gifts that are seemingly dictated by your chart. And then you transcend it completely by resting into that Mind which forever transcends all manifestation. For those that would use the language of the astrology, the window of astrology, we would say to be very, very careful. Are you looking to your intellectual understanding for the power you believe is there and giving your power to that understanding? Or are you merely allowing yourself to see certain patterns, to get a flavor for certain possibilities, inclinations, so that you can bring awareness to them and refine your mastery of them?

Dictate the effects of your astrological chart. Do not let the astrological chart dictate the effects you experience.

Question: I recently saw a friend's heart with my inner eye. And the symbol was a beautiful Cross of Light. I would like you to elaborate on the symbology of the cross.

Answer: Again, as we have shared many times, the cross symbolizes this: The vertical axis symbolizes the union of Creator and Created, of eternity descending into Creation or into time. The horizontal axis represents the extension in both directions; that is, that which embraces all of time—the past, the future. The horizontal plane is the plane of the Earth, the plane of space and time, the plane of created manifestation. The vertical axis represents, also, the pathway of ascending or turning your attention away from the horizontal axis, in order to access the guidance of the Comforter, the Mind of God, Herself. And to bring that Light, to bring that vision, to bring that Truth, down to the Heart where it can then be extended as far as from the east to the west—to join eternity with the things of time. And, thereby, to *transform* what has appeared to be the imprisoning of space and time.

As you would look, then, upon the friend and see this cross, it means, then, that this one has begun to awaken to that consciousness; that it's not about living unconsciously, whereby the things on the horizontal plane dictate your reactions and your choices. But rather, it is to quietly go within, to receive vision and guidance, and then to learn how to *translate* that into the horizontal plane.

This cross is also the symbol of the Christed Consciousness, which is exactly That Mind that is committed and dedicated, not to escaping creation into some formless abyss, but rather, to access the Mind of God the Love of God, and to *descend* it, to bring it down into the mind—into the human mind, the human body—in order to extend it, to create in a different way ... not a fearful-based way, not a survival-based way, but a way based on revelation and vision and the willingness to receive the perfectly unlimited Thoughts of God, and then to extend them.

You can begin to look upon anyone in that way. Simply tune into their heart, which is their core or their essential vibrational pattern. And simply ask,

> *Well, Holy Spirit, is the Cross of Light awakened within them? And if so, to what degree?*

And you will find that you can come to see it that quickly. And then you'll know who to spend your energy with and who not to. Not out of judgment, but out of recognition that you can't put the Cross there yourself. You can only learn to recognize where it has awakened in others. And those are the beings you want to, shall we say, dance with as brothers and sisters upon this plane. Does that make sense for you?

Response: Yes.

Question: Can you talk about initiations, and passing through them, and, then, having similar energies represent themselves again at a different level of the spiral?

Answer: Beloved friend, you've already done all that needs to be said. Initiations are those experiences which you cannot formally set up ahead of time. You can have the commitment, the intention, the dedication to awakening and healing and birthing Christ. Then you let the Holy Spirit take care of the details. Those details become, at times, *windows, doorways, initiations.*

To use a very simple example, imagine one who is sitting at the feet of a master learning the grand art of deep meditation. Then, one day the master says,

> *Oh, by the way, I need you to fly from the Himalayas to New York City to delivery a letter. Would you mind doing that?*
>
> *No problem.*

And the student takes the letter and gets on the plane—after spending sixteen years in the cave in the Himalayas—and goes to New York City. *Initiation time.* Can that student draw on what he has learned to be at peace in this new world? Hmm?

Now, it is very true that the process by which you let yourself awaken to the reality that ascension is already over with, carries you through the spiral of time and through dimensions and worlds. And so you will often come back around to experience similar energies that you experienced before. But now *you* are *different.* There is more of *you* that can embrace those energies being presented to you. The initiation comes in that because the old energies presenting themselves once had a certain effect, the first thing that they will kick up in your consciousness is the old effect, as a memory.

237

The *initiation* comes in this: Will you recognize that you are free to choose *differently*, or will you let the *old* association, the *old* memory, *dictate* your choice of perception and behavior? When the old memory, the old reactive pattern, is that which dictates your choice, you have failed your initiation. And when you fail a course, you must repeat it.

But when you look at it and say,

> *Oh, there are those energies again. I used to be very judgmental here. I used to flee. This time, I'm going to stay. I'm going to breathe. I'm going to use this as an opportunity to teach only Love, to extend forgiveness, whatever the lesson may be. Because there's more of me available, I am safe to turn and embrace what once defeated me.*

Now, you may not break off the entire chunk. Or you may—you may be done with it. And you'll know that you're done with it, because the next time you come around in this spiral and the world presents to you that old energy, you'll see right through it. And there will be no reactive pattern, whatsoever. You'll merely look and say,

> *Oh, yes. I've been there before. It's boring to me now.*

The new pattern will simply guide your way—the pattern of forgiveness, the pattern of Love, the pattern of being at peace, no matter what the world seems to be doing. If one is projecting on you, whereas before you may have been in fear, then when you come around (you've succeeded in your initiation), and one projects their things on you, you merely sit and *see through* the delusion of consciousness that your brother on sister is living in. And you see the Christ within them. And quietly, you bless them, in order to bless yourself.

Initiations are what time is all about. Do you feel complete with that?.

Response: Uh-huh. Thank you. Done with questions.

Jeshua: Hmm! We will see. Remember, beloved friend, *there is a place within you that already contains all answers.* The day will come when you trust that *so much* that you'll no longer even be interested in spending the time to ask me. We speak of questions you would ask for yourself, not as a service to others.

And so, with that, we'll let your bodies have their "breaks," and then put them back together, and we will continue.

Amen.

Lesson Eleven

Now, we begin.

Indeed, greetings unto you, beloved friends. Join with me in this moment. Join with me in this hour. Join with me in the place where, alone, two minds *can* join. For the body cannot bring you to where I am, as it cannot bring you to where your Beloved is. Join with me, then, in the silent place of the Heart in which all wisdom already abides. Join with me, then, in this moment, in the place prepared for us of our Creator, before time is.

Join with me, by choosing *now* to allow your attention to relax from the things of the world. Allow the eyes to gently close, as a symbol of your willingness to set aside your involvement with, and your attachment to, the things of this created world. Join with me, by allowing the body to be set free. This requires only that you make no demands upon it. Indeed, let it settle in, as though it were becoming again the dust of the ground from which it came.

Join with me, as you let your attention recede from the world around you. Begin to notice the thoughts that seem to stream through the mind. Join with me by moving ever yet deeper, as though you were allowing your attention to settle down, down, into the Heart. And as the thoughts would seem to stream through the mind, can you tell from whence they've come? Can you tell where they've gone? They arise in a moment and fade away in a moment, while *you* continue to relinquish your attachment to all things of the world.

Verily I say unto you, even the thoughts that arise and stream through the mind, ceaselessly, are of the world. Settle down, then, abiding in the gentle quiet of the Heart. You do not cause the physical heart to beat and send the blood through the body. It simply knows, and it does. You do not cause the breath to flow through the body. It arises and passes away. It does not require your attention.

And in this moment, is it you that keeps the stars in the sky above you? Is it you that keeps your beautiful planet, your Earth, spinning, hurtling through space, around and around your central Sun, never deviating very much at all from the same orbit it's been in since its creation? Must you attend to the quiet unseen way in which the flowers outside your window are growing? Can you hear the sound of the grass as it grows?

Somewhere, in this very moment, a child has been birthed. Are you aware of it? Indeed, all of Creation continues to go on, an eternal dance, mystery giving birth to mystery, returning to mystery, without ceasing. And yet, you simply abide in a quiet place within the *sanctuary* of the Heart. Join with me now in perfect peace. Join with me where alone we can remember that we are together. Give up all hope of directing yourself to me by taking thought. Join with me in the simple understanding that *of yourself you can do nothing*. Join with me by surrendering into the Truth of a union beyond *all* comprehension. Settle deeply into the quiet sanctuary of the Heart *we share*.

That Heart is the depth and the essence of the Creator's *only* creation. And that creation is Pure Mind, Pure Being, Pure Intelligence, the fulfillment of all wisdom, the depth of all compassion, the *certainty* of every purpose under Heaven. Rest with me, join with me, and acknowledge that our minds are joined. And as you rest, again, you might notice that thoughts seem to arise and pass away. But do you not sense them, now, as though they were coming from a place where you are not, as though you had sunk more deeply to a place of quiet beneath the surface upon which thoughts flow back and forth without ceasing?

Are you, then, the thoughts? No, you are not. Are you even the thinker of the thoughts? No, you are not. You are merely that quiet, and that presence, that observes all of Creation flowing through a field of awareness which is the Mind of Christ.

Unlimited forever, are you. Unchanging forever, are you. Perfectly changeless, are you. And we are of one substance, one Light, and one Truth. Here alone, does reality reside. Here alone, is reality remembered. Here alone, Love reigns supreme. Here alone, is where you are.

And in this place, that is everywhere at once, and in this eternity, that embraces every moment of time, what do we discover? What is it that we share? It is not a body. For bodies are limited, being temporary expressions of the coalescence of thought. It is not the body that we can share. Look yet more deeply. Is it the thoughts that still dance upon the surface far above you? No. What is it, then, that binds us one to another, *as* one another? Is it not the *silence* and the *awareness* of the *One* Who observes the arising and passing away of all created things?

I share with you the depth of a perfect silence. I share with you a wisdom supreme. I abide *as you are*—the thought of Love in form. To be in form does not mean to be a body. It means only that That Mind, which is the reality of Love's existence, truly abides within each of us *equally*. And if this were not so, you could not recognize me. And when I speak a word, or a sentence, or a paragraph that resonates within you as being the Truth, you could not know it was so, if that Truth did not already live within you as the reality of your very existence.

Remain with me now. Heed not the call of that part of the mind that would distract you and lead you back to the illusions that comprise your world. Here, there are no mates, no careers, no loss, no gain, no pain, no suffering. Here alone, the Truth remains a shimmering within you. Here is where I am. And this Heart that we share is not contained within your body. Rather, the body has emerged from within the power that resides in this Holy Place. It has provided for you only a temporary learning experience. It will be there when you return, should you desire it.

But for now, give yourself permission to rest into the Heart of all Creation—the still and silent place of Perfect Peace. What is it that we share, if not awareness itself? For here, if anyone were to look, they would see there is no difference between you and myself. You are a Shimmering Field of Awareness. And that same Shimmering Field comprises the essence of *All* that I am.

And within this Awareness lies the answer to every question you might choose to ask. Within this Shimmering Awareness is the reassurance that the end of the journey is certain. Within this Shimmering Awareness do you abide *at One* with all minds and every aspect of Creation. Join with me here, often, in remembrance of me. For this is the secret of communion—to relinquish the perception of the world in favor of the acknowledgment of Reality.

Mind reaches out forever, but it reaches only to *Itself.* Therefore, every word that I share with you is already present within you. Here, does Love abide, alone. And there is no space for anything unlike Love. This is why every loving thought is true, for it arises not from the superficial or the surface level of the mind that generates thoughts merely in reaction to other thoughts. But Love emerges from the *depth of the Heart* that transcends what you know to be your body and your mind, your feedback mechanism.

When you think a loving thought, you have been caressed by the touch of God. When you hear not loving thoughts within yourself, this can mean only that you have returned to the surface, and have denied the depth within you. If you would, then, hear only loving thoughts, simply observe where your attention is, and allow it to settle deeply into this place, beyond time, beyond the body, beyond the dream of the world. For this place, the Kingdom of Heaven within you, is vast beyond comprehension. The world you know, when you take your attention to the surface of the mind, is contained within it and embraced within this Heart, like a dewdrop begins to be consumed by the ocean that receives it.

Here then, beloved friends, is the place of all certainty. Here, the place of perfect power to fulfill the loving thoughts with which your Creator has caressed you. Here, the way to fulfill each loving vision. Here, the source of all wisdom upon which you can draw to recreate yourself to *be* the presence of Christ Incarnate. Here then, is the straight and narrow path that leads unto Life. For Life is beyond every concept you have ever heard, even those that I have used to communicate with you. They have been like so many fingers, pointing at the moon that shines its light gently upon you. That Light lives in the depth of a Silent Heart. Therefore, *Silence is the doorway to Wisdom Divine.*

Remain with me here. Do not think on what you hear, but allow it to pour through you, knowing that the vibrations of Wisdom that these words carry will *leave their trace* upon you, without the least bit of effort on your part. You need only be as a *lover* to the Mind of God—*opening, allowing, receiving*—taking in that which your Creator would bestow upon you. Remain with me in the depth of this Perfect Silence. Notice how you begin to feel a gentle spaciousness, a peace descending upon you, like a gentle dove—and yet, you have done nothing. And again, should you feel your attention being pulled back to the surface of your awareness, merely choose again, and return to the quiet of the Heart.

I am loved; I am loving; I am lovable, forever.

Let this phrase be as a stairway that descends from the world of your making to the depth of Perfect Peace. You need repeat it only when you notice that you've become temporarily distracted by the sights and sounds and images of the world around the body, as well as the thoughts that seem to stream and dance along the surface of what you would call the brain center.

I am loved; I am loving; I am lovable, forever.

And as you come to feel grounded, rooted in, that deep and silent place, *ask whatsoever you will* and its answer shall not be hidden from you. Ask to witness my lifetime as I walked upon your Earth, and it will be shown you. Ask to be shown the vibrational field in which you were conceived in this life; it will not be hidden from you. Ask whatever you would about a friend, who perhaps has seemed troubled of late, and the source of what is occurring within them will be gently revealed to you. For remember that, in this place, you are Awareness Itself, merely becoming aware of Itself. And that Awareness, that Consciousness, lives *equally* as the *essence* of *each and every one* whom you know and love. And your love *of them* is what binds you *to them*, in the depth of a quiet Awareness.

But as you descend the stairway to the quiet place of the Heart, there are a few things to leave behind you: the need to be right, the need to be supported in your illusions, the fear of rejection, abandonment, denial, and death. Leave behind you every thought of what the world is and what it is for. Leave behind you every thought you have ever held of everyone and everywhere.

Surrender, relinquish the world of your perceptions, and come quietly to kneel before your Creator. And there, in the silent place of the Heart, unattached to whatever is given you or shown to you, *nothing* will be kept secret. Would you know the foundations of the world? The answer is here. Would you know how to best direct Love to a loved one? The answer is here. And a Voice will speak to you, like one crying from the wilderness. Pictures will be shown you, feelings enlivened within you, and you will know that way to extend your treasure.

Remain with me here, for here do I abide. And the only difference between us is that, occasionally, you believe that you abide somewhere else. And when you journey up those stairs, to begin to be distracted by the thoughts on the surface of your mind, and by the sensory feedback of the energy field that comprises your physical creation, I remain in our shared Heart, patiently waiting for your return.

Remain with me here.

> *I am loved; I am loving; and I am lovable, forever.* This is the truth that sets me free. *I Am That I Am. My awareness knows no limitation and all worlds arise within me. I Am That Mind, present in all beings when they descend the stairway and embrace the Truth that alone is true always. Here, perfect peace. Here, the recognition that nothing is lacking. Here, the embrace of the fulfillment of the Love I have sought in all the wrong places. Here alone, do I abide. Here alone, do I remain. I Am That One, existing before all worlds. This alone, is the Truth about me.*

These words are not mine, they are *ours*. And we share in them, equally.

> *I am loved; I am loving; I am lovable, forever. I Am That I Am.*

And out of the depth of that Perfect Silence, and the remembrance of that Perfect Knowledge, there comes the impulse of a loving thought:

Take Me into form. Take Me into space and time. Reveal Me to the world.

Your life can become, whenever you choose it to be so, merely the process of Christ's incarnation. Relinquish the world, even as you walk through it. Surrender it, with every breath. Learn to cultivate the depth of this *knowing* in the midst of all activities in which the body is used as a temporary learning and teaching device.

Beloved friends, abide with me in this Union. And regardless of what the eyes of the body show you, regardless of what the ears of the body hear, regardless of the "harmless" thoughts that seem to dance across the surface of the brain-mind, you abide where I am, in-formed by that Love from which there has been birthed the sun, the moon, and all of the stars of Heaven, the planets in their orbits, and all dimensions within our Father's Creation. You can realize the incarnation of Christ by coming to dwell in the Heart of Christ, until every step and every word and every gesture flows from this deep and silent and perfect place, until Its Voice is the only one upon which you act.

And even as the thoughts of the world stream through your brain-mind, and even as the sensory data are received through the cellular structures of the nervous system of the body, yet you can relinquish these things, and act only from that depth of Perfect Wisdom, Perfect Safety, and Perfect Peace.

This is the month of your "Thanksgiving" as it is called. Will it be that month in which you truly give thanks for the Grace that sets you free? Will you honor that Grace by descending the stairway to the quiet places of the Heart in each of your days?

I am loved; I am loving; and I am lovable, forever. I Am That I Am. Infinite Awareness—birthless, deathless—That which embraces the dream of space and time, and looks lovingly upon all harmless and neutral events. And even the body is no longer mine. It merely arises and passes away, while I, the Creator of all Creation, inform it with the awareness of Perfect Forgiveness, Perfect Peace, and the fulfillment of Love. Yea, though I walk through the valleys of space and time, fear arises not within me. For all good things are in my safekeeping, stored where moth and dust cannot corrupt, where thieves cannot break in to steal. Here alone, is the treasure that I seek no longer because I have found!

Abide here with me, until the hour comes when you know that you will go out no more from our Father's Holy Place. That Place is this Depth of Peace that abides wherever you are as the very Heart and Essence of your reality.

I am loved; I am loving; and I am lovable, forever.

This I give you as a divine meditation and way of prayer. Perfect it! Live it! Drink it in! Embrace it! Devour it! Become it! For in this *becoming* you will merely *remember* what has always been true since before the arising of all worlds. As a bird returns to rest in its nest, as the melting snow becomes a river that flows into the depth of a silent ocean, as the sound, the song of a flute descends gently upon your own ears—you, the creator of the notes—so too be you, therefore, wise as serpents and dissolve into this depth of the Truth of your being often, until you abide here in every *where* and every *when*.

And when the body steps upon the Earth, and when the vocal chords are used to form words, the touch of the foot upon the Earth will remind you of Christ's blessing. And the words that shape themselves will teach only Love. Here then, beloved friend, is the essence of all that I would extend to you in this day and in this hour.

Utilize the remainder of your time of this hour's communication to practice gently descending and ascending upon the Ladder of Awareness. Give yourself permission to ascend, to notice the thoughts that stream through the mind. Hear the sounds around you. Feel the weight of the body in the chair where you sit, and then descend again. And abiding yet a little while, then again choose to ascend. Listen to the sounds around you, the beating of the physical heart. Shift the weight of the body. Notice the thoughts that stream through the surface of the mind. Relinquish these things, and descend again, gently ascending and descending. For as you do so, you will join both poles together. And you will cultivate within yourself the awareness and the spiritual power necessary to be *in the world but not of the world*.

Can there be a greater accomplishment than this? Can there be anything that can offer to you a greater fulfillment than to be the conduit through which Infinite Awareness and Power flows with every breath, every gesture, every spoken word—to reveal Christ to the world through you? What could you ever value greater than this?

Enjoy, then, your hour. And know that when you descend to that place of the Silent Heart within you, I will greet you and I will sit with you, in the depth of that Silence. And our minds and our hearts and our souls shall merge as One. And when you ascend, you take me with you. And when you descend, you drink me into yourself, until finally there is no difference between us. And when the world looks upon you, they will say,

> *Behold, I am in the presence of something mysterious, something attractive, something vast and peaceful and filled with power. Surely, this is the Child of God!*

And now, from that Mind that we share as One, I say again unto you:

May peace walk with you. And my blessings I give unto you, not as the world gives, give I, the Voice for Christ that longs to be your voice. For the world gives and takes away, but my Love is with you forever. Let this Love become your very own. Claim it. Own it. Taste it. Drink it. Breathe it. Walk it. Talk it. *Incarnate* it!

And though I go now, to recede into Silence, yet do I walk with you on the way that you will choose, that it might become a way that extends the treasure of your Perfect Knowledge that you are loved, that you are loving, and that you *are* lovable, forever. That you are, indeed, That Which You Are, and you cannot be anything else! Gently touch each moment with what you bring from what you discover in the depth of your descension into the Heart of Christ.

Peace be with you always and light your way while yet you abide within the world. You are, indeed, sent forth as That One who holds all power to extend the treasure of Truth. Be you, therefore, That Which You Are—and you *are* the stars that light the heavens and bring radiance to the things of time.

Go you, therefore, into all the world and bless it with the Radiance of the Christ within you.

And if ever you need to know where you should be, descend to that Depth. And when you ascend, open the eyes and bless the place you are. And in this is your purpose fulfilled.

Peace be unto you always.

Amen.

Lesson Eleven
Question and Answer Section

Question: I would like to hear Jeshua address the following issue brought to my attention by one who does not embrace our path or beliefs. This person quotes, "The message from Jeshua tends to privatize spirituality and right action. One could easily forget or rationalize away one's responsibility to the poor and oppressed."

Answer: Indeed, beloved friend, it is with great joy that we come forth in this hour to address this specific question. For indeed, it is a question that has been brought forth by many, many minds in many epochs. For, you see, there is a tendency for the human mind to separate spirituality into two camps.

There have always been those that sought to *separate* themselves from culture, from community, from daily life, and to run off to their caves and their monasteries, in order to seek a purely interior relationship with God. Now, there's nothing wrong with creating a purely interior relationship with God, since that is the Truth of your fundamental Reality.

However, when the mind holds the perception that it must separate itself from what it perceives the world to be in order to discover God, that mind is already beginning its search on a futile premise. For this means that one is still a victim of the world, and that the world holds a power to separate you from awareness of Love's presence.

Now, in the other camp, there are those who would wish to believe that genuine spirituality means constantly being engaged in finding someone to help or to fix. But this, itself, is also but an expression of egoic consciousness.

If only I can do for others, then I will validate my worthiness—not just to myself, not just to God, but my neighbors will see all the grand works that I do. So let me, indeed, rush about to feed the hungry and clothe the naked and house the cold. And, of course, whenever I gather with my

253

friends at a cocktail party, I'll let them know what I've been doing all week.

Each approach is founded in egoism. Now, in the latter camp, there are those who would seek to render service to others and perceive spirituality to require *sacrifice* of time, of energy, of money—it doesn't matter as long as the idea of *sacrifice* is, shall we say, fulfilled. I want to share with you that none of these approaches is genuinely what could be called *spirituality*.

Anyone—*anyone*—who has ever come into contact with what I teach, not just through this, my beloved brother, but through any of the other numbers of channels or friends with whom I am communicating with your world . . . if anyone would but read *A Course in Miracles* . . . if anyone would but read the sentences printed in red in their Holy Bibles (some of those are actually genuinely what I taught), they would be hard-pressed to overlook the most fundamental of teachings that I've offered.

First, the greatest of gifts, the highest form of service that you can give to anyone is to *assume responsibility* for your underlying sense of separation from God and to *rectify* that mistaken perception. That is where spirituality *must* start. For, until that is accomplished, all of your doing in the world will be *clouded* with *egoism*. Those who strive for peace would do well to first become established in true peace within themselves.

Those that seek is to serve the hungry would do well to nourish themselves until they are filled, not with that which satisfies the body, but with that which satisfies the soul. For only when the soul is brought back into perfect alignment with its established unity with God can the Wisdom of God inform that soul, that person, in which actions truly serve the highest good. Without it, one will merely use ideas learned from the world and will try to be the *maker* and the *doer* of its service.

This is based on the assumption that one knows what their brother and sister needs. Therefore, if you see one who is hungry and sitting on the side of the street, saying,

> *Here, give me a few shekels of coins so that I can go and eat,*

. . . if you perceived spirituality as being a *duty* to the oppressed, the poor, and the hungry, you would immediately look about to see what you can do for that person, based on their request. And, more importantly, based on what *you perceive* is amiss.

But how do you *know* that there is something amiss because a soul has chosen to create a situation in which they have no job, no home and no friends? Remember always that each mind literally creates its lived experience in this domain. There is no such thing as victimization. And oppression does not come from without. Oppression is a perception created within that mind. Anyone who looks upon the history of humanity can recognize many instances in so-called oppressive situations where individuals have simply chosen not to be oppressed, and have moved with freedom and with dignity, even into what appears to be death.

Therefore, beloved friend, understand this well: Relationship is the means to your salvation. But the fundamental relationship that must be rectified, must be nourished, must be healed, must be cultivated, is your *direct* and *immediate union* with, and *communication* with, your Creator. When this is established, the soul rests in perfect peace. It has far transcended the impulse to be the doer and the maker. It looks out upon a world completely forgiven; in your language, "let off the hook."

One does not look out and see a world that must be saved. One no longer looks out and sees a world in travail. One merely becomes the servant of the extension of Love and makes no pretense that it knows beforehand what that should look like. But in every moment and with every breath, that mind merely asks within,

> *Father, what would you have me do this day? How might I be of service as your plan for the Atonement is achieved in human consciousness?*

One learns to listen to that Inner Voice that might very well say,

> *I want you to establish hospices in every city in the world. Begin now.*

That same Voice might say to you,

Go and sit by the park this day and forget the world. Breathe deeply of the Angel of Air. Let the Angels of Sound of the Running Waters fill your soul and heal your bodies. Nourish yourself today. Go watch a movie, play with your friends, read a good book, have a cup of tea.

Those that believe spirituality rests on how much service is given to the oppressed might never hear the Voice that says,

Include yourself in the circle of your Love.

Therefore, awakening requires that all vestiges of the world mind are cast aside and one rests in that Perfect Truth which can *in*form perfect action, *right action*, through you. Again, the fulcrum of what I am sharing rests on this: Without the interiorization process of cultivating the healing of your misperception that you've ever been separate from God, without cultivating deep Self-love—not love of ego, but love of Self—without that, the deep silence required wherein one hears the Voice of the Comforter is never achieved. And only that voice, the right-mindedness within you, can perfectly *in*form your actions in the world.

Therefore, he who follows me, indeed, journeys to the desert for forty days and forty nights, and leaves his friends and disciples and businesses and associates to go off and be alone for prayer, for cultivating daily the process of seeking first the Kingdom . . . that all things, including how you can be of service, might be added unto you. Think not for yourself, but love the Self enough to surrender the world into God's hands. And see it not as a place that needs you to fix it. For, of yourself, you can do nothing. "I am the vine and you are the branches." Remember always that, without the Christ Mind dwelling within you, that of yourself, you can do nothing. And your service, though laudable in the eyes of the world, means nothing.

Question: I understand that the path of the poor and oppressed is their path. However, when and how will they understand, comprehend, that they are not victims? And how can they, too, participate in embracing ascension? Do we have a responsibility to bring the message, help them spiritually and physically to throw off the bonds? I feel a need to share the Love. How is this to be done?

Answer: Beloved friend, when you look upon one who you would perceive as poor, hungry or oppressed, *first* pause and look within yourself. What part of *you* is feeling poor? What part of you perceives yourself as hungry? Where within your own being do you feel oppressed? And then take steps is to rectify these perceptions by healing your life of their energies. When you look, then, upon another again, always cultivate first the ability to see the very essence of their soul. For they are pure consciousness, pure divinity. They are like a sunbeam to the sun, yet given perfect free will choice. Their journey has been as long as yours and as varied. Therefore, when you look upon them, see them in, and held by, the Light of God.

Why is this important? It is not just mental gymnastics. For, as you see another, you will see yourself. And as you see yourself, so, too, will your brother come to see you. If you wish to help another be lifted up out of their misperception that suffering is a requirement, then be you, therefore, *committed* to being the *embodiment* of one who has awakened to the *Truth* and *lives it*, who *breathes* it, who *acts* it, who *thinks* it, who *talks* it without ceasing!

Now, when will they come, those that you perceive to be oppressed? And rest assured, in any given moment, when you look upon who's sitting by the wall on the sidewalk with a little tin cup, saying,

> *I need some money,*

you need only go within and ask the Holy Spirit,

> *Is it appropriate, now, for me to render any form of service to this, my brother or sister?*

The answer will not be hidden from you.

Again, that returns us to the point of not thinking for yourself. But turning all decision over to the one Teacher and Guide given unto you, the bridge between the Love of the Father and the place of your soul: the Holy Spirit. When will they arise from their slumber? Beloved friend, when did *you* arise from *yours*? You may not remember that hour and that day, but there was a moment from within your consciousness—it may not even have been in this incarnation—when something *changed*, and a decision was made not to accept limitation, not to accept the pain and the guilt of perceiving yourself as separate from the Source of your creation.

Therefore, know well that not you, *no one*, not even I, can force another to arise. And no one can do it *for* another. You can, of course, listen to the Comforter's guidance, so that Love is extended through you appropriately in each and every moment. And then, release yourself from being attached to that extension, whatever it may be—whether it be a golden coin, or a meal, or a new Mercedes. It doesn't matter. It might be just a gentle smile. For as you choose to extend Love, by first abiding in the Reality that you are the *presence* of Love, having been made in God's image, you provide for your brother or sister the *opportunity* to recognize the presence of Love and *decide anew* for him or herself.

And if you're guided to feed them, then prepare them a meal. Let them eat it, but be not attached to the fruit of that meal. See their essence, love them, and live *your life* in fulfillment. Far too many seek to assist others when all it does is truly *oppress* them, because it does not *empower* them to take responsibility for the choices that they have made and the effects that have come from them.

Do not just give money indiscriminately to those that say,

> *Oh, I'm broke. Do you have an extra $5?*

Go within and ask,

> *Am I just in my neediness to be a helper and a fixer? Can I surrender this and just ask Holy Spirit, "What would you have me do or say? I am completely unattached to my need to be of service."*

When will they arise and know ascension? When they decide to, just like you did. And how can you extend Love? Beloved friend, *by giving that Love first to yourself*. For, if you are not fed deeply, you cannot feed another. Therefore, lay up for yourselves treasures which are in Heaven. That is, cultivate higher consciousness. *Cleanse* and *purify* your communication device, the body. Make it as *radiant* and as *beautiful* and as *healthy* as you wish it to be. Create abundance in your own life. Feel rich and wealthy in God's Love, so that your cup can organically and naturally *overflow*.

If there are two that are hungry, it is wise that one arise and learn to feed himself. Then the Holy Spirit can use your gifts, use your power, to assist in *genuine service* to others.

Question: Jeshua, how does one teach a young child peace and Love when they're acting out their fear and anger?

Answer: Beloved friend, this could, indeed, be a whole year's tape series in itself. However, for the sake of this hour, we would say this unto you: Remember well that when you perceive a child acting out their anger, their fear, whatever it may be, first, ask yourself: Are you sure it's *theirs*, just because it is being expressed where their body seems to be? For be of assuredness, that children come into this world sparkling clean. They are very clear—*very clear* and *very, very sensitive*. Therefore, if there are emotions that the parents are not dealing with within themselves, if there is lack of communication between the parents, if there is anger that has been repressed in the mother or the father, then indeed, *the child will know it*, and often will begin to unconsciously act it out, since nobody else is bothering to, shall we say, "clear the decks" and be honest. Therefore first ask yourself: How do you know it's their anger? Ask the Holy Spirit,

What is the source of this?

The answer will not be hidden.

Now, how to help them? Where you perceive anger in another, first make sure that *you* are clear of anger within yourself. Then, as you look upon the child, remember that that child is *perfectly free now*. Ask of yourself: Does their anger, their acting out, push *your* buttons? Can you give them the space and the freedom to act out that anger, to move that energy in a way that is healthful and helpful? Can you allow them to do so? And convey to them that,

This looks like fun! Maybe I'll join you!

And start to move your body the way they're moving their body. Make the sounds that they are making. And tell them straight out like an adult. Stop talking gibberish to children, for they are as old as you are the moment they are born. Tell them in perfectly clear adult language,

Anger is perfectly okay. Let's get into it and see how it feels in the body.

Have fun with it. Make it as charged as possible. And you will find that, in a very short moment, the anger will shift, and the children will begin to feel a sense of play. For they will know that they have been *accepted*, and that there is nothing wrong with them the way that they are. Just because they don't conform to adult perceptions does not make them wrong.

How, then, do you teach them of peace? By being peace yourself. How, then, do you teach them to cultivate peace? By not hiding from them your own emotions, by living honestly—not hurtfully, but honestly.

Yes, I'm feeling angry right now! It makes my stomach tight and my shoulders crinkle up into my ears. It makes my knuckles get white. And I just want to stamp my feet!

Well, *do it* right there in front of the child! And, as *you* start to feel better, you can smile and say,

See how easy it is? I think I'll just be at peace now.

Therefore, always remember that the greatest of gifts you can give to a child is to be the living embodiment and model of one who does not deny or repress their humanity.

Beloved friend, each relationship is a teaching and learning relationship. Therefore, when a child seems to be acting out their anger, first give them the space to do it, and *observe* the child. How do they move their body? Do they just live in their head? Or is their whole being involved in it? What can *you* learn from the child?

And when the anger has subsided, *always, always, always* wrap your arms around them, at least metaphorically. Let them know that you love them. Let them know they're okay. Let them know that yes, you too know that sometimes it's a little hard to be in the world and that you thank them for being present in your life, because you are committed to learning *from them* as much as you are committed to *teaching them*.

Cease—everyone that could hear these words upon your planet—*cease treating children like second class, incapable people. Their consciousness is clear and bright!* Talk to them like an adult. Live like a mature adult in your relationships with them. Give this a try, beloved friend. There is much here for you, if you will but cultivate the treasure within these words.

Lesson Twelve

Now, we begin.

And again, greetings unto you, beloved and holy friends. Once again, we come forth to abide with you. Once again, we come forth to celebrate with you. Once again, we come to abide with the Holy Mind that *is* the Sonship. We come to abide with our brothers and sisters, and we come *as* brothers and sisters. And indeed, we come forth to abide in that process whereby the Sonship is remembering Itself as the Son—something to contemplate there. Indeed, beloved friends, I am one who comes forth in this *particular* work, to be as the primary spokesman, through this, my beloved brother, to share that with you which already resides within you.

I come forth—*we* come forth—to join with you who have chosen to answer a certain call to bring forth a creative expression that can signify, to the world, the Truth that alone can set this world free. Free of what? Free of *fear*, and all of the children that fear begets: guilt, dishonesty, unworthiness, limitation, the need for suffering, judgment, and the list goes on and on.

But ultimately, when a gardener seeks to improve the quality of the soil from which that gardener would want his flowers to bloom forth, the gardener seeks not to look upon the *effects* of a weed, that is, that which is above the surface, but rather, makes haste and goes for the root. And when the root has been pulled up, the effects of that weed can no more be seen.

Therefore, in Truth, we come, not to improve what you would be thinking of as the surface of the garden, the surface of the soil, but to strike at the *root* that resides *deep within the mind*, in the depth which I have called the *Heart*, or the *Soul*. All that we endeavor to do, then, is designed to *uproot* the weed of fear that has made a home in the depth of your being.

And in this past year, as you would know time, we have endeavored to share with you what we have chosen to call *The Way of the Heart*—which has required (for those of you that have *truly* participated in the devotion necessary to extract the wisdom which has been offered to you)—*The Way of the Heart* has been designed to bypass the cognitive, or thinking mind, and to strike at the *roots of fear* that abide in the depth of the mind, and therefore resides in a place that is, by and large, what you would call *unconscious*. *All* that we do seeks to dissolve *that root* from the depth of your being.

We cannot do this *to* you, we can only do it *with* you. For *never* can anything be forced upon the mind of the Son of God. The Holy Spirit makes no effort to usurp, or take from you, your freedom. For in your freedom, all power under Heaven and Earth resides. And Grace does not descend until your Father knows that *you* are willing to prepare a place to receive it. And this is why, in the process of healing and awakening, it is not necessary to *seek* for Love. It is only necessary to prepare the place, the soil, by choosing to discover the *obstacles* to Love, which all come down to fear, and to be willing to loosen that root, that it might be removed from the garden of your consciousness.

And then, that Rain of Grace that purifies, transforms, awakens, and brings Christed Consciousness to the mind, can descend gently. For when the rain falls upon hard ground, it strikes the soil and runs off, and the garden remains barren. But the wise gardener, who has softened the soil, who has reached in and begun to pull up the roots, to sift the soil and make it soft and open and porous, with the intent of bringing forth a beautiful garden, will indeed, then, be assisted by the Rain of Grace that falls gently, without it being earned—'tis given freely.

This year, *Drops of Grace* have been offered to you in each and every one of your months. Some you have received; some you have not noticed. Some are waiting to penetrate the deeper levels of your consciousness as you continue in your *willingness* to release fear. And suddenly, a *Pearl of Grace* that has not yet been received, will sink deep. And the recognition will come, the awakening will come. And suddenly you will find yourself saying,

> *Wait a minute. This insight, this vision, this realization I've just had, it sounds like something that was on tape number one. Hmm, I think*

I'll go back and listen. Yes, there it is! I wonder why I didn't notice it the first time?

It is simply the natural process in which the Drops of Rain of Grace had not yet a place to be received.

Understand then, and this is of great importance as we move into this next year, that all that transpires from *this* point rests on how well the gardener has cultivated the soil with the tools that have been given. If they have not been utilized, the soil remains hard, and the drops of rain run off and pool in the side of the garden, waiting for the soil to be properly prepared. Of all of these, that which can continue, and will continue, to serve you in the greatest, will be the simple five-minute practice of *abiding as Christ*, and observing all that you see, all that you feel, all that you think, as though a perfectly Awakened Christ was the only One sitting in that chair.

I know that this sounds simplistic for you, but the way *is* easy and without effort. Complexity is born of the world, and not from the Mind of God. Therefore, continue well in that practice, and *allow* it to be the foundation from which soil is prepared, the roots of fear are loosened, even in ways that you cannot comprehend with the *thinking* mind. For the roots of fear are not merely ideas. They are the *effects* of ideas. They've been allowed to penetrate deep into what you call the unconscious. This is why *The Way of Transformation*—which is, by the way, the entitlement, the title, that we will give what is to be shared during your next calendar year—it is why *The Way of Transformation* requires not striving, but allowing; not thinking, but letting go . . . *feeling;* not doing, but trusting.

Those roots of fear must be dissolved at a level that is deeper than the conscious thinking mind can reach. The mind was never designed to be your master, but to become aligned as a *servant* of the *Awakened Heart*, just like the flower blooms and sends forth its scent for all to see, from the depth of the soil that is unseen but has been well prepared, so that the only roots that gather nourishment from the soil are the roots of that which speaks of Life and beauty, not that which speaks of fear and unworthiness.

Seek you, then, to *seek no more.* For the place is prepared for you, and you need only go *to* it. Therefore, we will be cultivating more deeply the art of *surrendering,* resting ever more deeply into that place of silence which is the threshold to perfect Wisdom Divine. *The Way of the Heart* is the *preparation of the soil* which allows *The Way of Transformation* to truly occur. And transformation is not complete unless it envelops, encompasses, and is expressed through the very life you know, right there on your speck of dust, whirling about one sun in a small part of one universe—your Earth, your time frame, your relationships, your experience, your life as you know it, as you live it, as you breathe it, as you *feel* it!

So, to many of you that are listening (and the breath is beginning to stop), let the breath flow and realize that, with your grand technologies, you have the freedom to go back and see if there is anything you missed. As you do that, do it from a place of Christedness:

> *I am that one choosing to enter The* Way of Transformation *whereby human consciousness, the human lived experience,* becomes *the living expression, the fruit which has sprung forth from the soil in which the root of Grace and of Love and of healing has been well planted.*

Not from the perspective that you are doing something amiss, but out of the *desire* to be the *master gardener,* who brings forth that fruit which extends beauty and the scent of joy for all to be received, for all to see, for all to marvel at.

And yet, that beauty that springs forth from the gardener's beautiful garden does not build up the ego of the master gardener, for a master gardener knows that he or she has only been the keeper of the soil. But the magic that brings forth the flower is not his or her possession, it is merely that which you have been given stewardship over: *consciousness.* And consciousness is the gift of Life, streaming forth from the Mind of God. Your mind, then, is the soil of the garden. And all awakening, and all transformation, occurs nowhere save in that garden.

And right away, some of you are *still* seeking to understand the mind by seeing it as something that is locked inside the shape of your skull, and is somehow cohabitating with what you call the gray matter of the brain. Rest assured, your mind is *unlimited* forever. And the body that sits in the chair, in your five minute exercise, is as a drop of foam being expressed at the slightest tip of one wave in an infinite ocean. And that ocean is itself within the unlimited expanse of your Mind. You are Consciousness as such—*Pure Spirit!*

The only question, then, is: Are you willing to allow that drop of foam to be transformed into that which fully and always expresses only the Love of God, even though that expression is still temporary because the body has arisen in the field of time and disappears in the field of time? Are you willing to say, "What the heck!" and allow that Love to be as fully embodied as it is possible for it to be, for the split second that the body is in this world?

For rest assured, to the degree that you turn your attention to expressing mastery, which is the effect of *The Way of Transformation* in *this* world, in *this* time, in *this* little tiny moment—to the degree that you do that, to the degree that you use time wisely to be the embodied Christ, rest assured that when the body drops away, and it veils from you no longer the magnificence of the Light you are, the Light will not be blinding to you. And you will not contract in fear. You'll merely let this world go, gently, and as easily as a child has put away a toy that has been outgrown, because its usefulness is complete. *All* that you see—the body, your relationships, your devices, your stars and your winds and your waters—will eventually be put aside by you, not out of denial, but simply out of recognizing that their usefulness is over.

Indeed, beloved friends, as we then come to the completion of this one brief year together, look well to see that no Drops of Grace have been ignored. Open the heart ever more deeply. *Allow* those Pearls, those Drops of Rain, of Grace, to penetrate ever more deeply, not just as ideas in the thinking mind, but as *feelings* in the cells of the body. Let it create for you a sweetness in the flow of breath, a sensitivity in the way your foot rests upon the soil of the Earth with each step. Let it begin to transform the way in which you rest your hand upon the shoulder of your brother or sister. Allow that sweetness to permeate your gaze as you look upon another—seeing the Christ within them that is growing into a beautiful flower whose scent and beauty will be as a blessing to many. For there is no one among you who is not the evolving Christ. And remember always that what you *see* is what you *get,* in the same way that as you teach, you learn.

Look well, then, and ask yourself this:

> *Who do I know in my existence whom I have judged, and locked into a certain box, and I have decided that is all they are?*

There you will find a fruitful meditation for the remainder of your time until we begin that which will be called *The Way of Transformation.* In other words, you have about thirty days to take the time, and use it wisely, to allow the names, the images, the faces of those that you've done that to, to let them come back to you, to say,

> *You know, mother, father, ex-mate—whatever it is—I get it. I've placed you in a box and thrown away the key. You're stuck, so I have said. And now, I release you, that I might be released.*

And contemplate their image. Allow the memories of the experiences you have shared with them to come back. If there are feelings, by all means, let yourself *feel* them. Gaze upon them, in your mind, until you feel that sweetness that dissolves the imprisonment into which you've placed them. For as that imprisonment begins to melt, you will sense and know that *your freedom* is blossoming.

You cannot take fear into Love. You cannot take judgment into forgiveness. You cannot take limitation into unlimitedness. These things must be released *at the level* in which they were first created. Therefore, make note that this practice should not be *overlooked.* Give yourself thirty days with the goal to truly go back and—shall we say—mop up any forgiveness or releasing that you need yet to do. Don't let the mind say,

> *I don't know if I did that well enough.*

For understand, it is the Comforter that releases you and the other, through your *willingness* to allow it to occur.

Now there are some effects. This will mean that when you've truly done that, never again do you have any justification or excuse for attaching any experience you have had, any feelings you have ever felt, shall we say, to the hook on the side of their imprisonment that you've placed them in. Often, the human mind, the egoic mind, wants to hang the coat of its judgment on the hook just outside the bars in which you have locked someone.

> *That which I have experienced is the result of my father's alcoholism.*

> *That which I have experienced in life is the result of my mother having forty thousand affairs a week.*

> *That which I have experienced is the result of my business partner who has stolen my golden coins.*

and all of the rest.

> *That which has caused my suffering is the result of the position of the stars in the sky when I chose incarnation. If only they would have gotten it right, I would be okay.*

It is time, fully, as we conclude this year of *The Way of the Heart* (and to those who will be concluding it many years hence)—I say unto you, do not enter *The Way of Transformation* until you've *truly* and *fully* satisfied your awareness that you are not clinging to even the subtlest iota of perception that, in any way, you are a victim of the world you see. *Nothing* has been *caused by* your relationships. All of them have merely shown you what you have already decided will be true. The world, then, is not the cause of *anything.* You merely see what you have used the freedom of your consciousness to concoct about yourself.

Lack is not caused by taxation. Taxation is caused by the decision to need to believe that there is a power outside of yourself that needs all of your energy. Government does not cause you to be subservient. Your sense of being subservient, guilt-ridden, weak, and limited is what births the idea of government. And then some of you, as loving brothers and sisters, say,

> *Well, I'll play that part.*

And they become your politicians that, pardon the language, create the "pissing off" feeling that you have.

The world is *uncaused* by *anything*, save the *choices* you have made as a free consciousness. You've concocted the thought, immersed yourself in that which reflects back to you what you have already decided to believe. This means that *The Way of Transformation* is that way in which one becomes empowered, in every moment, to become fully responsible for clearly deciding what they will see, and that they will not settle for anything less. The better you get at this, the quicker it happens. Until one reaches the point where miracles occur.

And yet, they are only miraculous to those that do not understand how consciousness works. And you can achieve that place in which you hold out the palm of the hand and desire the sweetest tasting apple that has ever been created, and it will, literally, appear in the palm of your hand. Of course, at that point, you will be well beyond any need, whatsoever, to even hold the thought of requiring physical form.

You will begin, then, to get a sense of your mastery by being able to look at the world you are seeing and observing clearly what's been changing in it, and how quickly and effortlessly that which the heart truly desires, because it's in alignment with the Mind of God, becomes manifested, effortlessly. When the gap between the pure desire and the manifested reflection of it is smaller and smaller and smaller, you will literally sense in the feeling body that mastery is growing, and that you are merely a Child of God playing, without ceasing, in the sandbox of all possibilities called the Mind . . . and that there is, literally, nothing out there that is solid, nothing out there that is unrelated to you.

So! That's where we're going, if you wish to come along on the journey, if you are willing to truly become committed to uprooting every root of fear that has taken hold within the depth of the mind that has been rendered *unconscious* because of your hatred of yourself. It is called the *separation from God*. And therefore, because it has become unconscious, it has ruled you. Time to release the un-rule-able, by allowing that alone which can uproot the root of fear to come and take up its rightful place within you: Christ-Mindedness.

So! You have your homework before you, then. Go within and ask,

> *When that third tape came and I listened to it, but I was trying to watch the game of the football on the television, I wonder if I missed something? Hmm. When I listened to tape number seven, but was on the way to having the dinner date with that new body that looked so enticing to me, did I really sit with it and extract all of the pearls that were offered? Perhaps I will go back and really set aside an hour in which I deliberately set the world aside and—what you do when you call it, the* "hanging on every word."

And yet, with a relaxed body and a soft breath and a non-grasping mind, be you therefore like a sponge that allows the raindrops to be absorbed into the self, and that is all. *Knowledge is not a cognitive struggle.* It is not the arranging of ideas in some order that satisfies the thinking mind. Knowledge is the receiving of a vibration that begins to soften the soil of the heart and dissolves the root of fear from your being. Knowledge is that which is the result of the transformation of the garden that you have been given and entrusted with—the *field of mind* that is *you.* And that mind pervades the body. It pervades the space around you and melds and dances with other infinite webs of relationship called other minds—energy dancing into energy, unlimited forever, out of which all things of time are birthed and pass away.

So, you see, where I abide is everywhere at once. And so do you; you simply don't know it yet. I abide with an infinite array of friends who have *realized* the Truth and have been set free. They are infinitely creating, without ceasing, that which extends their treasure, which is the good, the holy, and the beautiful. Many have given you images of choirs of angels singing the praises of God. It's the same thing.

For when extension of joy becomes free to express only the good, the holy, and the beautiful, it is like a *vibration* of many notes, a choir of creative consciousnesses, sparks of divinity, who abide in perfect unlimitedness and *know* it, and ceaselessly extend their deepest bliss by allowing the good and the holy and the beautiful to flow through them from the infinite, mysterious, ungraspable, uncontainable

273

Mind That Is—God—as the sunlight of the sun creates and streams through many sunbeams that extend out to the far reaches of your universe as light, out of which planets are birthed, and animals and water and trees and birds and man.

Imagine, then, that *that* is your destiny: To take up your rightful place beside me, to join your brothers and sisters in infinite and perfect creativity, like a harp player would ceaselessly run the fingers across the strings, creating the most beautiful notes. And the combinations never cease. And in every moment, you experience the fruit of the flowers springing forth from the garden that you have well prepared to receive the Rain of Grace—evermore, evermore, *evermore*, the good, the holy and the beautiful flowing through your *unobstructed mind* that rests in perfect marriage, or union, with That which is your Creator, your Source.

Not a bad way to spend eternity! But if you look ahead, and feel that there is a distance between where you are and where that reality is, you will miss the opportunities required, right where you are, to practice where you're going by *being* it *now*. You have heard it said that a journey of a thousand miles begins with the first step. And the beginning is every bit as important as the end. For in the beginning, the end is already present. *The Way of Transformation*, then, asks you to truly become present where you *are*, to deliberately and consciously cultivate, with every thought and every breath, the willingness necessary that allows the root of fear to be dissolved, so that the good, and the holy, and the beautiful is *all* that emanates from you, like a beacon being sent out to creation around you.

Do not delay. Do not *waste* time. Time can, indeed, be wasted. But listen well, for time can also waste. You have a saying we would perceive in many of your silly little movies, where someone gets "wasted."

I'll go and waste Charlie.

How many times have you been the mafia leader that has said to yourself,

Well, I think I'll just waste myself?

How many ways have you gone unconscious? How many ways have you numbed your feelings? How many ways have you judged your brother or sister? How many ways have you decided to hold onto thoughts that say,

> *I could never do that. What's the point? It's a waste.*

Oh, yes! You just put a gun to your head and pulled the trigger. You've wasted *yourself* by wasting time.

Every moment is as a doorway through which the good, and the holy, and the beautiful can be expressed, the cultivation of the consciousness through which the power to do so grows. Oh, beloved friends, those moments of your time are *very precious!* Do not look out upon the world and go,

> *Well, what the heck, it's just the same old world.*

Remember, then, as you begin to come to the completion of this year's *Way of the Heart*, that what you see *outside* of you is only the reflection of what you have allowed to live *within* you. And simply ask,

> *Is this what I wish to continue? What do I truly want? What is this, my very consciousness, for? What do I commit myself to? What do I say I believe? Where do I freely choose to place the power of valuation?*

For what you value, you experience [snaps fingers] immediately. And the world will bow down and say,

> *Very well. You have let us know what you value. We will mirror it back to you, because we love you, because we're a part of you. And heaven forbid that we would take away your free will.*

So if you value hopelessness, the world will be a hopeless place. If you value lack of golden coins, you will continue to see lack of golden coins—flow of energy is all that means. If you value loneliness, you will continue to be alone. If you value the right to be in judgment of another, you will experience the fruit of separation.

If you value sweetness, sweetness will come. If you value *receiving* Love—listen to this carefully— if you value *receiving* Love, the world will begin to show up at your doorstep in completely different embodiments. Different vibrations, different thought patterns will be mirrored back to you that let you receive Love. For nothing can be received until the place is prepared for it to enter. And you can only *give* what you have been *willing* to *receive*. If you receive a drop of water into your glass, that is all that you can give to another. But he that receives all, gives all. And he that gives all, receives tenfold more.

So, it has been a good year. And we have watched with great amusement, at times, but always great compassion, and always perfect patience, and *always* perfect Love. We have called out to you across space and time, and if you have heard the call, the connection, the relationship with us is *already* established. There is, then, no bridge to cross, merely the willingness to receive what is true:

Jeshua is available for me always. Mary is available for me always.

The one you would call as my friend, as Germain, is available for you always. The entire family, lineage, of masters that have sought through time to create a frequency and a vibration that can dissolve the effects of the negative thinking that you have extended out of your mind, that creates like the smoke and the veil around you—to dissolve that—*all of us are available to you, and our number is legion*!

Rest assured, you are not alone. And in any moment, you need only call upon me, and I am with you. *And I do not come alone!* For some of you, then, we would highly suggest that in those moments when you feel like you need a little help, when fear seems to be coming up but you know you must go ahead, whether it be to spend golden coins to go visit some teacher, whether it be to tithe to some church, whatever it be, whatever you think you're fearing, simply say:

Legions of angels and masters and friends, whose number is infinite beyond comprehension, you who are sent directly of God to assist me over the ditch, come now, because I declare it and I receive it. And therefore it IS!

And then take the step that is necessary to take. It will not be your imagination. *We will be with you.* And the perfect end is *certain*. Fear is nothing more than the illusion you have chosen to value in order to experience what it's like to feel separate from Love. That's all. You merely waved your cosmic magic wand and said,

Let there be fear so I can experience it.

That's all.

We love you. Beyond your present comprehension, *we love you.* Beyond *all* comprehension, even at what you might perceive to be our level of functioning, is the presence of God's Love, which we seek to merely pour forth to you, that by *giving*, we continually *receive.* You see, the Laws of Consciousness work for us just like they work for you! We're just more aware of them, that's all.

That Love which God Is is *incomprehensible forever!* The Sunbeam can never comprehend the Sun. *I* am a Sunbeam to that Sun. *You* are a Sunbeam to that Sun. *We* are therefore made of One Substance, and that Substance alone sustains us throughout eternity. And the greatest of joys is to *surrender* fully into allowing That Light to light your way without ceasing.

And she that releases the world, embraces the Creator. And he that releases fear, remembers Love. She that embodies forgiveness, lives at peace. And he that relinquishes control, knows perfect trust. And that Awakened Christ that has surrendered the knot of fear, called "I," rests in unlimitedness forever, in perfect communion with all of Creation. And that union *never ceases.* It merely expands and extends as Life comes forth, Creation comes forth, extending the good, the holy, and the beautiful.

A flower that blooms in the spring for a day is the good, the holy, and the beautiful. The bird that alights upon your fence and sings its morning song has come forth from that infinite perfect Sun, and its notes extend the joy of the Son of God. The smile upon one of your brothers and sisters, who has received a Pearl of Grace through you, is Creation Itself and is the *presencing* of the good, the holy, and the beautiful. The rays of sunlight that dance upon the oceans of this world, creatively sing forth the good, the holy and the beautiful. Every loving thought that you allow to be cultivated in the garden of your own mind extends the *good*, the *holy*, and the *beautiful.*

Therefore, sing that song without ceasing. And be willing, as we close this year, to celebrate your willingness to *embrace*, with perfect deliberateness, *your* creativity and the power *you* have, the dominion over that which is planted in the soil of your mind. Prepare that soil well as you complete this year, that the Pearls of Grace might bring you into *The Way of Transformation*.

And with that, beloved friends, by the time you hear this you will have celebrated your birth date as those sunbeams which are expressed through these stories of the birth of Christ into the world. Seeming that it occurred two thousand years ago? For *me*. Is it not time now for *you* to let that same birthing be fully completed in *you*?

Therefore, we bring this message to a close, for now. Know that it has been our honor and our joy to abide with you. And there is a whole host of beings encircling you every moment you remember that you have chosen to answer a call that can be traced to the very Mind of God, Who has reached out to call His Creation, *you*, back to Himself, so that you can deliberately extend Love without ceasing.

Yes, we will have that which is called the question/answer period. But for now, we bid you peace. We give you Love. We hold you with perfect patience, knowing the Truth that is true, alone, about you. And *we will never leave you*.

Peace, then, be unto you always.

Amen.

Lesson Twelve
Question and Answer Section

Question: On the day of your crucifixion, it was told that you spoke the words, "Father, why hast Thou forsaken me?"

Can you elaborate on that? Will you?

Answer: That is always the proper question. First, I have, indeed, given forth this answer to a certain one that you're aware of. We would highly suggest that you merely obtain that answer, for it was not given to be kept and held in privacy. Now, we would amend it by saying that I've felt guilty about that statement ever since.

[Laughter]

Beloved friend, if I have not touched every kernel of humanity and the experience of it that you have known, it is useless for you to listen to me. And I have nothing to offer you. Therefore, to have come into your world and to have, shall we say, made myself impervious to doubt, pain, guilt, tears, anger, you name it—yes, even lust—to have done that would have rendered my relationship with you *meaningless*.

That is what we'll give as an amendment, a clarification, a driving home a very important point that can then be amended or added to the answer that you will extract, that has already been given. Does that make sense for you?

It is a very good question, but in the end, bring it around a little further and ask of *yourself*,

> *Why have I said, "Father, why have you forsaken me?"*

Something to be pondered.

Question: There seem to be many, many women who tap into memories and experiences of being Mary Magdalene. Can you talk about that, or the fragmentation of that one soul?

Answer: Beloved friend, we would suggest here there are many in what you call the male body that also hold secretly that very same thing, a little more deeply, because they would perceive that it would truly be seen or perceived as insanity.

Well, since I only have this kind of apparatus . . .

what you call the plumbing and that which helps to—in the procreation process of the body,

> *since it is of a certain type, surely I could not possibly have ever known incarnation in any other kind of form. So, if I say to another "I believe I've tapped into being—having been—Mary, the one that you speak of," but then I would certainly be laughed at. Because, after all, my chest has too much hair on it. But no, I don't believe I'm just the body!*

[Laughter]

Now, what occurs? In the beginning, Mind is One. You—we speak to all "yous"—were That Mind. A dream was dreamt in which fragmentation seems to have occurred. In that fragmentation, it is as though many individual Points of Light, Souls, Sparks of Divinity, call yourself whatever you want, call yourself a Burp in the Mind of God . . . it doesn't matter. That is the *result* of the dream of separation, which, in Reality, never occurred.

It does rather boggle the mind—thank God for that! In that process, many worlds have been birthed, and continue to be birthed, by Mind as It perceives Itself as fragmented. In one tiny, tiny, tiny speck of dust or speck of Light, a world was birthed that you call the Earth, and all life forms with it. And in that tiny speck, a time frame was evolved or created in which human bodies were given names. And minds believe themselves to be, much as you still do yet today, that you are somehow something other than the one who sits apart or across from you, just because there's a body that creates the perception that there's a distance from you.

One such very temporary illusory fragmentation is That One known as Mary of Magdalene, Mary of Magdala. Within that dream, one emerged known as Jeshua ben Joseph. And in the process of that expression of that dream, these two, shall we say, looked upon each other and went,

Oh, my goodness! How sweet it is!

That is, as souls, as yet still parts of that dream—it's not that we're from someplace higher than you. We're all in it together, since Mind is One.

In that dream, there was relationship, 2,000 years ago in embodied form, between two Sparks of the same Mind, manifesting as individualized consciousness. One is called Jeshua, one is called Mary. And a rather nice friendship evolved in which one seemed to serve as the teacher and the savior, and the healer of the other, who then, in turn, served as supporter, healer and awakener of the other.

Now here's the point: That individualized focus of Light lives within *everyone*. How could it be other than that? Just as I, as an individualized aspect of the dream, *abide wholly in everyone*. You, again speaking to all of you, could not begin to recognize me as Jeshua ben Joseph, that individualized Spark of Divinity that somehow got its "stuff" cleared up enough to remember the Truth and let it shine through—you could not know me or remember me, if I was not you. It takes *One* to recognize *One*.

So when you approach the question of Mary Magdalene from the perspective that there is something separate from yourself to begin with, you'll end up with all kinds of fantastic perceptions and philosophies. Now, within the dream, That One, who's really you, experienced a process of healing and awakening, a transformation, a healing of the heart, experienced relationship with me and many others, experienced passion and sensuality—what you call the little sparks that excite the cells. When This One died—and death is an illusion—that crystallized contraction of energy has, in itself, never incarnated again.

However, it has—in a sense, you could perceive it this way—extended or radiated aspects or strands of Light of its own being that have made a home in other individualized body-minds. And therefore, in the process of healing and awakening, This One needs to be looked upon as a *symbol* of an aspect of the part of consciousness that is awakening within yourself—that part that can recognize and love

Christ and take Christ into its arms, *your* arms, and embrace it as the *Beloved*.

It is time to release the insane perception that there is a separate you, distinct from all other "yous," that has incarnated over and over again. We talk this way because a teacher must have a form of language that the student can understand. But the point is to lead *beyond* that language and understanding, to release the attachment and the value that has been placed on an *individualized past*. And to anyone who feels that they *must* have been Mary: You're not special. Do not make the egoic mistake of claiming That One as yourself, in order to feel *special* or *closer* to God.

Your value is not found in the past. It is not found in who you *were*, but in who you are choosing to be *now*. And if your name is Fred or Ralph or Hazel, it doesn't matter. For Hazel can be just as Christed as Mary ever was. And indeed, Hazel *must* become Christed in order to be free.

It is the egoic mind that looks to the *past*. It is the egoic mind that *requires specialness*. It is the egoic mind that simply refuses to let you, so to speak, settle in to be Hazel, or Fred, or George, or Anastasia. These are merely sounds floating in the ethers that designate a temporary aspect of Christ's incarnation. So you're beginning to see, then, why there can be so many "Marys." Some are sincerely tapping into that aspect of the One Mind. Some need to create the illusion that they were That One because they refuse to heal the holes in their bucket where they are, and seek to reach back and find that energy in another and make it their own. It is called *special relationship*.

Look well, then, and see:

> *Is there anything lingering in me which needs to reach out to grab another part of myself in some ancient past so that I can finally feel I have some measure of worthiness?*

The only thing that defines your worthiness is how well you are choosing to be the embodiment of Christed Consciousness *now*.

This is why I once taught, and continue to teach, that belief in reincarnation is not necessary for awakening. And if you think it is, you may rest assured that, if there's anything unhealed from the past, it is with you now. Learn to look only to how you are *now*. For there you will discover the effects of what was not healed in what you perceive to be the past.

You need not go to the great Akashic Record Library and research yourself on the cosmic microfiche of the world in order to discover who you *were*, so that you will understand why you're such a schmuck now.

[Laughter]

> *There, I finally got it! Whew! Ah, that explains everything.*

As you down yet another beer. You are creating your schmuckness nowhere but right now. So, will you be the princess of schmuckdom? Or will you don the cloak of one who assumes complete responsibility for creating their experience?

To those that seem to feel an affection for the "Johns" and the "Marys" and the "Peters," the "Judases," notice that it's coming up in your consciousness so that you can make the decision to love that expression of the dream and see the Christedness that is its essence. Bring it into yourself. Love it. Let it go. Let it be assimilated to that which you are.

Therefore, for all of you, then, to contemplate, especially if you're feeling some affection or attraction or identification with this Mary, why not stop keeping Her at arm's length and, in your meditation, ask yourself,

> *What are the qualities of That One that make me feel so affectionate toward Her? What is it in Her that I desire to have within myself?*

And bring those qualities in. Again, as though you were a sponge. Make them part of your being. Overcome the fragmentation that has occurred in the dream of separation. Does that make sense for you?

Now, I know that what I've just shared might give a few a bit of a start when they hear these words. If it does, it only means that they're yet needing to perceive themselves as having some *special* form of relationship that somehow got lost in an ancient past. No. It is not lost. And they must take another step and realize that they have to start doing the work, if that is what it is perceived to be, of getting on with what has not been completed here and now.

Am I embodying Christed Consciousness?

Yes or no.

What steps do I need to take to do that?

That's all there ever is.

That should suffice for now. The only other alternative, of course, is to remain in the kingdom of schmuckness.

Question: You had mentioned you're coming through 2,003, or so, other people. And there have been several people out there claiming to have channeled St. Germain. And we have been told by Jonah that nobody does channel St. Germain. They only receive thought forms. So the question is: Are there people out there who are authentically channeling our mutual friend, St. Germain?

Answer: You're asking what is called a technological, philosophical question. You are doing what is called the "mincing of words." It is the *effect* that matters.

We would suggest here for you that This One, my friend who was once my—almost my—executioner . . . that, indeed, is symbolic for you. For who do *you* perceive as *your* executioner? That One communicates with many. For That One has long since learned to assume responsibility for those assigned to Him. That One does communicate through thought forms to a *multitude* of beings. That One, by the way, still pops in and manifests a body whenever He wishes—just to spend a few moments on a park bench with an old friend. This One lives in complete unlimitedness.

Therefore, to the degree that those minds receiving This One's thought forms are continually at work keeping their garden well-cultivated and free of egoism do, indeed, reflect very accurately that which This One would seek to transmit. As you would understand that which you are calling channeling, in which This One's consciousness blends with the temporarily-crystallized form that you call a certain individual, in order to speak through the mind, the mental field, the language structure of that one to others, This One, my friend, does indeed do that, from time to time. But as you would perceive it, the number of those through whom that effective blending is occurring is very, very small. We would say that you could count the number as less than the fingers on two hands.

But there are a multitude who receive This One's thought forms, and a multitude who do a very, very good job of transmitting those thought pictures, those images, those thoughts, into a language that conveys His message to those in your world. Does that help you in that regard?

Response: Much.

Jeshua: Always what matters is this: Anyone who serves as what your world is now referring to as a *channel* has the very same work in front of them, constantly, that anyone does—the work of constant self-cultivation, surrender, allowing, trusting, letting go, letting go of egoic consciousness, letting go of need for specialness, staying in observation of how one is truly being. Surrendering, surrendering, surrendering.

> *I'm not the maker and the doer.*
>
> *I'm not the one who knows anything.*
>
> *I need nothing from anyone.*
>
> *Who do I need to let off the hook?*
>
> *How deeply can I master forgiveness?*

And all of the rest. That is primary. And, in fact, the relationship, such as the one between my beloved brother and myself, is one that accentuates the need for that one to practice these things.

We would also say here that it is possible, and Germain is one of these who can overcome the impediments within the consciousness of another to get their thought form well planted, well received. So it's kind of a mutual thing. The channel must always be involved in the same work that everyone's involved in, because *everyone is a channel*. And nothing is manifested through them, save the frequencies that they are allowing to make a home in their mind . . . those that channel my beloved friend, as you would call Him, as St. Germain . . . although, where we abide, sometimes we joke about the "saint" part of that. Now, those that are channeling Him, then, are no different than you. They need to keep doing their own inner work. Their goal should not be to rest, but to continually desire to be the embodiment of Christ Itself. Not to rest on their laurels, so to speak.

At the same time, rest assured that we are capable of ensuring that the purity of that vibration be maintained. Because, when it isn't, we simply pull away. If egoic consciousness begins to take root in any channel, we simply, shall we say, "put it on a shelf" and wait until later. And it is only *you* who can discern whether what is being spoken is flowing from us or is merely the repetition of a record that has already been implanted in that one. Then they've reached a certain limit of their own growth and we have departed. And you are well aware of that. It is a vibration that you sense, even in the cellular structure of the body.

Does that help you in regard to that question?

Response: Yes. Thank you.

Jeshua: Indeed. So have you any other questions?

Response: No.

Jeshua: Rest assured, unto you we would say that, in the weeks to come, a multitude of questions you did not know exist will come into the surface of the consciousness.

Response: I'm sure.

Jeshua: For only one reason: so that you can embrace them with the answers that you already know. And, thereby, be freed of the past.

Response: Amen.

Jeshua: Very well then, as you have spoken: Amen.

The Way of Mastery PathWay

The PathWay offers a comprehensive roadmap if you have the desire to **grow, heal** and **know** yourself truly.

It includes **five core texts, additional materials** and a series of alchemical **living practices** which offer support that ideas alone cannot achieve.

The Five Core Texts

1 ~ *The Jeshua Letters*
2 ~ *The Way of the Heart*★
3 ~ *The Way of Transformation*★
4 ~ *The Way of Knowing*★
5 ~ *The Way of the Servant*

★Also available as the original audio.

Living Practices ~ additional material

LovesBreath, Radical Enquiry, the unveiled original teachings of *The Aramaic Lord's Prayer* and *The Aramaic Beatitudes,* meditations including the much-loved *In the Name,* together with the in-depth darshans of the Online Ashram—these are all key elements of the PathWay.

Living Practices ~ insight groups, workshops, retreats and pilgrimages

From small informal groups to our global pilgrimages, Friends of the Heart gather to grow together.

You can find out more about the PathWay and all that it offers by visiting our website, where a wealth of video and audio excerpts, and much more, awaits you:

www.wayofmastery.com